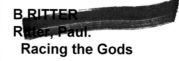

DISCARD

Racing the Gods

A Ducati Superbike Racer's Autobiography

PAUL RITTER

Foreword by Cook Neilson

DEDICATION

To my wife Dee,

who has put up with a lot
while I worked on this book.

Thank you, dear.

To the memory of my friend and
racing sponsor, Dale Newton.

Without him there would have been very
little worth writing about, and my life
would be much less interesting.

Regarding names: The names of the professional racers are real. Unless the author was given permission to use their full name, others are referred to by first name only or by nickname.

Regarding photos: The author tried to credit the photographer whenever possible. When Paul Ritter was actively racing, many people would give him pictures. He doesn't remember who gave him certain shots and there is no name on the back of the prints. If there is no photo credit, the picture was taken by the author or is from his collection.

Copyedited by Steve Casper
Proofread by Leah Noel
Layout by Tom Heffron
Cover Design by Tom Heffron

octanepress.com

Printed in the United States of America

CONTENTS

FOREWORD

by Cook Neilson

I remember it like it was yesterday: arcing into Sears Point's downhill, off-camber Carousel turn, my bike working beautifully, only a few laps to go, the situation relaxed, comfortable, and secure. Then, out of the corner of my eye, a black-and-yellow blur whipped past me on the inside. It was Paul Ritter, doing everything I was doing, but doing it much, much better, booming off into the middle distance, demonstrating a connection not only with his bike but an almost psychic link with the man who engineered the track. This was Paul's first AMA National event, and all the Superbike big names were there: Reg Pridmore (the biggest name of all), Ron Pierce, Steve McLaughlin. On his first try, Paul had dispatched them all.

I shouldn't have been surprised. We came up to Sears for an AFM club race two weeks before the big AMA National, and Paul had beaten the tar out of me (and everyone else) then as well. Not only was Paul fast, he was graceful, precise, and intelligent. And not just at Sears Point, his home track, but also at Riverside, and Laguna Seca, and everywhere else he took his Dale Newton-tuned Ducati. His first National go (and win) at Sears happened in 1977; he defended his win there with another in 1978, almost won his third National at Laguna Seca, and finished third in the National AMA Superbike Championship that same year.

Superbike racing, an outgrowth of Production racing, was growing fast all over the country in the early '70s as the major manufacturers continued to make bigger and better equipment. By 1976 the class was firmly established as a fan (and participant) favorite. The GP class was populated by identical Yamaha two-stroke TZ750 four-cylinder machines, while the Superbike class offered Moto Guzzis, BMWs, Laverdas, Ducatis, Suzukis, Hondas, snarling Kawasaki Z1s and H2s, and even the occasional British bike. Meanwhile, competitor Steve McLaughlin, a born promoter if ever there was one, would soon take the American idea of Superbike racing to Europe; World Superbike was created, and flourishes to this day. Paul Ritter was right there at the creation of what was then, and arguably is still today, America's favorite class of two-wheel road race competition. A classic underdog (journalist Larry Lawrence nicknamed him "The Ringer" in a lovely *Cycle News* piece published in 2006), Paul accomplished what most underdogs merely dream of: weaving reality from the threads of the impossible.

Having had a brief but spectacularly successful career in AMA Superbike racing, Ritter moved on to other things. But leaving motorcycle racing doesn't mean motorcycle racing leaves you. More than any other activity I can think of, motorcycle people use their particular passion to define themselves *to* themselves, and to the world outside. Motor racing in any form demands this: all you've got. All your talent, all your dedication, all of your focus, and all of your time and money. To the people who take it seriously, nothing else is as disruptive, as consuming, as greedy, as involving, as inclined to break in to your life at odd moments and rearrange the furniture. It was Steve McQueen who said, "Racing is life. Everything else is just waiting." So when racing–the bitchiest Bitch Goddess of all–beckoned to Paul 20 years after his spectacular 1978 season, it isn't surprising that Ritter answered, and found his life thereafter challenged in almost unimaginable ways.

How he answered the challenge is the substance and soul of Paul's terrifying, and ultimately life-affirming, story. It was a nothing bike event, really, and Paul was riding a nothing motorcycle on a nothing track in Steamboat Springs, Colorado. Then–early on–disaster (not of Ritter's making), and the beginning of a completely different existence, with a completely different vocabulary: weight shift, autonomic dysreflexia, busted aorta, aisle chair. None of us knows how we would deal with the sort of total physical destruction visited on Paul Ritter, but with this book we know how Paul is dealing with it, and that alone gives us courage, and hope. As much as I admired him all those years ago as a beautiful motorcycle racer, a sweet guy, and a good friend, I admire him so much more now as he is wrestling to gain a meaningful life from the flames and ashes of near-total destruction. His tools: courage, curiosity, optimism, the love of a wonderful woman (Dee, a damn fine motorcycle racer in her own right), and the confidence and determination that had to have come from his amazing success on the track way back in the '70s.

The story's framework is motorcycling and motorcycle racing, but this is much more a human story than a biker story. As effective, lyrical and fluent as Paul Ritter was as a racer, this story reveals how far he has journeyed beyond those happy, easy, sun-washed days. Paul Ritter, more than anyone I know, has stood in the fire. And triumphed.

— Cook Neilson

Cook Neilson was the editor of Cycle *magazine in the 1970s. His writing and editing and ability to attract the best moto-journalist talents helped* Cycle *become the largest subscribed motorcycle magazine in the world. Cook was also a very competitive racer, missing the Superbike Championship by only 4 points in 1977. He is one of the most respected men in his field.*

PREFACE

This book began with stories from back in the day. Whenever a group of motorcyclists gathered and someone would eventually ask what it was like in the old days, I would say, "If you insist," but in truth I liked telling these old tales. My wife, after hearing several, said, "You ought to write these stories down while you still remember them. After all, you're an engineer who can spell!"

I thought, *Why not, I'll write a book. It should be quick and easy—just start writing down my motorcycle and racing adventures in chronological order.*

I soon found out it was quick and easy to write a *bad* book. Starting with my first motorcycle and proceeding, by the time I got to 1980 I had 100,000 words. I showed it to a trusted friend who asked a few key questions that brought me to earth with a thud. The book was awful. The stories were OK, but the "glue" I used to tie them together was not OK. I look at that now and wonder *what was I thinking?*

So I re-wrote it and it became a history book, an insider's history of the first four years of Superbike racing. It still stopped in 1980, now with about 80,000 words. It was better than the first one. I showed it to another friend whose response was, "I don't care who won what race in 1978, I want to hear *your* story, especially how you ended up in that wheelchair."

Sigh. I told him he was talking about a complete second book and many more hours at the keyboard. So I removed or severely shortened all the stuff I wasn't personally involved in, and added the story of my accident and recovery. The book now ended around 2010 and had ballooned to more than 100,000 words—which was way more than I ever expected to write.

I sought more advice, this time from some published authors. I was told I had a nice journal—this happened, then I did this, then that happened, and so forth. But it wasn't a memoir yet. It needed more of me in it—what were you thinking when that happened, how did you feel about this, what were your emotions? Time to edit, edit, edit. I took out a number of stories, good racing stories and rehabilitation stories, and added more of me. Then I did something smart–I had the book professionally edited. More stories disappeared, a few more good stories but ones that didn't move the main focus forward.

So here we are—several years and many, many hours at the keyboard since I first wrote that "quick and easy" book. In the end, I feel it was well worth all the extra effort as I am extremely pleased with the final product that you are now holding. It's my story, and I hope you enjoy it.

ACKNOWLEDGMENTS

Several people not only helped get me started on this project but kept me going when things seemed stalled. Writing a book takes a lot of time and finding a publisher can take just as long these days. First and foremost was Dee, my wife. She not only encouraged me to start this book, but also kept me going during the search for a publisher, saying, "Do not self-publish this book." She assured me that the book was worthy and a publisher would turn up. She was right. Both Cook Neilson and Phil Schilling lent encouragement. Cook graciously wrote a fine foreword, and when it looked like I might never find an agent or publisher, he said, "Keep knocking on doors."

Thanks to Ed Milich for recommending Charles Everitt as editor, thanks to Charles for providing many good ideas that tightened up the book and also for suggesting Octane Press as a publisher.

Many people read portions of the text and made good suggestions for improvements. Keith Underdahl, Jack Lewis, and Virginia Aldrich contributed. Lill Ahrens and her critique class read portions of the text and made many good suggestions for improvements. Lee Klancher of Octane Press had several ideas that streamlined the book and improved the flow. Dee, again, spent many hours going over the text, providing comments that ran the gamut from "this is really good" to "there's a run-on sentence in this paragraph" to "I'm falling asleep on this part." Many improvements are her fault.

I was able to contact many of the "Superbike Pioneers" who each read their vignette page and approved it or requested changes: Reg Pridmore, Cook Neilson, Phil Schilling, Steve McLaughlin, Keith Code, Harry Klinzmann, Erik Buell, and John Long. Dave Emde is no longer with us, but Don Emde took a look at Dave's page in his stead. Thanks guys.

Conversations with Shasta Willson and Jennifer Lauck's seminar "Finding the Hero Within" helped me understand the difference between a memoir and a simple diary.

Many people contributed photographs, but especially Virginia Aldrich for the 1970s and Dee Ritter for the 2000s. Thanks to Russ Granger for the work he did in converting the color photos to black-and-white.

INTRODUCTION

The winter night in Oregon's Willamette Valley was clear and cold, below freezing. The parking lot pavement had been wet all day from melting snow, and the dampness had frozen in a thin frost-like layer. It was just enough to make traction slightly tenuous. *I wonder if I can slide my wheels?* I charged the frosty surface at full speed, then shut off quickly. Hmm. Nope, try again. I went back to top speed, but this time I threw it into reverse instead of just shutting off. Better. The drive wheels broke traction and I got a nice little slide. A few more runs and I discovered if I started to turn just before breaking the wheels loose, I could slide through the turn like a flat-track racer, like Mert Lawwill on his Harley-Davidson at the San Jose Mile.

Well, not exactly. My power wheelchair wasn't a motorcycle.

I was a motorcycle racer for a time in my life. Not a champion flat-tracker like Lawwill, but an American Superbike road racer, and a pretty darn good one. In July of 1977, I did something noteworthy. I won the first professional road race I entered, defeating some of the best Superbike racers in the country: Reg Pridmore, Cook Neilson, Wes Cooley, Steve McLaughlin, Erik Buell, and others. It caused a shock in the motorcycle racing world–novices weren't supposed to do things like that.

I competed for three years in Superbikes and retired from motorcycle racing early in the 1980 season. This is part one of my story, the journey from a novice street rider to a Superbike race winner, and my three years of Superbike racing at the very birth of the Superbike class. It is a story filled with passion for riding and racing, with victories and failures, with joys and sorrows, with life and (sadly) death.

Nearly 20 years after retiring from top level Superbike racing, I entered a just-for-fun vintage race and got swept up in the accident that put me in the wheelchair. That is also part of my story, building a different, but satisfying life after that near-fatal incident. It too is filled with passion, with successes and failures, with sorrows and joys and romance and, finally, with triumph over tragedy. It's a long story, but it's a good story, some might say compelling or inspiring. And as memory serves, it's all true.

PART I

FROM TYRO TO
SUPERBIKE PRO

CHAPTER ONE

Falling in Love
with Two Wheels

Some people see motorcycles as a symbol of rebellion: anti-establishment, renegades, outlaws. Others see the motorcycle as a metaphor for freedom: the open road, wind in the hair, nobody to answer to, no required place to be. Nice images, but they were not mine. I liked motorcycles because they were fun, inexpensive transportation. It was that simple, I told myself and others. But it really wasn't quite that simple.

———

I call it the Close Second Child Syndrome. I've seen it in my nieces and nephews: if two children of the same gender are born fairly close together, and the first child is talented, the second child spends his or her early years in their shadow.

My brother, Phil, is 18 months older than me, which is close enough that as kids we played together. Through no fault of his own, Phil is brilliant. For example, when he was five, he invented a super hero, Super Cowboy, who was a blend of Superman, Hopalong Cassidy, and Roy Rogers. Phil drew complete comic books of Super Cowboy's adventures, with his hero always wearing a cowboy hat and a cape. He had a sidekick, a cat named Dynamite, drawn in the comic book as a man with a cat's head. Dynamite wasn't very bright, but was very strong. When muscle was required, Super Cowboy called on Dynamite.

At that age a year and a half is a big difference, and Phil was always better at *everything*. He would organize the neighborhood kids, six or seven of us, and direct us to act out his comic book adventures. He was, of course, always Super Cowboy. I was always Dynamite, always the sidekick, like Robin to Batman, Festus to Marshal Dillon.

Don't get me wrong. I loved my older brother (and still do), and aside from the typical sibling rivalry, we got along well (and still do). But I wanted *so much* to find something I could do better than he could.

When I was around five, I found it. We had gone to visit my mom's cousin's family, the Carters. Phil went inside with my folks, but adult conversation bored me, so I asked if I could stay outdoors. It was a nice day.

"Just stay within hollerin' distance," my dad said, and I was left to entertain myself.

The Carters lived in a quiet semi-rural area just starting to turn from farmland to suburb. Their house was a former farmhouse, two-story and square, with a large, covered front porch. It had been built on a slight rise on the corner of two streets. I wandered around the house, looking for something to do.

I found a kid's bicycle in the side yard and I tried to ride it. I took it down to the street but didn't have much luck. I was able to get it going once and I found that just above a walking pace the bike was pretty stable. Getting it up to speed was the tricky part. I fell down many times. Then, somehow, my pre-school mind figured out how to put it together by learning one thing at a time. The side yard was grass, a short slope down to the street where the grass smoothly gave way to pavement—no sidewalk or curb. I used the slope to the street to help me get up to stable speed quickly.

I started astride the bike at the top of the slope, pushed off, and coasted down the hill, into the street and stopped. I fell over many times, but the grass was fairly soft and I was determined.

Once I mastered that I started beside the bike, pushing off and swinging my leg over the rear tire to get on the seat, the way I'd seen older boys do it. This was difficult—swinging my leg over the bike upset the steering. Again I fell a lot, but with practice I learned to mount the bike while starting.

Then I added a 90-degree turn at the end of the coast, so I would be pointed down the street instead of across it when I stopped. On the next run I added a few pedaling strokes after the turn but before stopping. Once I was good at that part, I added a U-turn and pedaled back to my start point.

Finally, I forsook the assistance of the slope and started in the street. That took a little time to learn and a few falls, too, but by then I was starting to get a feel for the bicycle. After a couple hours I was riding up and down the street with confidence. It was pretty exciting, being able to go to the end of the block and back in only a few minutes instead of 15, and swooping through the corner was downright thrilling. I wasn't doing anything fancy, but it sure was fun. And there was a bonus: Phil didn't ride a bicycle yet.

When the visit was over and my folks came out to collect me, I yelled, "Hey, Mom, watch this!" and rode the bike up and down the street, around the corner and back, while everyone watched from the porch. My mom just said, "Huh." Dad didn't say anything, nor did Phil.

Our family finances at the time meant Phil and I got a bike to share and Phil learned to ride pretty quickly, but he never showed the enthusiasm for it I did, even after we both got our own bikes. We were beginning to form different areas of expertise, allowing each of us to excel without directly competing. The bike helped established a pattern of sorts that lasted until our college ages. Phil was the scholar, the bookish type, and the creative one. I was more the athlete and became more outgoing. Even with this, however, Phil cast a pretty big shadow and I was still growing up in the shade, becoming a follower, not a leader. I was content to do what my parents, my teachers, and, eventually, what my boss told me to do.

But two-wheel vehicles were forever holding a special place in my heart and in my life.

Growing Up in the Shade

Having a smart older brother makes life difficult. I followed Phil by only one grade in school so there were built-in expectations of excellent scholarship. I didn't want to compete so I was an indifferent student for most of grade school–in fact one of my teachers wrote a note on my report card, "Just plain lazy!" It made my mom laugh, bless her heart. I think she knew about the Close Second Child Syndrome, realized I was smart, and was fine with waiting for me to emerge on my own time.

There were moments when I caught a glimpse of sunshine. There was the above-described adventure with the bicycle, and there was eighth grade. Between seventh and eighth grades, my family moved from upstate New York back to the West Coast, to a small town near Redding in Northern California. Phil was in high school and I was in intermediate school, so no one expected me to be special.

The New York curriculum was ahead of California's. I could get high scores without much effort since it was stuff I had already seen. I made a remarkable discovery–when I performed well and the teachers thought I was smart, they treated me better. The surprising thing was, so did my classmates, including the girls! Now I was motivated and applied myself, no matter what Phil did, and my grades shot up. My mom was right–I *was* smart. After realizing this in eighth grade, I discovered it was an advantage to perform well, and I actually started studying in high school.

Such moments as this and the bicycle were the exception, however, and I grew to young adulthood with the mindset of a follower. Being a leader, setting a path for others to follow, was beyond my experience. In fact I found it scary, something to avoid. Don't get me wrong–I wasn't a sheep afraid of adventure. Think of it this way: on the wagon trains going west in the 1800s, I probably wouldn't have been on one of the first 10, but I would quite likely have been a part of the next 10. Being a scout, a front man looking for passes through the mountains, would be unthinkable for me.

A Motorcycle Obsession

I was barely aware of motorcycles when I started high school. I knew they existed, but they didn't touch my life directly–I still loved riding bicycles. Motorcycles were very far from mainstream American life, and were unpopular with most citizens. Honda almost single-handedly changed the American world of motorcycling. Their massive ad campaign in the early 1960s, "You meet the nicest people on a Honda," and their cute little 50cc single-cylinder motorbikes changed the public's mindset. Surely owners of those little bikes weren't like those greasy, brutish gang members who rode big cubic-inch Harley-Davidsons and British bikes, roaring up and down the highways terrorizing honest citizens. It became acceptable to own a little Honda.

But Honda didn't stop at 50cc. Soon there was a 90, then a 160cc twin-cylinder model. Other Japanese small bikes started arriving on U.S. shores. By 1965 the 250cc Honda Hawk and the 305cc Super Hawk twins–to many the first real motorcycles Honda made–were selling well. American attitudes toward motorcyclists were changing, at least in some places.

In high school I realized I needed a motorcycle. *Needed*, not wanted. One day a friend let me ride his Honda Sport 90 for about an hour and that was enough for the hook to be firmly set. However, parental permission was not forthcoming. Mine was *not* a motorcycling family and Honda's advertising had made no impression on my folks. Getting a motorcycle would have to wait until I was on my own.

Why such an obsession? No one else in my family showed much interest in motorcycles. As described above, two wheels and I had long had a special relationship. Swooping through corners on a bicycle was thrilling. Adding a motor made it downright addicting.

When I went off to college, I subscribed to some motorcycle magazines and read them cover-to-cover when they arrived. I was especially drawn to road racing coverage, and racers Mike Hailwood and Cal Rayborn became my idols–Hailwood because he could get on just about anything and ride it fast, and Rayborn because he could win road races on a Harley-Davidson when nobody else could.

After a couple of years I had saved enough money to buy a used motorcycle. I had been out of the family home, working part-time while I attended the University of California, Berkeley. I was relatively clueless regarding motorcycles, but I knew a few classmates who rode and they gave me one really good piece of advice. They said to start with a small bike for learning and use it for a year. If I still wanted to ride, I should get a bigger bike, otherwise get a car. That's still good advice.

I saw an ad for a low-mileage Honda CB160 in my price range. The owner was keeping the bike in his apartment's living room, so it was in as-new condition, completely unmodified. The 160cc motor was just big enough to make the bike freeway-legal. It was a perfect beginner bike for me.

There weren't any New Rider classes in those days, and nobody told me a Honda CB160 wasn't a dirt bike, so I occasionally rode it in the dirt. It was OK on dirt roads, but not on trails. I once took a downhill trail I couldn't ride back up. The bike would either stall or spin its rear wheel. That trail was the only way out of the riding area, so I had to push the CB160 back up the hill, walking alongside it, revving the throttle while the rear wheel spun, spitting dirt clods to the rear and trying to dig a 3-inch-wide trench. It wasn't a dirt bike!

Nobody told me a Honda CB160 wasn't suitable for long rides either, so I took it touring. I rode from Berkeley to Bakersfield to see my folks. The short way was about 270 mostly freeway miles, but I thought that would be boring; with motorcycles the fun is in the curves. I planned a trip that included more interesting roads, which then made it a 350-mile ride. The ride there on the curvy road was fun. I wasn't a very good rider yet and kept my speed reasonable, but I really liked swooping through the turns. I took the short freeway route home and it *was* boring. Miles of holding the throttle wide open to keep up to freeway speeds while fighting the wind was *not* fun. I was very sore after that trip, the first and last long trip I took on that bike. It wasn't a touring bike.

Nobody told me a CB160 was a good choice for getting around town, but I figured that out quickly. I rode it to school, to shopping, to work, and to visit nearby friends. I added a luggage rack to strap down my books or groceries. The little Honda worked well for those tasks or for getting from Berkeley to other Bay Area cities. It was an excellent small urban motorcycle. I also rode it on the back roads on weekends, searching out twisty tarmac. There were many nice curvy roads in eastern Alameda and Contra Costa counties I enjoyed riding.

The movie *Easy Rider* came out during the time I owned the CB160 and I rode over to San Francisco to watch it on a super-wide screen. The travel scenes–where Captain America and Billy were winding through the mountains or rolling on the open road through the desert with the Byrds' song "Wasn't Born to Follow" on the soundtrack–were inspiring. To this day I can't hear that song without getting the urge to hit the open road on a motorcycle.

I knew my little Honda was nothing like the Harley choppers in the film, but on the ride home I felt sorry for all the people stuck in their cars and trucks. I was riding a *motorcycle!*

Moving Up

For me, buying a motorcycle is a battle between logic and passion. I want something that is a good fit for my type of riding, but it also has to stir my soul and make me smile when I look at it.

———

After a year I did sell the CB160. I wasn't soured on riding at all–I simply needed a bigger motorcycle. There were some very cool, very fast bikes available by this time: Triumph Bonneville, Norton Commando, Kawasaki Mach 2, Honda CB750, and others. The passionate devil on my left shoulder whispered in my ear, "Buy one of those fast ones. They're chick magnets." The logical angel on my right shoulder said, "You'll hurt yourself on one of those. Buy something sensible." This time logic beat passion and I bought a new 1969 Honda CB350. Today a 350cc motorcycle is seen as a beginner's bike, but in the late 1960s a 350 was considered a middleweight, suitable for adults. I can't say it was very soul stirring, but I did like its looks.

I still had a lot to learn. I figured the 350 would have plenty of power to make it up that dirt trail the CB160 couldn't climb, so I rode it down that hill. And guess what? The CB350 couldn't get back up either. I had to push it up with the rear wheel spinning and spitting out clods of dirt, just like with the CB160, thinking, *I'm an idiot*. I had learned the hard way one basic truth about motorcycles: it's not just the amount of horsepower a bike has, but also how the power gets to the ground by way of tires, frame, and suspension. I had watched a pal with a little Bultaco 125, a proper dirt bike, putt up that hill no problem. The CB350 was not a dirt bike.

Nobody told me a 350cc motorcycle was too small to be a long-distance touring bike, so I went touring with it. I rode that "too small" motorcycle all over the West Coast. Here are a few examples.

When my New York cousin Patt came to visit, we went to Bellingham, Washington, me on the 350 and she in her late 1960s Mustang convertible. We took Highway 101 north, so we could see the redwoods on the way up. It was a 950-mile, three-day trip to get there and we played leapfrog on the way up. We agreed upon certain rendezvous points, but would run at our own rate. The 350 could run 65-70 mph easily, but strained to go much faster, and when the road was mostly straight, she would blow by me. When the road got twisty, I was the quicker one and I'd slip past her. I remember it as a pretty fun trip. After the visit with our Bellingham relatives, Patt headed east to her home and I went south to mine. I took I-5 back in two days, Bellingham to Portland and then Portland to Berkeley, about 880 miles. (An aside: If you like palindromes [words that read the same forwards and backwards] and are travelling on I-5 near the California-Oregon border, you should stop and visit the Yreka Bakery in Yreka, California.)

One Saturday morning I loaded some camping supplies onto the bike and rode south along the coast to Big Sur, camped for one night near the beautiful Bixby Creek Bridge, and rode home the next day. It wasn't a long trip, but the CB350 made possible such spur-of-the-moment trips I would not have done on the smaller 160, and the Big Sur area is achingly beautiful.

I made another trip to Bakersfield to visit my parents, selecting a different non-freeway route than the one I took with the 160. By then I had added some accessories to make high-mileage trips more comfortable. My mom insisted on taking my photo. I think she secretly understood the allure of motorcycles and appreciated I had chosen an unconventional mode of transportation. My mom, rest her soul, was pretty cool about certain things. After visiting my folks I went farther south to see some friends in the San Fernando Valley, then back home on Highway 101.

With the CB350 in 1971: fairing, water-filled seat cushion, and a luggage rack.
Enid Ritter

The CB350 was an even better around-town bike than the CB160. I rode it to school, to the store, to visit friends. I even took my cat to the vet with it once (he didn't like it). I spent a lot of time studying maps looking for good, short rides that were nearby–the more curves the better. I developed a collection of about a dozen favorite local rides I would zip along. Some were short enough to squeeze into a lunch hour while others were half-day or full-day rides reserved for weekends.

Why All the Miles?

What was it with all this riding? Short trips made sense, but 1,800-mile multi-day journeys on a bike that wasn't really suitable didn't. At the time street bikes did exist that could be ridden all day in comfort, but the Honda CB350 was *not* one of them. The 350cc motor buzzed and sent vibrations to the foot pegs and handlebars, the seat padding was too thin, and there was no protection from the wind.

There is, however, something about travel by motorcycle that appealed to me. I loved riding and was quite happy spending many hours in the saddle. Melissa Holbrook Pierson describes it well in her book *The Perfect Vehicle.*

You may have to take my word for the fact that traveling by bike is superior to traveling by car. All right–I will allow that it's very, very different. Especially in the dark; the road seems to tilt ever upward, and you start imagining things. There will be rivers rushing in the blackness near the roadside; there will be a cliff looming overhead. You can ride into imaginative space, which is real traveling, because you are not anchored by anything. Look around. There is nothing between you and the weather, the smells, the color of the sky. All impress themselves on your consciousness as if the ride had turned it to wet cement. And there they will stay, apparently forever, so you can recall those sensations with an almost frightening precision years later.

Perhaps the best way to demonstrate this is to take you for a ride. Join me on this trip.

One Exceptional Ride

Roads have a rhythm. Often it's due to the terrain–roads will go around and between hills rather than straight over them. Sometimes it's due to the road designer, who can force a different rhythm onto the road, cutting and filling the earth to make the road more level or terracing a hillside to make it straighter.

For a relaxing ride it's best to discover the rhythm and adjust speed to match the pace of the road, and not try to rush through turns as fast as possible. Think of it as a dance. If the road wants to waltz and you try to jitterbug, things will not go well.

Even riders in sync with the road best not get too complacent. Roads cannot be trusted. They can suddenly change the pace, or throw in just one turn that isn't in sync with the rest of the miles of curves. Other traffic likewise cannot be trusted. One ought to be able to assume others on the road know and obey the rules, but it isn't so. You must pay attention.

––––––––

If you take Beegum Road west out of Red Bluff, California, there are two road signs that will get the attention of any motorcyclist. First is a sign advising trucks, RVs, and those towing trailers to select an alternative route, followed shortly by a sign warning of twisty road for the next *140 miles.*

With the Internet and today's nearly instant communications, any road with these signs will not go unmentioned for long and today this road is well known among motorcyclists. A recent vote by members of the

No, it's not Photoshopped.

American Motorcyclist Association ranked this road eighth out of the 15 best motorcycle roads in the U.S. It's the section of California Highway 36 that runs between Red Bluff and Fortuna. That's pretty much from no place special to nowhere in particular, and it wasn't so well known in the pre-Internet days.

I discovered this route by chance one summer day in 1970. I was planning a trip from Berkeley to visit friends in Oroville, a small town north of Sacramento. The quick route from Berkeley to Oroville is Interstate 80 to Interstate 505 to Interstate 5, then a few miles east on two-lane farm roads. I had already done that ride a couple of times and found the 170 miles or so to be very hot in summer, mostly flat, mostly straight, and mostly boring. I looked at the map and decided to ride north on U.S. 101, head east at Fortuna to Red Bluff, then take Highways 99 and 70 south through Chico to Oroville, about 460 miles in all. A good summer day ride, I figured.

You might wonder why an otherwise sane person would swap a ride of less than 200 miles, a perfectly reasonable distance on a 350cc motorcycle, for a trip of nearly 500 miles. There are advantages to travel by motorcycle, even one like my Honda CB350.

First, I'll be exposed to the elements. You might think having the comfort of a car's climate control would give it the advantage, but no. One of the best things about travel by motorcycle is that you are *in* the environment you are traveling through. You can feel the temperature rise or fall, sense changes in the direction of the wind, and detect subtle differences in the smells in the air. All these things give the trip more depth, more texture, if you will, and that makes it all the more memorable.

Second, there's the view. There is no way any car, even a convertible, can compete with the view from the saddle of a motorcycle. Left, right, ahead, behind, up in the sky; it's all right there.

There was one disadvantage with the CB350. I was going to spend 10 to 12 hours in the saddle and I would be tired and sore by the end of the trip. But sometimes the journey can be as important as the destination. I was young and recovered quickly from this form of self-inflicted abuse.

I'm describing this ride from the distance of 40 years and Ms. Pierson's "wet cement" of my consciousness set very long ago, leaving these impressions. I got up before daylight that Friday morning, eager to get on the road. I showered, shaved, dressed, made and ate breakfast, packed some clothes, an apple and a sandwich into my tank bag, grabbed my jacket, helmet and gloves, and was on the road about 20 minutes before sunrise.

While I rode west over the Richmond-San Rafael Bridge, the sun popped up in my mirrors and everything in front of me glowed in the morning light. The bay below was calm and Marin County looked inviting—in the early morning light the sun-dried, brown grasses on the low hillsides actually did look golden. I merged onto Highway 101 in San Rafael and headed north.

As I rode north the environment changed, but so slowly it was easy to miss. At Benbow the highway started playing with the Eel River, crossing and re-crossing as it followed the waterway north. In a few more miles the environment had become moist enough to support the giant redwood trees. They were *not* easy to miss. The trees are majestic and it felt like I was in a cathedral as I rode among them. I rode slower than usual, looking around and up.

I was nearly to Fortuna, passing through some low hills, when the west hills flattened and I could smell the ocean. The Pacific was 10 miles to the west and not visible, but the land between was level farmland. There was a slight on-shore breeze and the air held the pungent salty odor of the sea as I rode into Fortuna to stretch my legs, eat my lunch, and get gas.

Fueled and fed, I turned my back to the ocean, and the air soon lost its salty tang. Highway 36 went east through the Van Duzen River valley for several miles. The valley floor was farmland, but the foothills ahead were forested. The river meanders through a wide, flat valley and the road meanders with it, nice lazy flowing curves. My speed was moderate and I was practicing the classic turning technique I had read about in a motorcycle magazine: start near the outside edge, slow as necessary, lean into the turn trying to touch the road's centerline at the exact middle (the apex) of the curve, then return to upright while accelerating gently, ending up near the outside again at the end of the curve. When I got it right, it was a very smooth flowing process, very satisfying. When I got it wrong, mid-course corrections were needed: slowing to avoid running off the road, or changing direction slightly because I misjudged the turn's radius. These adjustments in the middle of the turn spoiled the smoothness and made me feel klutzy. I was dancing, really, dancing with the road. With the large-radius turns and my moderate speeds, it became a kind of waltz. I could be very graceful, making smooth, swooping paths along the pavement, or I could figuratively trip on my own feet. Like any other dance, it takes practice.

After 15 miles on Highway 36, I was in the forest. This section of the road runs through very lush vegetation–tall redwoods, alders, maples, and firs with a thick fern understory, the products of abundant moisture from rain and frequent ocean fog. The air smelled green, fecund. The forest was dense and trees came right down to the road's edge. I found myself humming the Byrds song "Wasn't Born to Follow." It has a nice, rolling rhythm that goes well with the thrum of turning cycle wheels.

The valley was getting narrower and the road was starting its climb into the foothills, but still followed the river and still had those nice, waltzing large-radius curves. About then my dance practice was rudely interrupted. I was leaning into a left turn with my Honda's wheels on my own side of the road, but with my head about even with the centerline. The trees blocked my view around the corner, and as I rounded the turn, I found myself staring directly into the grille of a logging truck that was straddling the road's centerline. *Yow!* Instinctively, I jerked the bike upright, missed the truck, and found myself hurtling through gravel, desperately struggling for control at 45 mph. I was trying to slow down, but I locked up the front wheel and the bike started to tip–I had to release the front brake and kick the ground with my boot to stay upright. After a couple of scary near falls, I was able to stop, using the rear brake, just before the gravel ended and the shoulder reverted to trees and shrubs.

I was shaking so hard I had trouble getting the bike's side-stand out. The shot of adrenaline I got when I saw that truck was starting to fade and my legs felt like jelly. I finally got the side-stand out and slid off the bike to sit on the ground. I felt a short moment of relief, quickly replaced by anger. That damn truck driver ran me off the road! For a moment I considered chasing him down and giving him a piece of my mind, but sanity prevailed. He was in a loaded logging truck and I was on a motorcycle. What could I do to him?

As the anger faded it was replaced by a sense of astonishment as I reflected on what had happened. By pulling the bike upright to keep from becoming a Peterbilt hood ornament, I had missed the truck, but it meant I was going straight while the road continued to turn left. I ran off the right edge of the pavement. There was a rare graveled pull-out at this turn; if not I would have been dodging trees and brush instead of struggling for control in the gravel. I definitely preferred the gravel.

In a period of approximately five minutes, I went from terror to panic to relief to anger to astonishment and finally back to relief, with all my dials pegged to their max. Until my heart rate returned to normal, I sat staring at my tire and boot tracks in the gravel and thinking how lucky I was.

On hearing this story some have suggested that I was being reckless by riding with my head near the centerline. In my defense I point out that there would have been no problem if the truck had been on its own side of the road—it would have taken a small adjustment to avoid it. That being said, I *did* change my riding style to avoid any recurrence of that type of problem. For the rest of the dance I stayed on the outside part of my lane until I could see *all* the way through the corner, and then aimed for the apex while opening the throttle. I found out years later that this technique actually has a name: "late apex" or "late entry." Using this approach on the blind turns allowed me to finish my trip safely, and I was able to re-focus on the aspects of travel by motorcycle that make it so pleasant.

Thinking back on this very close call from a more, um, *mature* perspective, I imagine if I had been in my 40s when this happened I might have considered giving up street riding. But I was 20 and still felt immortal, as 20-year-olds often do, and the logging truck became yet another experience woven into the fabric of the trip. In fact, it may have been my first real experience with adrenaline dependence; the first hit was free. Who knew I would eventually become fully addicted?

In a few more miles the valley narrowed and the river became hemmed in by the foothills, no longer meandering. The curves were slightly tighter and more frequent, and the waltz became more like a foxtrot. As the road left the fog zone behind, redwoods gave way to dense stands of mixed firs and deciduous trees and the understory became scattered shrubs and grass. Instead of following the river, the road started its climb into the coast range, gradually at first.

Just past the village of Bridgeville, the road started a steep climb. Highway 36 was no longer a river road but a serious mountain road and I needed to stop admiring the beauty of the forest and focus fiercely on the pavement. We weren't foxtrotting anymore; it was more like a quick two-step. The road climbed up the side of a mountain using linked hairpin turns (switchbacks) to gain elevation rapidly. The first few were tight, marked at 10-20 mph. The following curves were not so tight, but there were many of them in quick succession and still steeply uphill. After climbing from 800 to 2,400 feet in just a few miles, the road leveled somewhat and stopped throwing curves at me in such rapid succession; I could relax, catch my breath, and look around. The forest had changed during the rapid ascent. The deciduous trees, the oaks and alders, had faded away leaving a dense coniferous forest, mostly firs with some cedars in the mix.

This requirement for sudden intense focus is not scary or unpleasant, quite the contrary. When the road requires attention in this way, everything else is driven from my mind—there is only my bike, the pavement, and me. Problems at work? Gone. Trouble with my girlfriend? Vanished. The nagging ache between my shoulder blades? What ache? Worries about running out of gas? Forgotten. It is almost a form of meditation.

Highway 36 crossed the Coast Range, but it didn't simply climb to a summit and drop down the other side. It gained and lost elevation, swinging left and right as it wandered eastward through the heavily forested mountains. After entering the Trinity National Forest, the road crossed a ridge, dropped into the Mad River valley, and then climbed steadily to more than 4,000 feet, dropping back down to around 2,000 feet before it climbed again, slowly this time, back above 4,000 feet.

The woods were really beautiful. The trees were dense and I could not see very deeply into the forest, just a thin strip along the roadside. I could easily imagine Bigfoot being able to hide out in the many miles of forested mountains with very little human presence.

The road curved back and forth while dipping up and down, but stayed above 4,000 feet for miles, passing through some very rugged mountains. These were mostly large-radius curves, a few tighter ones marked for 45 mph, connected by short straights. The road and I were waltzing again, with a little bit of quick rhythm thrown in here and there.

After about an hour at this lofty elevation, the road turned left and figuratively dropped off a cliff. I was rapidly losing elevation, facing switchbacks with yawning drop-offs on the outside of the curves. Again my focus snapped sharply onto the road. In a few miles the descent became more gradual and I could pay some attention to the surroundings. The land was now drier, the air warmer, the shrubbery more sparse, and pines had become the dominant tree. The smell of pitch was in the air. I had passed the peak of the Coast Range and was now in its rain shadow. Manzanita and sagebrush began to appear among grasses in the open spaces between the less densely packed pines.

Around 3 p.m. I reached the small town of Platina, where there were a few buildings and a general store/restaurant/gas station. I had been on the road about eight hours total by this time and the break was welcome. I took a seat at the counter and put my helmet next to me. The pie looked good so I asked for a slice and a cup of coffee.

I was the only customer at the counter, and the waitress, a dark-haired woman of indeterminate middle age, chatted with me. "Not many people come through here. Where are you headed?" she asked.

"I'm on my way to Red Bluff, then south to Oroville."

"Do you live in the Eureka area?"

"No, I live near San Francisco."

"Oh. Did you have had some business, or a friend to visit, along the North Coast?"

"No," I replied. "I looked at a map and this road looked like it might be fun."

She paused for a while, apparently mulling this over. "So let me get this straight," she said. "You're riding a motorcycle from San Francisco to Oroville, taking this route, for no particular reason?"

"I guess you could put it that way," I replied, "but it *has* been fun." I neglected to tell her about the logging truck. She gave me a strange look, moved away, and started wiping down tables that were obviously clean.

Sigh. Some people just don't get it.

Refreshed and refueled, I continued east and the road soon made another rapid elevation loss, descending quickly out of the pine forest and into the oak grasslands of the Coast Range's eastern foothills. The terrain was now gently rolling hills instead of rugged mountains; think of an ocean with swells of 10 to 20 feet. When this part of the highway was made, the pavement was poured directly onto the ground; the builders wasted no energy in cutting and filling to level this road. The narrow band of tarmac rolled down into the troughs and up over the peaks, running left and right while bearing mostly east.

I was traveling in four directions now, working rapidly–left, right, up, shifting my weight in the saddle, down, left again, pressing down on the outside foot peg, up, then down and right at the same time, levering the handlebars to force the bike to change direction quickly. This was no waltz, the road and I were jitterbugging and my partner was an expert, throwing new and different steps at me to see how I would respond. I hustled to keep up, and it went on like that for miles. I was having the most fun of the whole trip, yet I had been on the road for nearly 10 hours. My arms were sore, my butt was hot, and my legs were aching, but my mind was sparkling.

My shadow stretched long in front of me, disappearing and reappearing as the road swung back and forth; I chased it not expecting to catch up. I was almost to Red Bluff when the sun set behind me and the air started

Highway 36 in the eastern Coast Range foothills. Note how the centerline disappears and reappears, each time going in a different direction.

to cool, but not evenly. I felt the coolness, almost a chill, at the bottom of the dips and the day's lingering heat at the peaks.

I stopped in Red Bluff for a late dinner as darkness fell. The remaining hour to Oroville was on mostly straight roads and I was enjoying the afterglow of a great ride. I rode rather sedately, following my headlight beam as it pierced the darkness.

The Girl in the Langlitz

Some women are attracted to men who ride motorcycles. I don't really know the psychology of it, the good girl/bad boy interaction. But that's not the point of this story. The point is that the attraction also works in the other direction.

———

I would see her from time to time at the campus computer center. She was small and cute, holding her helmet under her arm while telling slightly risqué jokes to the center staff. What really caught my attention was her Langlitz motorcycle jacket. Langlitz jackets were the best you could buy–black leather, handmade to measure in Portland, Oregon. The jacket fit her like a glove. She rode a Honda CB350, one model year earlier than mine.

Long story short, we started a relationship. Virginia, also known as VA, was a few years older than me, and had been married and divorced. She claimed she was the wicked divorcée out to debauch young men. At the time I was perfectly willing to be debauched–by her, at least.

Virginia was a bit of a character. She liked motorcycles, sheep, rubber duckys, and telling and hearing off-color jokes. She had a degree in math from Radcliffe and had come west a few years earlier with her now ex-husband. She worked as a computer programmer for the University's Graduate Division, which is why we met in the computer center.

VA rented a nice one-bedroom cabin high in the Berkeley hills, with a great view and lovely deck, but she wanted her own home. She had a good job and made a decent salary but couldn't get a loan.

"You could become pregnant at any time and quit your job," she was told. Bankers didn't give loans to single women in those days. To get a loan she needed a source of income from a "steadily employed" male. That would be me. She invited me be her "tenant" and rent the downstairs room. This satisfied the banker and I liked the idea as well. We moved into a nice house in a good part of Oakland near Lake Temescal. And, yes, I paid rent every month.

Virginia at Sears Point, wearing the noted Langlitz
jacket, leaning on her BMW.

Time to Try Racing

The incident that finally prompted me to go racing is still clear in my
memory. I was taking one of my favorite lunchtime rides through a place
simply called Canyon. As I entered the route that day, I saw a sign saying,
"Warning, Road Closed 1 Mile Ahead." I thought, *OK. I'll ride to where
it's closed then turn around and ride back.*

I was riding slower than usual, watching for the closure. After well
more than a mile, I had seen nothing and assumed the road had reopened
and they hadn't removed the warning sign yet. I started riding at my
normal too-fast rate. After another mile or so, I rounded a curve and saw
the barricades blocking the road. I just touched the brakes and *bam!* I went
down so fast I didn't have time to blink. I wasn't braking hard as there was
plenty of room to stop before hitting the barrier.

The bike made it through the fall better than I did. The front brake
lever was broken but still usable and the right-side turn signals were
scraped. I ripped my jeans and got some nasty road rash on my right knee.
It hurt a lot.

Looking around at the site, I saw that drivers had rounded the same corner, spotted the barricade, and made a U-turn. They used the shoulder of the narrow road to make their turn and some roadside gravel had been scattered onto the edge of the pavement, right where I applied the brakes. The front wheel locked up because of the gravel.

On the way home, nursing my cut-up knee, I thought things over. I'd had a few close calls and a couple of slow speed tip-overs, but this was the first time it really hurt. I decided to take my desire to speed to the track, where I wouldn't have to worry about gravel, oil, police, dogs, cars, etc. Tracks were safer than the street.

Virginia and I joined the local racing club, the American Federation of Motorcyclists (AFM), which had just started running races at Sears Point Raceway near Sonoma. I began planning what to race.

The Canyon crash was one of the last adventures with the 350. It was time to move up, and this time my passion and logic really had to fight it out. I thought the Norton Commando was the best looking bike in the world, but going from 350cc to 750cc was a concern. Also there were tales of unreliability, oil leaks, and poor quality Lucas electrics. It was a tough battle, but in the end logic prevailed and I bought a new 1972 Honda CB450. I didn't ride the 450 as much since I was spending lots of time racing and preparing to race. It did get ridden—I have a photo somewhere of the odometer with 10,008 miles on it.

CHAPTER TWO

Taking It to the Track

When I started racing, I had a simple agenda. I wanted to ride quickly without having to worry about street hazards, and I wanted to learn more about tuning and maintaining a motorcycle. There was no grand plan, no intention of making a name for myself or collecting trophies for the mantel. I still had a "follower" mindset and didn't imagine I'd be winning races, although I wasn't opposed to the idea of competing. I stuck pretty close to this agenda for my first three years of racing before circumstances stepped in and things changed.

I wanted to start racing in one of the small-displacement production classes, which were for slightly modified street bikes. Choosing to race a 250cc Ducati Diana in 1972 was, admittedly, an odd choice. It would have been a good choice in 1966, but in 1972 there were many better options. My reasons for selecting the little 250cc Ducati have more to do with my own biases than anything rational. I thought the Diana would be easy to work on.

I found a Diana for sale that looked dirty and pretty tired, but it started and had all its parts. The first teardown was pretty interesting. The inside of the bike matched the outside—it was very worn and dirty. I had fun during the winter of 1972-1973 tearing the bike apart, inspecting everything, and creating a shopping list of parts. Making the parts list was easy, but finding them was a challenge. Ducati had introduced its 750 GT twin to the U.S. in 1972, and the smaller single-cylinder models were being phased out. Finding a good parts source was a continuing problem, but I did get the bike running by the beginning of the racing season.

First racing photo. I'm not that big; the Diana was small even for a 250cc bike.
VA

How *Not* to Start Racing

The photo shows me in 1973 in my original racing gear on the Ducati Diana. This is a very good example of a disaster waiting to happen. When I first started racing, I tried to be, um, thrifty. It was actually more than thrift. I was, frankly, a cheapskate.

I got a black leather jacket designed for street riding that had no padding; a proper race jacket would be padded at the elbows and shoulders. A friend using a blue jeans pattern intended for denim made blue leather pants, without the padding that would be at the knees, shins, and hips of proper racing pants. On my feet were street shoes with duct tape covering the laces so they didn't catch on the foot controls. My gloves were street gloves that offered adequate protection, but were rather thick and didn't provide good feel. The only smart piece of race gear in this photo was a decent, Snell-approved full-coverage helmet.

Continuing the theme of cheap were the tires. Instead of good racing tires from a reputable dealer, I ordered "racing" tires from a mail order catalog. The rest of the bike was OK considering it was some six years old at the time.

Looking back at it now, it's amazing the club allowed me to race like this. It certainly wouldn't happen today.

First Time on the Track

My first 250cc practice at Sears Point International Raceway (now Sonoma Raceway) was, in a word, terrifying. I didn't know which way the track went and I kept finding myself in the wrong spot or at the wrong speed, or both. The track was hilly and there were many blind corners. The racers who raced here the year before were zipping past me at a remarkable speeds. I tried to keep up, but I wasn't good enough.

After that initial practice session, I realized that the first thing I needed to do was learn the track. For the second practice I used the late-apex technique I learned from that logging truck incident on Highway 36 a couple of years earlier. I would start a turn on its outside edge and stay there until I could see which way the track went. Only then would I aim for the apex and start opening the throttle. More experienced racers were still zipping by me on both sides, but I kept reminding myself that I wasn't racing, I was learning the track. By the end of the second practice session, I had a pretty good idea which way to turn.

The next thing was to find a fast path through the turns. Racers call this path a "line," as if the tires were ink rollers drawing an actual line on the pavement. Most corners have very few fast lines, sometimes only one, and a racing skill is the ability to find a fast line. During my first race I resisted the urge to try to keep up with the others and started looking for the good lines. I figured out a few things. Sears Point has a series of linked turns called the esses. If I tried to take the first turn fast, I would end up at the wrong place to negotiate the next turn, and I had to slow down there to go fast. Other racers were still zipping past me, but I tried to ignore them. I don't remember where I finished, but I may have been last in the 250 Production class.

At my second race I continued to use the practice sessions and the race to try out different lines through the turns. I remember trying an inside line the Carousel turn, finding a series of vicious bumps and thinking, *This isn't going to work.* Before the race finished I crashed in turn 11, but I had enough track time to figure out a few things. For a number of corners the late apex worked pretty well. Eventually I found a decent line around the track, at least for the 250cc Ducati Diana I was riding at the time.

Racing and Tumbling

It was strange waking up after being knocked out. When I wake up after sleeping, even a short nap, I know some time has passed. I didn't sense the passage of time while unconscious so I found myself suddenly surrounded by people who seemed to have materialized out of thin air. My senses were telling me something impossible had happened. It took a few moments to realize I must have been out for a while.

————

When I started racing, there was a shallow pothole in Sears' turn 11, the slow hairpin near the pits. I hit the pothole and the front tire lost traction and I crashed. As I watched the bike sliding away from me, I remember thinking, *I've got to get to the ignition key and shut it off.* The very next thing I knew I was being picked up by the ambulance crew.

"You guys got here fast," I said. I was a little disoriented.

The paramedic said, "Yeah, we've been watching you."

What? Did I look so bad that the ambulance crew knew I was going to crash? I felt insulted but held my tongue. It turns out that wasn't what he meant. When I crashed, the rider behind me hit me and knocked me out cold. A witness said I laid motionless on the track. The ambulance was parked where the crew could see turn 11 and they saw the crash and my

The Ducati Diana and I in turn 11 at Sears Point.

motionless body and started rolling even before they got the word from the race director.

It was a slow speed tip-over and normally I would have rolled along the pavement until I stopped. Being unconscious, I slid instead of rolling, and my cheap leather pants tore open at the knee. I lost some skin and picked up some gravel, not really a fair trade. One of my duct-taped shoes came off and I had bruised my big toe. They took me to the hospital where the doc shot my knee full of Novocain and took a hemostat and started plucking pebbles out. Ironically it was the same knee I damaged that day in Canyon when I decided to go racing.

The main cause of the injury was my penny pinching. The cheap mail-order tires I bought didn't grip very well. Except for my helmet, my gear was outrageously inadequate. Proper racing leathers would not have opened at the knee. Proper racing boots would not have come off. I vowed to stop racing until I was able to afford decent leathers, boots and gloves, and real racing tires.

While my knee healed, I did find roadrace leathers, a decent used set from an ex-racer that fit me well enough and didn't break my wallet. I bought some new boots and gloves—no more duct tape covering the laces—and got some new Dunlop KR proper road racing tires. After putting good tires on the Diana, I was able to actually finish some races and started to figure things out and go a little faster. This would have happened sooner and with a lot less pain if I had just spent the money in the beginning.

Racing and Relationships

Racing takes time, sometimes *lots* of time. It becomes your mistress, stealing not only time, but also attention and passion away from your partner. Many of the racers I knew had girlfriends or wives who were part of the crew; scoring, recording lap times, even doing mechanical work. It was rare for a racer to have a girlfriend or spouse who wasn't interested in the racing and few of those relationships seemed to last.

I'm a real dim bulb sometimes. Soon after VA and I moved to her new house in Oakland, I started building the 350cc Desmo GP racer described in the next chapter. On a typical day we would come home from our day jobs, fix and eat dinner together, then chat for a bit. I would then say, "I'm going to go work on the bike," and disappear into the garage, emerging in time to wash up and go to bed. Virginia didn't say anything at the time, but told me later that this wasn't quite what she expected when she invited me to live with her.

Because the conversion of the 350 Desmo was so much work, I spent more time with my "mistress" than average. Virginia, however, wasn't the type to settle for helping with scoring or taking lap times. She bought her own bike, a Yamaha RD125, and started racing in the 125cc Production class. "I'm going to go work on the bike," became, "Let's go work on our bikes," and we spent many evenings together in the garage. She was a competent mechanic, so sometimes we'd just work on our own racers, or I'd help her with the Yamaha, or she would help me with the Ducati. We made a good team and I remember it as a happy time in my life.

CHAPTER THREE

Learning the Craft

Toward the end of my first year of racing, I concluded that riding the Ducati Diana for another year was pointless. In spite of my outstanding lack of success with the Diana, I wasn't turned off on racing. I was able to satisfy both items on my original agenda, but I wanted to improve and expand on the second item —working on motorbikes. I needed a new race bike. With the new motorcycle I was able to learn about fiberglass fabrication, automotive painting, and oxy-acetylene welding in the next two years. I also became a much better racer, but that was a side effect.

Instead of getting a current model to run in a Production class, I decided to shift into the Grand Prix classes. The GP classes were for bikes that were produced as race bikes and for street bikes so heavily modified they were no longer legal on the street. There were several GP classes, based on engine displacement, and this gave me the opportunity to learn new skills.

During the winter of 1973–1974, I bought a 1968 Ducati 350cc Mark3D and converted it into a GP-style race bike. Why did I stick with Ducati? I was intrigued by the idea of a desmodromic valve system where the valves are closed mechanically instead of by springs, and I wanted a project that would let me learn some new skills.

The first year I made a lot of changes to the 350's chassis, taking a lot of weight off the bike. I made a light fiberglass fuel tank and a fiberglass racing seat. The seat was good, but the tank was really ugly. I also added a disc front brake and a Ceriani racing fork. I left the engine alone except for fitting a more free-flowing carburetor and exhaust system. The result was a quick (on takeoff), but slow motorcycle that was reliable, lightweight, sounded good, and handled very well. Making the bike very light and adding free-flowing intake and exhaust systems allowed it to accelerate well, and the disc brake slowed the bike quickly. Top speed was not good, but it was fast enough for my skills at the time. The little Desmo turned well and was very stable both in the corners and through the few straight stretches of Sears Point. It finished every race I entered in the 1974 racing season with no crashes.

Although I didn't change the engine much for 1974, during the racing season I was asking about modifications. There was a lot of knowledge about what had worked in the past. I started making a list of upgrades to make over the winter of 1974-1975.

The riding position on my GP bike was very different than on a normal street bike. From the seat there was a long reach to the low clip-on handlebars, so called because they attached directly to the front fork tubes. It left my elbows only slightly bent. The footpegs and foot controls were set higher and more to the rear than their street bike positions, and were called rear-sets. They positioned my feet fairly close to my backside, putting a tight bend in my knees. It was a position that would have been quickly painful on the street, but it allowed me to tuck in tight behind the fairing, making the bike and me more aerodynamic. It also made it easy to lift my weight off my rear and onto my feet, which was important when the track was bumpy.

The main competition in the 350cc GP class was the TZ350 Yamaha, a purpose-built race bike that handled well and had an amazing top speed. My Ducati handled better, but had nowhere near the top speed of the Yamahas. I couldn't even keep up with the smaller TZ250s over a full lap. There were two areas where the TZs dramatically pulled away from me, across the start/finish line area, and the stretch between turns 6 and 7. Against much faster machines, I had to work on keeping up a high corner speed. As I improved as a rider, I was able to keep up with them in the twisty parts of the track, where stability and the ability to turn quickly and precisely mattered more than speed, but there wasn't much I could do about their superior horsepower on the straights. I was becoming a better racer, but nobody noticed, as my finishing positions were always downfield.

A Visit to *Cycle*

While I was asking people about alterations to the 350 Desmo, Phil Schilling's name kept popping up in conversation: "You should ask Phil Schilling," people would say, or "Schilling would know." As the assistant editor at *Cycle Magazine,* I figured he would have little

The 350 Desmo in turn 2 at Sears Point. I had read how Mike Hailwood used his toes as lean sensors. I copied him. *Mush Emmons*

time to help out an unknown club racer, but I mailed some questions to him anyway. He answered promptly and we began a semi-regular correspondence. He invited me to stop by the *Cycle* office if I was ever near Westlake Village in Southern California.

Early in the 1975 race season I took a couple of days off work and traveled to Southern California to meet Phil. I took my Desmo racer's cylinder head with me hoping he could show me how to get a bit more horsepower out of it. We took it into the *Cycle* workshop and Phil began unscrewing the valve cover's bolts. "I wish I had a nickel for every time I've done this," he said with a chuckle. "I'd be a rich man."

Phil was an average-size guy, with brown hair cut slightly shaggy and heavy-framed glasses. I thought he looked rather bookish. His voice had a slight nasal quality and he was a bit of a slow talker as well. He was wearing a white T-shirt and blue jeans and both were spotless.

While Phil was undoing the valve covers, I took a look around. There were several work areas, each equipped with a full set of quality tools. There was a motor disassembled on one workbench. At the far end of the shop were a number of motorcycles. Some were new models probably there for testing–shiny new street bikes, dirt bikes, and dual-purpose bikes. Some were older models, most likely bikes owned by the staff.

Phil told me I was on the right track concerning the Desmo head. He said I needed to do some work with the intake port, but he liked the other modifications I had done. He warned me about certain maintenance requirements of some items that wore during operation. We chatted a bit about this and that. I whined about how hard it was to get Ducati singles parts, especially racing parts. He mentioned Vic Camp in England, whom I knew about. He also told me about Richard White, a Ducati dealer in Canada who might be able to help, and gave me White's phone number before I left.

I was introduced to Cook Neilson, *Cycle's* editor, during this visit. Cook was slender, very blond, and awfully young to be running the largest-circulation motorcycle magazine in the country. He was sitting at a large desk and we talked about his experiences racing one of the new twin-cylinder Ducatis, a GT750. As we chatted, people kept coming in with publication questions. Cook took a glance, made a quick decision, and returned his focus to me. A guy brought in a photo of the new Honda 550cc four-cylinder motorcycle, Cook looked at it, and said, "Too much red. Rebalance the colors." Others showed him sample page paste-ups for the magazine. "Make the lead photo three columns wide and at the top left," or "Yes, that's perfect." He was clearly in charge and at ease with it. He could have easily said to me, "I'm kind of busy right now," but he was happy to talk to me for a while.

Phil, Cook, and I kept in touch from then on. I would sometimes see them at the club races in Southern California. Phil and Cook were racing a Ducati GT750 in 1974, Cook riding and Phil tuning. Phil was a great source of information about the singles and was becoming a Ducati twin expert as well. A good man to know.

Sometimes It Pays to Do the Right Thing

ZDS Motors, in Glendale, California, was the West Coast distributor for Ducati during the time I raced the Ducati singles. By 1973 there weren't many dealers still stocking singles parts in the Bay Area, so I made plans to visit ZDS Motors. I needed parts for the 350 Desmo I was building for the 1974 season. Also, I hoped to establish an account that would allow me to mail order parts directly from them. I got up very early one November Friday morning in 1973 and drove from Oakland to Glendale, arriving about 2:30 in the afternoon.

When I walked through the front door, I was in a large empty room finished in a South Seas island motif, with lots of bamboo and artificial palm trees along the walls. It was *not* what I expected. Was I in the right place? It must have been a Polynesian-themed restaurant at some time in the past. There was an opening in the back wall with a counter where I found the parts department and I asked for the various things I wanted. The parts guy pulled out a medium-size cardboard box with a bunch of crumpled newsprint in the bottom and filled my order, adding some more newspaper for padding. I asked about setting up a mail order account, but was told they only did that for dealers. Shucks. I paid the man, stuck the box in the back of the van, then spent the weekend with some friends in Costa Mesa.

At home a few days later, I unpacked the box and started to toss it out, but it felt too heavy. In the newsprint in the bottom of the box were eight metal rods, about 10 inches long and an inch in diameter with splines on each end. I wrote a letter back to ZDS telling them what I had found and asking if they wanted me to ship the rods back or toss them out. A packet arrived shortly with a letter, a check for $5 to cover shipping, a Ducati singles parts book, and a list of parts with dealer prices. In the letter they said the rods were Moto Guzzi driveshafts. The ZDS folks had been looking all over for them, and yes, please send them back–they were worth well over $1,000! That's in 1973 dollars, mind you. The letter finished with this:

"In the future, when you need parts for your Ducati, please write directly to me and I will see to it that you receive a dealer discount on them. It is truly a pleasure to receive a letter like yours and know that you cared enough to inform us about the parts and return them."

Score!

I sent the driveshafts back and told them I would take them up on their offer, but as I was racing a Ducati, they might be sorry they ever made it. They stayed true to their word, however, and I bought many parts from them at dealer cost during the 1974 and 1975 racing seasons.

The Desmo 350 Racer 1975

Between the 1974 and 1975 racing seasons I made one change to the chassis. I rerplaced the ugly fiberglass fuel tank with a nice looking fiber-glass fuel tank. I made a bunch of changes to the engine. The work really pepped up the motor. Both top speed and acceleration were improved, but reliability was compromised, as we shall see. Top speed was still nowhere

The 350 Desmo race bike at Riverside Raceway's esses.

near that of the TZ350 or TZ250 Yamahas, but it was very good for a 350cc, four-stroke single.

The 1975 season started out well as I finished all the early season races with no crashes. As my racing skills continued to improve, I took the 350 to Southern California and raced in an AFM event at Riverside, a high-speed track where my bike was at even more of a disadvantage than at Sears Point, but it was actually competitive on certain twisty sections of the track. I got clobbered on the straights, but I still enjoyed myself.

Retiring the 350 Desmo Racer

The mid-winter changes to the 350 Desmo were good, but I wanted to get some more horsepower, so I made a couple of changes in the middle of the 1975 racing season. They both caused problems; one was solvable with reasonable effort, but the other wasn't.

One of the approved modifications for racing singles was a high-compression piston. In spite of the bike's age some aftermarket piston makers still had a Ducati piston in their catalogs, and midway through the 1975 season I bought one from Arias. It came complete with rings, wrist pin, and wrist pin clips. To a gearhead like myself, it was a beautiful piece of machining.

I took a stock cylinder and the piston to my local machine shop and asked them to bore the cylinder to the tolerances listed in the Ducati shop manual. I got it back and assembled the motor in time for a race at Sears Point.

I took it easy during the morning practices to give the rings a chance to seat properly and checked the spark plug to see if any jetting changes were needed. Everything was going along nicely so I upped the speed a bit in the actual race. I was running past the start line on full throttle when the motor suddenly stopped—the rear wheel locked up and started sliding to the right. I quickly pulled in the clutch lever and the bike straightened out. I couldn't believe it. The motor had seized! Somehow I had managed to make my modest-horsepower four-stroke single act just like a high-horsepower two-stroke that had been jetted too lean.

Monday I called Arias and told them what happened. The guy asked me what cylinder-to-piston clearance I had used. I said I used the standard clearance Ducati specifies, which was 0.004 to 0.005 inch.

"Well, there's your problem," he says. "That's a forged racing piston; you need at least nine thou clearance."

"Huh? The stock Ducati piston is a forged piston and it only needs 4 thousandths," I replied.

"That's not enough clearance for our piston," he said. "They must be using some low-expansion alloy or something."

"Why didn't you send some set-up specifications with the piston? There was nothing telling me what clearance the piston needed."

"We figured you knew what you were doing," he said.

How do you answer something like that? Apparently, I didn't know what I was doing. I assumed the Arias piston would use the same clearances as the Ducati piston, or they would have told me what clearance to use. I was able to salvage the piston and successfully used it again with no trouble after boring the cylinder to the Arias piston clearance specification.

Connecting Rod Failure

It was known that over-revving the Ducati 350cc motor could lead to damage to the connecting rod and/or big-end bearing. Yes, it happened to me, as the photo on the next page shows. I honestly don't remember the incident, but I can't argue with photographic evidence. It happened toward the end of the 1975 season.

The broken connecting rod. *VA*

The approved fix for this was to replace the Ducati rod with a high-quality Carillo rod, so I sent Carillo some money and a brand-new 350 Ducati connecting rod, and asked them to make one to match. They did, and the new rod looked great. I took the rod, a new big-end bearing, and a good crankshaft to my favorite machine shop and had them install the rod. I was pretty excited about my new Carillo rod, so I took the 350 Desmo to the next AFM race, which was at Ontario Motor Speedway (OMS) in Ontario, California. This was my first time at Ontario. It was an experience.

I had quite a bit of trouble learning the track. There were 20 numbered turns, and there were two sets of left-hand sweepers that were nearly identical. I kept getting them mixed up. Then I made an important discovery—I could look ahead and see what the next couple of turns were. The track didn't disappear around a corner or over a rise like it did at Sears. I could actually see what was next. I started looking ahead and my riding smoothed out and my lap times dropped. Racing at OMS taught me something I couldn't learn at Sears Point.

The 350 Desmo wasn't really suitable for Ontario. Two long straights meant the faster TZ350s in my class disappeared quickly. There wasn't enough curvy track for me to make up the lost time. But I wanted to see how the new rod worked. The answer was it didn't.

At some point early in the second practice, the motor began making some very loud knocking noises and started running badly. I shut it off and got a ride back to the pits in the rescue truck.

I pulled the head and cylinder from the crankcase. There was a *lot* of movement at the rod's big end–bad news. The top of the piston had been hitting the valves–more bad news. I pulled the crankcase drain plug partially out and let some engine oil drain into a catch pan. There were lots of tiny silver pieces of metal in the oil–*really* bad news. The valves were bent from contact with the piston, and the camshaft and the rocker arms would need careful examination. I was done for the day, as the motor needed to be split and the crankshaft taken out and examined. All the top-end pieces, and there are many pieces in a Desmo top end, would need to be inspected.

The shop pressed the crank apart and we found the Carillo rod no longer had a smooth, round hole at the big end–it had been seriously chewed up by the big-end roller bearing. There were metal shavings from the rod in the engine oil and those shavings had been pumped throughout the motor. It was a complete mess. Every bearing would have to be cleaned and examined, and probably replaced. All the oil galleys would need to be flushed.

I called Carillo and I described the situation to the guy on the phone in some detail. Finally he asks, "What sort of bearing inserts are you using?"

"Inserts? The Ducati singles use caged roller bearings at the big-end," I replied.

"Oh," he said. "That rod is for a plain bearing. It needs a hardened steel insert to work with a roller bearing."

"What? The Ducati rod I sent for you to copy didn't have an insert."

"It must have been hardened by some process. I guess we never checked."

I'm getting a little peeved at this point. "*All* Ducati singles have a roller bearing at the big end. You guys ought to know that. You've made rods for Ducatis in the past. Why didn't you send installation instructions with the rod? Or ask me about the application? I gave you my phone number."

"We thought you knew what you were doing," he replied.

Oh crap. I've been here before. *I thought you guys knew what you were doing popped* into my mind, but I held my tongue.

"I tell you what," he said, "send me the rod back and I'll put an insert in, no charge."

"It's not just the rod at this point," I told him. Then I described what happened, the shape the motor was in, and what it would take to fix it. He refused to take any responsibility for the other problems the rod had caused. The conversation went on for a while, but in the end his offer to put the insert in the rod was the only one he made.

I sent the damaged rod back and it returned with a hardened steel ring inside the big end. There was no other damage I could see, but when it was pressed into a crankshaft, it just lightly brushed the crankshaft's left counterbalance cheek when I spun it. The rod was ever-so-slightly bent. I never did use it again.

A Eulogy

It was time to stop racing the 350 Desmo. I had developed it about as far as reasonable and further attempts to get more power from the motor would clearly be at the expense of reliability.

I had raced the bike for two seasons, from 1974 through most of 1975. It was never going to challenge the faster bikes in the class, but I learned a lot while building it, had fun racing it, and I grew quite fond of the bike. It was very reliable for a year and a half and I started to develop some skill riding it. My finishing positions were always downfield so no one noticed, but I could tell I was getting better. During the time I raced the bike, I never crashed it.

Racing against much faster bikes forced me to focus on cornering. Keeping up a high corner speed was crucial to getting decent lap times. I didn't set any records or turn any heads with the 350 Desmo, but I became a better racer.

CHAPTER FOUR

Meanwhile, Back on the Streets

I didn't stop riding bikes on the street when I started racing, but two things happened. One, my street speed slowed, which was the intention. Two, I did ride less as racing and preparing for racing started taking up more and more of my spare time. There were some interesting things happening outside of racing, however.

——————

I didn't really want a Ducati 750 Sport. After two years with the Honda CB450, I was ready for a new street bike. When I saw photos of the 1974 Ducati 350 Desmo single, I wanted one of those, bad. Logically it was *not* a good choice, but, man, it looked so good! The little ochre bike looked to me like a nearly perfect motorcycle. To my dismay none of the Desmo singles were available in the U.S. I decided to settle for a 750 Sport instead, a much larger two-cylinder bike. It was also a beautiful motorcycle, with the same bright yellow-orange bodywork, but I wasn't sure about the motor's gangly look. It was a 90-degree V-twin, with one cylinder pointing up and one cylinder pointing forward, making the motor rather long

I knew that some of the staff at *Cycle* had bought Ducati twins. These guys got to test ride every new bike that came out and they were spending their money to purchase Ducati 750s. Reviews in other motorcycle magazines were quite positive. There had to be something special about these bikes, so I decided to get the Sport in spite of my reservations.

I picked it up in February 1975. I was nervous because I had never ridden a bike that big and powerful. In those days 750cc motorcycles were the *big* bikes. It was also raining just a little, enough to make the streets slightly damp. Not a good combination for riding a large, unfamiliar motorcycle. I bought the Sport in Berkeley and had to ride the bike east on busy Ashby Avenue a few miles to highway I-580 to home. On a completely new, powerful motorcycle, I needed to deal with new bike issues, such as a different shift pattern on the other foot, traffic, and wet streets to boot. Ugh.

The east end of Ashby Avenue enters the Berkeley hills, becomes Tunnel Road, and gets quite curvy. At the end of this curvy part, the road splits and the right fork leads to an on-ramp to the freeway. It had a set of awful ripples–the summer heat and the cars accelerating had really wrinkled up the pavement. This turn upset my Hondas something fierce. I would point the Honda in the desired general direction and make mid-corner corrections as needed to keep on course.

I approached the turn with trepidation, not knowing what would happen on the slightly slick road. I slowed and leaned the Sport into turn. The bike floated through the ripples, keeping *exactly* to the line I had started it on. I distinctly remember thinking, *Oh, so* that's *what all the excitement is about!*

My Sport in street bike trim in the summer of 1975. Note the low-rise handlebar in place of clip-ons.

I'm not kidding. It took one turn, one particular turn, for me to realize how good the Ducati was. It was *way* ahead of the Hondas in handling. I fell in love with the Sport on the exit of that corner and my concerns about making the purchase disappeared.

Younger riders can't appreciate this. Virtually every sport bike today has excellent handling in stock form. That wasn't the case in 1974. Even though the Honda CB twins were considered good handling bikes at the time, the Ducati was stunningly better.

I did eventually get the Ducati 350 Desmo I lusted for, but that's another story.

Two Notable Rides on the 750 Sport

The Ducati Sport soon became my everyday street bike. It was good on my commute and really good on some of my short lunchtime or weekend rides through the East Bay Hills. It wasn't so good in town. It was flashy and loud and attracted a lot of attention, sometimes not the kind of attention I wanted. Still I did have some interesting rides on it.

The Sport Is Not a Touring Bike

One of the first rides I took on the Sport was to San Simeon with Virginia to take a look at Hearst Castle. I knew the Sport was not a touring bike (the Sport is a sport bike, duh), but I thought there would be enough curvy parts of the coast highway to make it tolerable. The northern part of the trip was good, especially through the Big Sur area. As we went farther south, there were more and more straight sections and I began to feel pain in my back, right between the shoulder blades, and in my wrists. As the hours built up, the pain increased correspondingly. By the time we got to Cambria, I parked the Ducati at the motel and rode to dinner on the back of Virginia's BMW.

I somehow survived the trip home. I replaced the very racy clip-on handlebars with a slightly racy set of low-rise handlebars. They raised the position of my hands about 3 inches and it made all the difference in comfort. No other changes were necessary.

The Caldecott Tunnel Stall

The Sport had the turn-signal switch on the right handle bar, along with the horn button and the engine shut-off switch. Japanese bikes had the turn signal control on the left handle bar. I was riding the Sport to work one morning and had just entered the Caldecott Tunnel heading east. I switched over into the right-hand lane and the motor died.

This was a long, busy freeway tunnel with two lanes of traffic and *no shoulder*. There was a narrow raised catwalk on the right side and I was standing on the catwalk trying to kick-start the bike back to life as the freeway traffic bore down on me. The catwalk was preventing me from getting a full swing on the kick-start lever, which was also on the right side. A truck driver blew his air horn at me, as if I wasn't already doing everything I could. Bastard. I got this terrifying image of everything going up in a huge fireball when I noticed the white Gen indicator light wasn't lit. I looked at the engine stop switch and saw it had been flipped! I flipped the switch back and the bike fired on the very next half-kick. I used the Sport's considerable acceleration to *quickly* get out of that tunnel and took the next exit.

Once off the freeway I stopped to figure out what had happened. Apparently when I switched the turn signal off after the lane change, the thick leather on my glove's thumb also hit the engine stop switch. After that, I took the turn signals off and a bit later I replaced the control sets with more conventional, Japanese-style switch gear.

Getting the Sportling

Phil Schilling gave me the phone number of a Ducati dealer in Canada named Richard White. Phil thought White might have some go-fast parts for my 350 Desmo racer. I called Mr. White at his shop in Quebec and we talked about oversized valves, high-compression pistons, big-bore kits, and so on. At some point in the discussion, I told him I had a 750 Sport as a street bike even though my dream bike was the 350 Desmo single, which was not available in the U.S. Then I heard him say these magic words:

"I can sell you one."

Logic and passion went at it again. Logic said, "You already have a semi-exotic street bike and you don't need a second one." Passion said, "I don't care, I want *that* motorcycle!" Passion pinned logic to the mat in about three seconds and I said, "Tell me more."

It was expensive, but about three weeks later a large crate arrived. In about an hour I had a beautiful little bright ochre motorcycle on my garage floor. I put oil and gas into the bike, acid in the battery, and kicked it to life. Now I had two yellow-orange Ducatis, a 750 Sport and a 350 Desmo. Life was good.

Some people name their motorcycles, but I normally don't. My Hondas were the 160, the 350, and the 450. The Ducati 750 Sport was called the Sport. I considered calling it the Ochre Duke, but it just didn't

The Sport (left) and the Sportling.

feel right. The exception was the Ducati 350 Desmo. It seemed completely natural to call it the Sportling.

Unfortunately, the first ride on the Sportling was disappointing. The bike didn't handle as well as I expected. My 350 Desmo racer was much better. The Sportling didn't handle badly; there was just a bit of vagueness when cornering I wasn't expecting.

I took a long look at the differences between the Sportling and the 350 Desmo racer, which handled superbly. They were the same frame and basically the same motor. The suspension was also similar. The tires were different. The Sportling came with old-fashioned tires, a rib pattern on the front and what was called a universal tread pattern on the rear. Even though there was plenty of wear left on the original tires, I bought a pair of Dunlop K81s, which were the top choice sporting street tire at the time. I removed the original tires and installed the K81s and took the bike out for a ride.

Ah-hah, now *that's* the way it should work. All it took was different tires to give the Sportling the handling I expected. The bike was cutting through the corners with precision, going exactly where I wanted it to go, and with remarkable stability for such a light motorcycle. I rode home with a big grin on my face.

After the tire swap the Sportling became my main street ride. It was my commuter bike, my shopping bike, and my around town bike. Occasionally I would take the Sport to work, but it was ridden mainly on the weekends when there wasn't a race. For most of the riding I was doing at the time, the Sportling was a better choice than the Sport.

Acquiring the Sportling made the Sport a bit redundant, and it saddened me to see it sitting idle in the garage so much. A solution to that problem popped up later that summer. I had some mechanical problems with the 350 Desmo racer so I prepped the Sport for racing and took it to Ontario Motor Speedway.

CHAPTER FIVE

The 750 Sport Becomes a Race Bike

When I bought the 750 Sport in early 1975, I intended it to be my street bike since I was still racing the 350 Desmo GP bike. Later that year, however, when I got the 1974 350 Desmo street bike through a dealer in Canada, the 350 became my daily rider. The Sport became available for track use.

When I first started racing the Sport, I started a racing journal. It was a good idea, but I only kept at it for a few races as I didn't have the discipline. The journal vanished for many years, but I found it while looking for reference material for the book. Here's the first journal entry from 1975:

> "Took the Sport to OMS just for fun. Put the clip-on handlebars back on. Only other mods were a racing KR76 [tire] on the front and a set of high header pipes. Left the Pirelli MT11 [tire] on the rear, even left the air cleaners on! Bike gave indicated 120 mph before the wind came up (stock gearing). Ontario is a hard track to learn. Got off the track once on 1st lap but no fall. Finished 7th in class out of 14."

Seventh out of 14 is not a very auspicious beginning. Every journey starts with the first step. On the facing page was written:

> "Costs for Ontario: $42 KR76 front tire, $50 headers."

The Sears Point Three-Hour Endurance Race

Toward the end of the 1975 season, the AFM scheduled a three-hour endurance race at Sears Point. It was the Northern California equivalent of the very popular Ontario six-hour endurance race. The club knew better than to try running for six hours at Sears Point, feeling correctly that three hours at Sears was at least as exhausting as six hours at Ontario. The rules were simple: production class bikes, 250cc and bigger, minimum two-person teams, maximum of one hour of racing per turn.

I mentioned to a couple of racing pals I was considering racing the Sport in the three-hour and before I knew it plans materialized. Mush would be my co-rider with Jack and Ted working as pit crew. Mush was a top-five finisher in the very competitive 350 Production class with his RD350 (and a really good action photographer). I was the weaker rider on the team, but I owned the bike.

I bought a Dunlop KR91 long-distance racing tire for the rear and a fresh Dunlop K81 street tire for the front and a new drive chain. We geared for Sears by replacing the 40-tooth rear sprocket with a 42-tooth one. The crew installed all the new parts and tires, checked valve clearances, installed number plates, and declared the bike ready.

During practice Mush said the bike was sliding the rear tire on acceleration, but we didn't think a stickier tire would last the distance. We would have to use the traction control in our right wrists to limit tire spin. The gearing was just right.

Our plan was to each take a one-hour turn and we would fuel the bike at each rider change, and we would split the final hour. The Sport had a 5-gallon gas tank that would give us a full hour of racing. I had the first turn in the race and surprised everyone, even myself, by running with the leaders.

There were three of us up front for the first 30 minutes or so, with me being in third position but close behind two others. My lap times were consistent and quick at the 2-minute, 4.5-second to 2:06 range. At about the half-hour mark I made an attempt to get into second place and over-cooked it going into turn 11, ran wide, and let the first two get away a little bit.

The team saw my error and the next time I came past the pits Ted held up a sign with "HOLD POS!" written on it. That settled me down a bit and I caught back up with the other two but didn't try to get around them.

Somewhere near the 50-minute mark, I tried to lap a slower rider in the turn 7 hairpin by riding around the outside. Traction was poor off line,

Jim (8), myself (71), and Mike (51), early in the three-hour race. Contrasting racing styles in turn 11.

and when I got on the gas, the rear tire spun and I crashed, falling onto the right side. It was a low-speed get-off so I wasn't hurt and the bike was in good shape except for a bent shift lever. I picked up the bike and dashed into the pits where they fueled the bike and straightened the shifter. We lost about one and a half laps during the crash and repair.

My turn was nearly up anyway, so I got off and Mush took over. He flew around the track, laying down laps of 2:03–2:04; his fastest was a 2:02.8. In about 10 laps Mush caught up to the leader; then the next lap he didn't come around. He had crashed unhurt in the fast esses section of the track just as he was about to pass to get back on the same lap as the front runner. The bike had slid tail-first into the hillside and the seat was smashed and the rear sub-frame was bent. We didn't have a spare seat so our race was over after one hour and a few minutes.

When we got the bike back, the problem was obvious—the rear tire was shredded. It was more than half gone after only about an hour of racing. Even if Mush had kept it upright, we would have had a tough time finishing the full three hours.

I was hooked, though, really excited. I liked being competitive for a change. I continued racing the 350 Desmo in the GP class until the disaster with the Carillo rod, but I started making plans to race the Sport in the 750 Production class in 1976.

The 1976 Championship Challenge Begins

When I raced the Sport in the three-hour endurance race near the end of the 1975 race season, something special happened. I was competitive. I discovered I liked being able to run with the leaders. I decided to make the Sport my racer and compete in the 750 Production class, maybe even try for the class championship. I had caught the fever. I wanted to win races.

Still, it was a modest ambition. I really didn't expect to win the club's 750cc Production championship, but I intended to have fun trying. Looking back at this now I think this was an early step toward losing my follower attitude.

———

In 1976 the man to beat in the AFM's 750 Production class was a young San Franciscan named Ed, Eddie to his friends. I had gotten to know Ed when we were both working on the AFM's board of directors and we had become friends. Eddie had raced a Honda CB175 in the 200 Production class in prior years and did really well. In 1976 he was a really good racer on a decently fast CB750 Honda his dad tuned. It was a true family activity as his mom also came to the some of the races. His parents were well known, well liked, and affectionately called Pops and Moms.

Ed and I competed on the track, but we also worked together as club officers and he helped me with my first edition of *The Lap Times*, the club newspaper I edited for three seasons. He was a tiger on the track, but a really nice guy off track, and I was pleased to consider him one of my racing buddies. We both wanted to win the 750 Production class title and we were racing at Sears Point and traveling to Southern California to race at Ontario and Riverside.

I spent the first part of the season playing catch-up as I needed experience with the Sport after several years of racing Ducati singles. Ed's Honda and my Sport were pretty closely matched for speed, but he had considerably more skill than I did. I was earning second- and third-places to Ed's wins, but I was improving and the gap between us was shrinking.

In spite of the competition, we respected each other and wanted to win in a fair fight. One spring race at Ontario, Ed won and I finished third with another Honda CB750 rider in second place. After the race, someone told us the other CB had an 812cc big-bore kit installed, which would make it illegal in the 750 class. Ed and I together went and talked to the rider, explaining we were battling for the class championship and wanted a fair competition between us. We were very polite and said that we weren't going to protest this time, but if the rumors were true and he was running an oversized motor, we would appreciate it if he ran in the Open class. The fellow listened quietly and never admitted his bike was over the 750cc class limit, but at his next race, he ran in the Open class.

Ed Shows Me How

One day at Ontario I was able to hang just behind Eddie for the first half of lap one, up to the turns leading to the back straight. The entry to the straight was a series of fast left-hand sweepers, and the bevel-drive Ducati twins did fast sweepers really well. I was able to pass Ed by going around the outside. I remember thinking, *I hope I don't get in his way too much.* The Ducati held the lead all the way down the back straight, topping out nearly 125 mph.

I reached my brake marker for the rather tight right-hand turn at the end of the straight, sat up, and got on the binders when *whoosh!* Ed zipped past me and went at least 30 feet deeper into the turn before he applied his brakes.

It was one of those moments of enlightenment that happens now and then. I thought, *Oh, so that's how it should be done.* I finished in second place that day.

A rare photo of me leading Ed at Ontario in 1976. Usually the order was reversed. Number 214 is a Triumph Trident. *John Ulrich*

We talked later in the pits. "How did you do that?" he asked.

"Do what?" I replied.

"I'm going through the corner with my rear tire at least 2 inches out of line and you rode around me on the *outside!* That's what."

"Oh," I said, grinning. "The Ducati does fast sweepers really well. By the way, you sure went into turn 10 a lot deeper than I did."

He laughed and said, "You made me feel it was necessary."

My Worst Day

About 25 years later, my future wife asked me a question while we were getting to know each other, "What was the worst day of your life," she asked. By then I was already using the wheelchair and she expected a particular obvious answer. She was surprised when my answer was completely different.

"The day Ed died," I said.

This happened in July 1976, about midway through the racing season. I don't talk about this and I don't like writing about it, but it is part of the story and it would be wrong to omit it. Ed and I were competing for the 750 Production class title and up to that point Ed had won every encounter while I was getting seconds and thirds. I was improving, though, and getting closer and closer to keeping up with him. We had gotten to be pretty good friends, as competitors often do. There was a race at Sears Point and the second Heavyweight Production practice had just started. I was following Ed closely to try to pick up some better lines or braking points. The bikes were still pretty bunched up because we had all left the pits together.

The track does a little left-right wriggle between turns 7 and 8. Ed tried to go around another rider there, but the guy moved to his right, cutting Ed off. I'm sure he never knew Ed was there. Ed went into the grass in the narrow gap between the pavement and the Armco fencing. There was a rock or a curbstone or something hidden in the grass and when Ed hit it the back wheel kicked up and sent him into the air. He came down on the track directly in the path of my front wheel.

There was nothing I could do. I had no time to react.

I stopped at turn 8, dropped my bike on the grass, ripped off my helmet, and started yelling to the corner worker to send an ambulance. Then I ran back uphill toward the accident scene. I got close enough to see that the corner workers were already working on Ed. One of them was giving him mouth-to-mouth resuscitation. That stopped me. I had no real first aid training and would only be in the way.

Of course I was worried sick. After standing in the middle of the track for a while, I went back to my bike, picked it up, and coasted down the hill and into the pits. Word of the accident had already spread through the pits, and Virginia met me with a big hug while I shed some tears. She and I immediately started packing up. We were no longer interested in racing. As I was putting stuff away, I heard the ambulance and looked up to see it leaving the track with lights flashing and siren wailing.

VA and I ran into Pops and Mom at the hospital as they had both been at the races that day. We sat with them as we waited for word from the doctor. After about an hour the doc came out and quietly told Ed's parents that there wasn't much hope. People don't usually recover from the sort of head and neck injuries Ed had suffered, he said. Each word felt like a dagger into my heart.

Ed died the next day, having never regained consciousness.

I was shattered, completely inconsolable. It was then, and still remains, the worst day of my life. I considered giving up racing. If this was the price to pay for the fun, it was not worth it.

There were a lot of people at the funeral. The family was well-known and popular with both the Northern and Southern chapters of the AFM and in the San Francisco Italian community. I met Ed's sister at the funeral. She said it was a good thing that if Ed had to die he went out doing something he loved. She was trying to help me get through the grief, I'm sure, but I didn't agree with her. Why did he have to die? I just nodded my head and kept quiet.

A couple days after the funeral, Ed appeared in a dream. He told me it was OK. He knew it wasn't my fault, and it was time to stop grieving and get on with my life. He also told me I shouldn't stop racing.

"If you love to race, you need to keep at it. I would." Then he said goodbye.

I don't know if it was Ed's spirit in that dream, or if it was my own subconscious telling me what I wanted to hear in a form I could accept. Whichever it was, it worked. I got up that morning, dried my eyes, made my goodbye to Ed, and got on with my life.

I can't say the death of Ed matured me, but I certainly lost any innocence that may have been left from my childhood.

I have a photo of us racing down the main straight at Ontario in front of empty grandstands. It's an eerie photo as it looks like Ed and I are the only two people in the world. In my mind's eye, this is how I see us still, me giving chase and Ed staying in front by just enough. I never did catch up to him.

Ed leading me at Ontario.

The Ducati Sport Wobbles, and Cook Lends a Hand

The 750 Sport was a good race bike. It had decent speed and very good handling. The bike went where I pointed it and was extremely stable, except for one place. Going through the start/finish straight at Riverside, the bike would wallow from side to side. The throttle should be wide open during this stretch and the odd behavior was giving me pause. It happened only at this one spot at Riverside.

The entry onto the start/finish straight was turn 9, a very wide, fast sweeping right turn of more than 180 degrees. The turn was slightly banked and had an intimidating solid steel wall on the outside, intended to keep the cars on the track if they lost it there. The Sport's behavior in the turn itself was perfect, but on exit it would start this slow wobble that continued until the turn-in for turn 1. It wasn't just my bike, either. There was another racer who had the same model Ducati as mine, and I would watch his bike do the same thing.

One afternoon I had just finished the Production race when Cook Neilson came up to me in the pits.

"Hi, Paul. Your exit from turn 9 could be better." This might have been the second time I actually talked with Cook, and I'm sure it was the first time not in his office.

Initially I was defensive and replied, "Well, I won didn't I?" Then I bit my tongue, thinking to myself, *This guy knows stuff. Shut up, listen and learn.*

He said, "Yes, but you could have been faster. Let me show you. Come on."

"Sure," I said and followed Cook over to the pit wall next to the start line. Cook pointed left to the exit of turn 9.

"You need to open the throttle sooner and exit the turn closer to the wall, on the left." Then he pointed to the checkerboard start line by our feet. "Then cross over to this side of the track and pass the line between the second and third white squares here."

"OK," I said. Then Cook pointed to the right toward turn 1.

"Then as soon as you cross the line, you should start banking into turn 1, aiming at the apex there next to the traffic cone." I squinted off into the distance between the start line and the cone, many yards away from where we stood. It was barely visible through the smog.

"You start turning left way back here?" I asked.

"Yes," he said.

"OK. Thanks, Cook. I'll try it next time."

At the next AFM race at Riverside, I tried Cook's line. Big improvement! I was able to exit turn 9 at a higher speed and carry that extra speed all the way to turn 1. At the higher speed just past the start line was indeed the right time to start leaning into turn 1, so I was faster through that turn and down the straight between turns 1 and 2 as well. As I recall, I dropped more than a second off my lap time, a significant change. And as frosting on the cake, the wobble went away. Gone without leaving a trace. Thanks, Cook!

Dale Newton Joins the Fun

It was right around this time, late July of the 1976 season, that I noticed another Ducati 750 Sport like mine appearing at Sears Point. The rider would be dicing it up with Vance Breese's Moto Guzzi 850 Le Mans a few positions back from me. I made the point to visit him in the pits one morning. His name was Dale Newton, and he was an older man, maybe in his mid-50s. He was also a big guy, well over 6 feet tall and at least 200 pounds. Not overweight but not skinny either. It was not a typical road racer build.

We chatted for a bit. He told me he was having a blast with the Ducati. He had raced British bikes when he was younger and was amazed at how much better the Ducati behaved. I also learned he lived in Chico, a college town a couple hours north of Sacramento. I told him I had graduated from high school in Oroville, a smaller town about 30 miles from Chico, but I had managed to escape. He chuckled at that, saying he had been to Oroville a few times and he knew exactly what I meant. We got along well and I always tried to visit with him on race days to chat, but also to compare technical notes. Maybe we could help each other figure out ways to go faster. You never know.

Shift When It Gets to F-Sharp

While I was racing my Ducati 750 Sport at club races in 1976, Virginia was racing a Yamaha RD125, a nice little air-cooled, two-stroke parallel twin with a five-speed gearbox. It was a good bike for the 125cc Production class, quick and reliable if you didn't mess with the motor too much.

Near the end of the season Virginia took a tumble at Sears Point's turn 11 and hurt her knee. Because she was going to miss the last two races of the year, one at Sears Point and one at Riverside, she offered to let me race her bike. I said, "Sure, thank you very much." So at two events I would be racing bikes that were wildly different. A tiny two-stroke with right foot rear brake and left foot shift, press down to shift down; and a big four-stroke with left foot rear brake and right-foot shift, press down to shift up. I could imagine making the wrong move on the Yamaha and jamming on the rear brake instead of upshifting, or shifting down a gear when trying to use the rear brake. I would need to keep my head clear.

On race day morning at Sears Point, I was asking VA about what gears to use in which turns, and where the shift points were, and so on.

"You weigh more than me. You'll have to figure it out for yourself. Just remember to up-shift when it gets to F-sharp."

The Yamaha RD125 racer. Pops the polar bear is keeping an eye on things. *VA*

Huh? I put my hands on my hips and looked at her, waiting for her to realize what she had just said. She looked at me puzzled for a moment and then broke into laughter when she got it.

Virginia, you see, has an uncommon talent called perfect pitch. She can hear a tone and recognize what note it is. "That's the G above middle C," or "That's a B-flat." So when she says to shift up when it gets to F-sharp that's exactly what she means. The problem is that advice doesn't help most of us. I was going to have to watch the rev counter to figure it all out.

Practice went OK, but I was still trying to figure out what gear to use in which turn. At least I didn't confuse the brake and shift levers. I didn't slip the clutch enough at the start so I got off the line slowly. The lightweight race included 125cc and 200cc Production and also 50cc and 100cc GP classes, so it was a good size field that zipped past me as I staggered off the grid. I finally got rolling, picking up speed through the hill section. I got through turn 5 pretty well and crested the hill for the Carousel at a good speed.

Have I mentioned the entry to the Carousel is blind? When I topped the crest and leaned left, I came upon *three* racers side-by-side going a lot slower than I was. There was no way I was going to be able to stop without crashing and I couldn't go around the outside without running off the track. I tucked my knees and elbows in as tight as I could and aimed for the gap between the middle and the outside rider. To my relief, I got through clean and got away from those three.

I was trying to figure out what gear to use in each corner. Going into turn 11, the slowest turn on the track, I down shifted into first gear. I discovered that if the bike got into first it wouldn't shift up to second gear until it had slowed down a lot. Pulling in the clutch lever didn't help. The rear wheel had to be turning below a certain very slow speed. I had to get off the racing line and slow down until I could get into second gear, and then try to catch up. It happened again in turn 4. *This is no way to win a race,* I thought. I realized I needed to *know* what gear the bike was in and to avoid first gear at all costs. Bikes didn't have gear indicators back then.

Heading up to turn 7, I up-shifted until it wouldn't up-shift anymore. Now I knew I was in top gear. I started actually counting my shifts up and down. From top-gear braking into turn 7, I down-shifted three times, saying out loud in my helmet, "four, three, two." Then accelerating through the esses, I up-shifted and said, "three, four ... five" as I got back into top gear. My riding smoothed out. Still counting gear changes, I picked up speed and began passing some of the other 125 Production bikes. On the last lap I came up on Greg, another RD125 rider, just going into the last turn. I was right behind him exiting the corner, but he got a really good drive out of the slow turn and easily beat me to the checkered flag.

Once I got a handle on the shift points I was having fun. When I got back to the pits I was told I took second in class. I was a little surprised. "You mean Greg got the win? I was right behind him at the checkered flag!" I said to Virginia.

"I know," she said. "I thought you were going to catch him."

"He got a lot better drive out of turn eleven, and beat me to the finish," I said.

A week later we went to Riverside for the season's final race. Again I bogged at the start, but I began counting gear changes almost from the beginning, avoiding the early lap problems I had at Sears Point and keeping away from first gear.

A SoCal rider named John with a strong 125cc dual-purpose bike kept passing me between turns 6 and 7. I'd draft him down the back straight and pass going into turn 9 to lead across the finish line, but the next lap John would pass between turns 6 and 7 again. This was fun! This happened several laps in a row, until the final two laps when I was able to keep in front the entire circuit.

At speed on the RD125 at Riverside. *VA*

After the checkered flag, I sat up and looked back. There was John, not very far behind. I waved and he put his hands together as if he was choking something, a racer signal for "the motor tightened up." Later we got together in the pit area to swap stories about what a fun dice we had. John first congratulated Virginia on how quick her RD125 was. I asked him, "Were you catching me going into turn six or coming out of the turn?"

"Coming out of the turn, definitely," he replied. I told him about the first-gear problem with the bike and how I would count to keep track of what gear I was in:

"By the start line I'm in fifth, then fourth for turn one, third for the esses, down one more to second gear for turn six, then counting up as I up-shift between turns six and seven." I thought it was a pretty good story. Virginia was listening to all this and when I finished she said,

"You know, this bike has a six-speed gearbox."

We had a good chuckle after that.

I wondered why John kept catching me coming out of the slow turn 6, and why Greg got a much better jump out of turn 11 at Sears the week before. Finally it dawned on me. Both John and Greg were little guys, around five-foot, seven-inches tall and slim. I probably outweighed them by 15-20 pounds. That much weight mattered with a 125cc motor. He was in second gear while I was in third.

In spite of the goof, I got the class win at Riverside that day, to go along with my second place at Sears Point. Maybe two-strokes are OK after all.

Dale Newton's Ducati Superbike

When I was racing, the majority of club racers were doing it for the fun of it. There were a few who had bigger goals, and saw club racing as a step towards a career as a professional racer. The dream of both types of club racers was a sponsored ride—the chance to race with someone else's motorcycle was a goal of many but achieved by few. I wasn't looking for a racing career as I had already started a career in computers, and I wasn't actively seeking a sponsored ride. When opportunity knocked on my door, however, I answered.

Near the beginning of August, Dale told me he was working on a special Ducati, a 900SS tricked out for the AFM's Open Grand Prix class. He wanted to know if I was interested in racing it. I thought about it for about a 10th of a second and said "Yes!" so we shook hands on the deal.

The Golden Gate Challenge

The bike made its first appearance in late August at the Sears Point club race called the Golden Gate Challenge, a special two-day event put on by the AFM North Chapter. The GGC was a non-points race that had contests for all the normal AFM classes, plus a special North-South Match Race for the faster riders, based on practice lap times, no matter what type of bike.

The star of that weekend was Dave Emde, son of Daytona 200 winner Floyd Emde and younger brother of Daytona 200 winner Don Emde. Do you think maybe racing was in his blood? Riding at Sears Point for the first time, he set a new motorcycle lap record of 1 minute, 56.1 seconds on his Yamaha TZ250. Emde won the 250GP event and the Match Race with ease.

Back to Dale's special Ducati: when he showed up with the bike on Saturday morning, I got my first look. Dale had started with a standard 1976 Ducati 900SS and turned it into a very sweet race bike. He had been in contact with Cook Neilson and Phil Schilling and was duplicating much of the chassis work they had done on their Ducati (known as

Dale's Superbike in its initial form at turn 11 at the 1976 Golden Gate Challenge.

Old Blue, or the California Hot-Rod), making improvements where possible. For example, like Old Blue, Dale's bike had Morris magnesium wheels front and rear, but Dale had engineered a way to adapt the normal Ducati cushion hub to the cast magnesium rear wheel, which gave much more shock absorption than the standard Morris setup.

The tank and seat were painted the bright ochre of the 1973-1974 Sport with Sport-style decals. Everything was clean and polished, and there was safety wire everywhere it needed to be. The whole thing looked professional. It was gorgeous.

The motor had only a few changes. Dale changed the foot controls back to the pre-1975 Ducati standard of right-foot shift, up for low, left-foot rear brake, so they worked the same as my own 1974 Sport; no mental conversion needed.

On the track it handled great—better than my Sport. The chassis felt stiffer and more precise. The motor had a lot more grunt off the corners than my Sport. It pulled like a tractor with a really strong mid-range, but with the stock ports and valves, it ran out of breath at about 7,800 rpm. It made sense to up-shift before hitting 8,000. The Sport, on the other hand, gained speed more slowly but made power until near 8,400 rpm.

Saturday of the two-day event was reserved for practice and heat races. At the end of the second practice, I set the bike against the pit wall and had just taken off my gloves when Dale came trotting up. He didn't say a word, just smiled and handed me a slip of paper listing my lap times. On the third lap he had written "1:59.4." Holy shit! I actually threw my gloves up into the air.

A little background information is needed to understand why this was special. When the track reopened to motorcycles in 1972, a lap time of less than two minutes was a goal. Nobody went that fast for the first year or two. When the Yamaha TZ250s, with the water-cooled engine appeared, the really fast riders started getting under that time, but it was still rare. Dale and I were the first to put a street-bike-based machine under that threshold since the AMA National event in 1969.

The rest of the weekend went really well. We qualified for the Match Race along with a bunch of TZ350 and TZ250 Yamahas and a couple other modified street bikes. I got a good start, but had to dodge another rider who fell trying to pass me in the turn 3-3A combination on the first lap. It meant a brief off-track excursion for me and I finished fifth behind Emde and three other TZ250 Yamahas. We won the Open GP race after Emde had to drop out with a broken gear shift lever on his TZ750, and I won the 750 Production race on my own Ducati 750 Sport. It was a good weekend.

Two Late-Season Races at Sears Point

I rode the proto-Superbike three more times in 1976 with somewhat less success. In September we ran a race at Sears Point, but the bike oiled a plug in the race for a DNF. The bike was having some ring seating problems. October at Sears was a bit more memorable and the occasion of a good story about Dale's attitude toward bike preparation. He was a perfectionist. I think it came from his business, which involved maintaining piston-engine aircraft. When there is an engine failure on an airplane, you don't just coast to a stop at the side of the road.

I was getting faster on the bike, turning times between 1:58.5 and 1:58 flat. We had a plug oiling problem in practice but got that sorted in time for the race. I was going well when the bike started running on only one cylinder on the second lap. It wasn't making any bangs or clunks and continued to run smoothly, but it made for a rather slow and heavy 375cc single-cylinder race bike. I rode it into the pits, got off the bike, and told Dale what happened. Suspecting a fouled spark plug, Dale immediately started to remove the plugs while I got out of his way by moving to the other side of the bike.

"Uh, Dale? I think I see the problem," I said.

"What?" he asked.

I said, "Look over here," and pointed to the front cylinder's right side. He leaned across the tank and looked. The front carburetor was no longer connected to the intake manifold, but was dangling by the throttle and choke cables. Apparently a backfire on closed throttle blew the carb off the manifold.

I started to laugh, but Dale got this strange expression on his face, a look I hadn't seen before. He was *angry*, really mad, not at me, nor at Ducati or Dellorto carburetors, but at himself. He really hated to lose because of poor preparation. The next time I saw the bike the carbs were safety-wired.

Halloween Race at Riverside

There was one more AFM race for the proto-Superbike in 1976, at Riverside Raceway on October 31. Dale brought the 900SS down from Chico while Virginia and I trucked our bikes south from the Bay Area. Practice went well, and although I wasn't near Yamaha TZ750 times, I was going faster than I'd ever gone there before and having a lot of fun.

Because it was the last race of the season, there was a pretty good grid for the combined 350/500/Open GP race. I got a good start and had just gotten through turn 1 when something hit the back of my bike and ripped it away. Mind you, I was still in my racing tuck, pointed down the straight toward turn 2, but I had no motorcycle under me. It happened that quickly.

I hit the track and started sliding. Two other riders were involved, the one who hit me, and a third unlucky rider, who ended up with a broken leg. Bikes were dodging every which way and slowing down in avoidance mode. I was sliding on my back, trying to become very small as most of the field was still behind me. Everyone missed, thank goodness. My bike, in the meantime, had landed on its side and was sliding down the track ahead of me. My friend Mike, racing in the 500 GP class, said he recalled being *passed* by a rider-less motorcycle on its side and thinking, *Was that Paul's bike?*

The race was restarted, but not with me. I had a hand injury that needed looking at, although it turned out to be minor.

1976 Season Summary

There had been a transformation somewhere during the 1976 racing season. It didn't happen all at once but gradually over the summer. I started the year still being a follower, chasing my pal Ed. After Ed died, I started winning, and by the end of the season I discovered I had the skills, but more importantly I had the drive and the attitude. I had learned to lead. It seemed natural to me to be in front of all the other 750 Production class racers.

———

The 1976 racing season was a great success marred by tragedy. It was my breakout year at the club level. Here are the crucial points.

- I won the 750 Production class championship, winning races at Sears Point, Ontario, and Riverside. The only downside was the death of Ed, which hurt a lot.

- When the 750 class points were combined with the points from my two good finishes on the Yamaha RD125, I had the second-highest point total for the Production classes. The top-five production riders got to use the numbers 6-10, so my second-place ranking meant I would be number 7. Pretty lucky, huh? I went from number 171 in 1974-1975, to number 71 in 1976, to number 7 for 1977.

- I had broken through the magic two-minute lap time at Sears Point, getting several laps in the 1-minute-58-and-a-fraction of a second on Dale Newton's bike.

- I had earned a sponsored ride. This is the goal of many club racers. Dale had started developing a Ducati 900SS into an AMA Superbike and asked me to race it. If that wasn't enough, Dale was also preparing a Ducati 750SS for me to ride in the 750 Production class in the AFM to defend my class title.

I was really looking forward to the 1977 season.

CHAPTER SIX

Dale's Ducati 750SS

At the end of the 1976 season, I retired the 750 Sport from racing and returned it to the street. For 1977 I would be racing someone else's motorcycle. Correction, motorcycles. It was a club racer's dream come true. In the AFM's 750 Production class, I would be riding Dale's Ducati 750SS, one of the renowned desmodromic V-twins Ducati produced in 1974. Ducati made approximately 400 of these bikes and only around 200 had come to the U.S. Getting to race one of them was a rare treat and a real privilege. I would also be riding Dale's Ducati Superbike, helping him develop it. I was a lucky guy.

The first AFM race of 1977 was at Riverside Raceway. Dale and I arrived separately and met at the track on Sunday morning, when I got my first look at the 750SS. It was beautifully prepared and looked very purposeful. The AFM's Production class rules enforced an as-sold look but allowed for lots of internal tuning. Dale's bike, however, was changed only a little from stock. He had installed a set of Imola cams from the race kit that came with the bike, done a very mild port job to the heads, and re-jetted the carbs. The rest of the motor was stock—gearbox, crankshaft, rods and pistons, cylinders—all stock. A high-rise exhaust system, also from the race kit, had been installed, but we used the stock Conti silencers as required by the rules. The headlight had been removed and the taillight was taped and disconnected, also required by the rules. We were using Goodyear racing slicks with the stock wire-spoke wheels—aftermarket cast wheels were forbidden.

Practice went really well. The bike's chassis was pretty much the same as the 750 Sport I raced in 1976 and the handling was the same. The SS was a lot faster than my Sport. The Sport stopped making power around 8,400 rpm, while Dale's Super Sport continued to pull for another 1,000 revs. It had a higher top speed by a considerable margin but seemed about equal to the Sport in the mid-range. I had to make adjustments to my brake points because of the increased speed.

Because it was early in the year, there was a rather thin field for the Heavyweight Production race featuring the 550cc, 750cc, and Open Production classes (the bikes raced together but were scored separately). The competition in the 750 class would come from my pal Mark who was riding the Mr. Jags Norton. Mr. Jags was a British gent living in California who seemed to know how to get the best out of that long-stroke push-rod motor, and with a good rider, it was very competitive.

At the drop of the flag, Mark on the Norton, I on the Ducati, and Terry on a Suzuki GS750 with an 884cc big-bore kit took off at the front. We were having a nice three-way dice swapping the lead back and forth. On the third or fourth lap, Terry was in the lead, Mark in second, and I was in third going through the esses. Then, exiting turn 6, Mark had to make a sudden move to keep from running into Terry. I think Terry missed a shift or found a false neutral because he slowed suddenly, then got back up to speed. I decided it was time to clear out, passed Mark going down the back straight, and then ducked beneath the Suzuki in turn 9. I put my head down, as they say, holding the throttle open a little longer

Dale's Ducati 750SS at Sears Point. He didn't paint this bike ochre like the Superbikes; he left it the original gray metal-flake but with a black frame.

and braking a little harder and nailing the turns. The bike responded eagerly; the harder I pushed it, the more it liked it.

We took the win in the 750 class, finishing first overall, beating even the Open class motorcycles. Mark also got by Terry to take second overall and second 750 on the Norton while Terry finished third overall and first in the Open Production class. It was a good start to the year.

Raising the Bar at Riverside

For the second Riverside race, the AFM had hired professional announcer Larry Huffman, known as "The Mouth That Roars" by virtue of his enthusiastic and colorful announcing of motorcycle speedway events in nearby Whittier. He was not taking the job lightly and he worked the pits during the morning practice, getting to know the racers. He passed out questionnaires for us to fill out so he could identify us by number from the announcing tower.

It was still pretty early in the season, but I had four wins with Dale's Ducati 750SS, the first Riverside race in March and three Sears Point races. The Sears Point wins didn't surprise anybody and the first Riverside win was against a relatively small field so it didn't raise any eyebrows. This day was different as there was a full grid of over 40 Heavyweight Production bikes.

The 550cc, 750cc, and Open Production bikes were lined up on the starting grid by class: Open bikes in front, then 750s, and 550 bikes in the rear. The grid was organized with the first row bikes about 6-7 feet apart, with the second row gridded about two bike lengths back, offset to face the gaps in the row one bikes. Row three was similarly offset. As the first 750cc class bike, I was gridded in the third row, directly behind Vance and his Moto Guzzi 850 LeMans on the first row, in front of me by four or five bike lengths.

The starter's sign went sideways and the revs came up. I was leaning forward intent on the green flag. It waved and everyone took off, er, except for Vance, who didn't budge. I'm stuck! Vance begins doing this little foot dance—start with your shifter foot on the ground and your brake foot on the peg, then you put your brake foot down and lift your shifter foot up …

Oh my God. He staged in neutral! I was yelling in my helmet, "Come on Vance! *Move!*" as bikes zipped past us left and right. Then a sudden thought came into my head—I could get run into from behind! I thought, *later Vance,* and did a quick flick with the handlebars as I passed him with no room to spare. I swear I ran over his toes, but he denied it.

I was well in the back of the pack at this point, behind everyone else in my class and surrounded by 550cc bikes. I was in a big hurry to catch up. I cut through a number of 550cc bikes going through the esses and I was beginning to catch up to some of the larger bikes. I took a chance in turn 7 and snuck inside a 1,000cc Laverda. The rider saw me at the last minute and jerked his bike more upright. I rudely stole his apex. I thought, *Sorry, buddy, but I'm in a hurry.*

I got a good drive out of turn 7A and I passed a few more bikes going through the dogleg and lined up with everyone else for the long right hand turn 9 sweeper. I felt I could go faster than the bikes right in front of me so I very carefully tightened my line up a little and edged past the inside of the first bike. The next guy was holding a tighter line so I edged a bit to my left and went around him on his outside. It suddenly occurred to me, *I'm passing bikes left and right in the middle of a turn! That can't be normal.*

On the second lap, bikes were getting more spread out and I was not catching them in bunches but rather one at a time. I was still running hard trying to catch the leaders and not paying much attention to which rider or what bike I passed. When I got even with one, I was already looking to see who was next ahead and how far. Then, on lap four of the six-lap race, I passed a rider I didn't know on a Kawasaki Z1, looked ahead, and saw … a clear track.

I was surprised. It took a while for it to sink in. *I'm leading? Not just the 750cc bikes, but all of them?* I could barely believe it. In another half a lap I started catching some of the slower 550 class bikes, lapping them, and I had to concentrate on that and stop thinking about what had just happened.

I took the checkered flag and looked back to see who might be close behind, and saw only the bikes I had just lapped. I rode back to the pits to meet a beaming Dale and handed the 750SS to him. People were collecting around to congratulate me, telling me what a performance, great ride, and such. Then riders in the race started dropping by. Leroy, who won the Open class on his 850 LeMans, came up laughing and said, "You ought to get down on your *knees* and apologize for passing me *that fast* down the back straight!" He meant it in a good way and I thanked him. I was enjoying all the attention, but I was a little mystified. You'd think I'd won a big deal event, not just a club race.

I found out a bit later that Larry Huffman noticed my progress through the field early in the race and was talking me up through most of the event. A buddy told me Larry said, "The only way they're going to stop Ritter is to shoot him!" He had found the little bio sheet I had filled out and told everyone my age, where I lived, how long I'd been racing, etc. For an afternoon I was a minor celebrity, and I liked it.

It wasn't just that I had won, it was the way I had won. Starting from near the back of the pack at Riverside, I had caught and passed a full field of 750cc and Open class bikes. Dale and I were going to be tough to beat in 750 Production this year.

Win Follows Win

The next AFM points race was also in SoCal, this time at Ontario Motor Speedway. The OMS track features lots of fast, sweeping turns, and the bevel-drive Ducatis did fast sweeping turns really well. The result was another overall win. It wasn't as dramatic as the come-from-way-behind victory at Riverside, but still notable. OMS featured two long straights and one might expect the larger-displacement bikes could use those to stay ahead of my 750. However, the Ducati 750SS was nearly as fast as the 1,000cc bikes, and it had a big advantage in the turns. I was usually in front by the end of the second or third lap.

Two races at Sears Point followed, which took us into July, roughly mid-way through the season. So far I'd been in eight races and gotten eight overall wins at the three different tracks. At one point someone asked me, "Don't you get tired of being out front by yourself all the time?" I thought for a moment and said, "Well, now that you mention it, no." It was a flippant, but honest answer, and the question made me think.

Being in a close race with lots of dicing is exciting and fun, but there was more to it than the competition. There was also the artistry—being able to find the perfect line through a combination of curves, then to hit that perfect line lap after lap was deeply satisfying, like a painter making the perfect brush stroke or a writer crafting the perfect sentence. When there was nobody to dice with, I would work on the art of making fast laps.

Years later a friend compared my riding with the East Asian art of Sumi-e. I had to look that up. Literally *ink painting*, Sumi-e is an art form that strives to distill the essence of an object or scene in the fewest possible strokes. The artist has a brush, a supply of black ink, and a blank piece of white paper, and tries to draw as few lines as possible yet still clearly identify the object being drawn. That's close. I was trying to define the essence of the particular racetrack by drawing the quickest possible line.

I Spoil a Perfect Record

Dale and I were having great success with his Ducati 750SS in the club races. From the very first race in 1977, the bike carried me to the win in every race, until the September 5 race at Sears Point.

From March through August, the bike had won 10 races, 10 *overall* wins, beating the Open class bikes as well. The Ducati 750SS was a great race bike, but ours had been worked hard and was beginning to show some signs of fatigue. In the two August races I occasionally found a false neutral when shifting from third to fourth gear. Something in the transmission had worn enough that the gearbox needed adjustment. This was done using shims of various thicknesses, a long and complicated process that required the engine cases be split. Dale and I talked about it and we decided it wasn't a serious problem; I would just up-shift again and get on with it. He could concentrate on the 900SS-based Superbike for the upcoming AMA Superbike races at Laguna Seca and Riverside. It wasn't a bad plan, if only I had kept to it strictly.

At Sears Point there were a few spots during a lap where I used engine braking to slow down. One of those spots was in the short space between the left-hand turn 8 and the right-hand turn 8A, the middle part of the downhill esses. I would accelerate hard out of turn 7, up-shifting from second gear into fourth by turn 8, and then I would roll off the throttle during the transition from left to right lean, which would give me the correct entry speed into 8A.

On that day I was in the overall lead on the last lap, and I found that false neutral on the shift from third to fourth as I entered turn 8. When I rolled off the throttle, the bike didn't slow down but continued to gain speed. I was entering turn 8A at too high a speed and I, um, well, I panicked. I tried to get back in gear quickly so I *down-shifted* and dropped the clutch. Instead of getting into fourth gear, I went back into third gear. I had already started banking into turn 8A, and when I released the clutch lever, the rear end lost traction and I crashed. The bike and I both ended up in the tires on the hillside outside of turn 8A. I was unhurt but not able to restart the bike.

The frustrating thing was I didn't have to crash. I could have just eased on the brakes and slowed enough to get through turn 8A, then gotten the gearing sorted out before turn 9. Alternately, if I had up-shifted to fourth

The 750SS exiting turn 11 at Sears Point. This was after the crash as Dale didn't have time to paint the fairing. *Anna Vallerga Homchick*

instead of down-shifting to third, I probably would have managed to get through the corner. It took a combination of a mechanical flaw and rider error to crash the bike.

After that incident, Dale split the cases and re-shimmed the gearbox. By the late September race at Riverside, the false neutral had been vanquished and we finished the season with two more overall wins.

1977 Season Summary (Club Level)

At the club level, 1977 was an even better year than 1976. With the Ducati 750SS, I was able to dominate the heavyweight Production races, keeping the AFM's 750 Production class title for the second year running. We entered 13 of the 15 points races, earning 12 overall wins and one crash. We did not race the last two races of the year at Ontario and Riverside. I don't recall the reason we skipped those events, but I suspect it was because we were just tired. It had been a busy year for Dale and me, racing both AFM and selected AMA Superbike races. The Ducati 750SS was retired after the 1977 season. We had nothing left to prove with that bike, and racing it again in 750 Production would be cherry picking.

Dale and I also collected the AFM's Open GP class title. We ran the Superbike in the class for testing and as warm-up for the AMA Superbike events. We had more good finishes in the class than others, scoring points in seven Open GP events.

I wasn't able to keep the number 7 plate in the AFM. I had more wins than in 1976, but racing in only one class, my points total made me the fourth-ranked Production racer, which earned me the number 9 in the AFM. It was a good thing, though, as the AMA gave me the number 96 for 1978. Nine and 96. There's some sort of cosmic unity in that.

CHAPTER SEVEN

Dale's Ducati 900SS Superbike

This chapter and the next two are about AMA National level Superbike racing. The racers and tuners who made up the early years of the AMA Superbike series were a rather remarkable group. During my three years competing in the series, I got to know several of these pioneers. I've included a short vignette of each of the ones I knew, plus a little bit about what made each one unique. Many of them are in the AMA Motorcycle Hall of Fame.

———

At the same time Dale and I were racing the Ducati 750SS in the AFM's Production class, we were developing a Ducati 900SS-based Superbike. The AFM didn't have a Superbike class so we raced it in the club's Open GP class. If the bike (and rider) performed well enough, we planned to enter the three California Superbike races scheduled that year, one at Sears Point, one at Laguna Seca near Monterey, and the third at Riverside. The first AMA race was the Sears Point race in July, several months after the opening of the club racing season, so we had some time for development.

Defining AMA Superbikes

In 1976 the American Motorcyclist Association created the Superbike class. It used street bikes, motorcycles you could purchase from a dealer, as the starting point. It was a silhouette class. The bikes had to look similar to the stock bikes, but quite a few alterations were allowed under the rules. As just one example, the stock muffler shell was required, but you could gut the insides and turn it into a racing megaphone.

There was a pretty good mix of bikes in the Superbike class. With a 1,000cc engine size limit, the Kawasaki Z1 was an ideal starting point. Other bikes already close to the limit were the BMW R90S, the Moto Guzzi 850 LeMans, and the Laverda Jota 1000. There were some over-bored 750cc class bikes, notably the Honda CB750 and the Ducati 750SS.

Points were earned at each race depending on the finishing position, with the high point scorer declared the class champion at the end of the year. Points for Superbikes in late 1970s paid down to 14th place:

1st	–	20	8th	–	7
2nd	–	16	9th	–	6
3rd	–	13	10th	–	5
4th	–	11	11th	–	4
5th	–	10	12th	–	3
6th	–	9	13th	–	2
7th	–	8	14th	–	1

There were no bonus points for earning pole position or for leading the most laps. You had to finish above 15th to earn points.

AMA Superbikes Year One – A Summary

The AMA had only four National road races in 1976: Daytona Beach, Florida; Loudon, New Hampshire; and Laguna Seca and Riverside in California. The other road racing classes, 750cc and 250cc, had become Yamaha-only classes and people were looking for a way to get more brands into competition. It was a good plan. I paid attention to the races and attended the Laguna Seca round, using my position as editor of the AFM's newsletter to finagle press credentials to the event.

Butler & Smith, the BMW importer for the U.S., stole a march on everybody by showing up with a professional team of three expert-ranked riders on R90S models with support from a professional race crew. Rumors were that Butler & Smith dropped $100,000 (in 1976!) on the effort. It paid off as BMWs won three of the four races. Steve McLaughlin at Daytona and Reg Pridmore at Laguna Seca and Riverside. The only non-BMW win of the season was Mike Baldwin on a Moto Guzzi at Loudon. Besides Baldwin's Guzzi, the only other bikes that could run with the BMWs were Cook Neilson's Ducati and Wes Cooley's Kawasaki, but both had some mechanical problems and the Kawasaki didn't handle very well. The first AMA Superbike champion by a wide margin was Reg Pridmore on

Steve McLaughlin's BMW R90S at the Laguna Seca Superbike race in 1976.

Mush Emmons

his BMW R90S. Reg finished on the podium in all four races, with a second at Daytona, a third at Loudon, and wins at both California races.

The 1976 Laguna Seca Superbike race produced one of the most iconic crash photos ever, a Mush Emmons' shot of Steve McLaughlin's number 83 BMW emerging from a cloud of dust, seemingly undamaged but completely upside down.

Superbike Pioneer - Reg Pridmore

Reg was the first AMA Superbike champion. He was from England, but had immigrated to the United States years earlier. When I met him, he owned a BMW motorcycle shop near Santa Barbara, California. He won the 1976 championship riding a Butler & Smith-sponsored BMW R90S.

Reg is a proper British gentleman. In spite of his good manners and gentlemanly ways, he gave no quarter on the racetrack. A rumor at the time was that he had been a military policeman in the British army during his military stint. He was tough when he needed to be and nice when tough wasn't needed.

As a BMW shop owner, it made business sense for him to be racing the big boxer-twins and he was very successful with them. He knew the

Reg Pridmore with son Jason and me, Laguna Seca 1977.

motors inside and out and seemed to know exactly how much racing abuse they would take. In 1976 Butler & Smith had a team of three excellent racers, yet only Pridmore finished all four races, and he was on the podium each time.

Off-track he was one of the nicest guys; his friends call him Reggie. He had a delightful British accent that was very effective with the ladies and a great sense of humor. One time as we were getting ready to go out for a practice session at Sears Point, I saw his bike's saddle was covered with a white powder.

"Is that chalk?" I asked.

Reg gave the seat a whack, raising a fragrant cloud of dust, and said, "It's baby powder. Nothing but the best for me!" It helped him shift his weight from side to side in the turns.

He wasn't just a fast racer. During his racing career, he began giving lessons, teaching riding and racing skills. After he stopped racing competitively, he founded the CLASS Motorcycle Schools. The company has been given high marks by the students and is still going strong after over 20 years in business, having helped thousands of students become better riders.

Superbike Pioneer - Keith Code

I knew Keith from club racing in 1976; we would meet at AFM races at Riverside and Ontario. He was one of those brave, smaller guys who manhandled a big Kawasaki Z-1 motorcycle around the racetrack, usually scoring well. He could be depended upon to be bright and cheerful, and he clearly enjoyed the racing. He was at the time a cobbler, of all things. He made his living by making custom shoes for celebrities and other wealthy folk.

Keith always struck me as a thinking racer. Some riders, especially younger ones, improved only by experience and had a crash record to show for it. Keith seldom crashed, but would think about his riding, analyze where he thought he was going slower than he should, and figured out what it was that slowed him up. And next time he would be faster. When a few years later I saw he had written a couple of books about how to race well, and started the California Superbike School, I thought, *Of course!*

Keith didn't win an AMA Superbike race, but he got a well-earned second place finish at Laguna Seca in 1976 and had several other top-10 finishes. His racing experiences allowed him to conceive and establish his racing school and author his books.

Before the California Superbike School, there was the Keith Code Rider Improvement Course. This image is from an April 1977 AFM program.

Superbikes 1977 – The Second Season

In 1977 the AMA had seven road race events scheduled, a big improvement over 1976's four races. Formula 750 or Class C was the main event with 250cc GP and Superbikes as support races. The Superbike schedule was:

Date	Location
March 11	Daytona Beach, FL
March 20	Charlotte, NC
June 19	Loudon, NH
July 17	Sears Point, CA
Aug. 21	Pocono, PA
Sept. 11	Laguna Seca, CA
Oct. 2	Riverside CA

Dale and I had looked this over and decided to contest the three California events if our pre-July club racing showed potential. The club racing started in March so we had four months to get ready.

The lead-up to the first California race, Sears Point, was pretty interesting.

Daytona Beach, Florida

Cook Neilson's Ducati won Daytona by a healthy 28-second margin over the Kawasaki Z1s of Dave Emde and Wes Cooley. The big four-cylinder bikes had handling problems on the Daytona high banking. The BMWs weren't as dominant as in 1976, with Reg Pridmore's fourth place the only finish for the team.

Charlotte, North Carolina

The Charlotte course was like Daytona, but smaller and bumpier. The top spots were taken by Mike Baldwin and Kurt Liebmann, both riding Moto Guzzi 850 LeMans. The banking proved nearly unmanageable for the big four-cylinder bikes if the rider tried to apply full throttle, although Wes Cooley took third on the Yoshimura Kawasaki Z1. The BMWs were absent as Butler & Smith had abruptly dropped their race effort.

Loudon, New Hampshire

The win went to one of the ex-Butler & Smith BMWs, now sponsored by Johnny's of Bakersfield and ridden by veteran ex-factory racer Ron Pierce.

Last year's winner Mike Baldwin was also a factor on his Moto Guzzi, and Reg Pridmore was now riding a Kawasaki Z1 sponsored by Racecrafters. Those three raced closely in the early laps, each one leading at one time or another. Toward the end Pridmore slowed with brake problems. Pierce had a one-bike-length lead going into the last corner and Baldwin made a last-ditch attempt to pass and fell. Pierce won with Pridmore taking second.

The first three AMA Superbike races had resulted in three different winners on three different brands of motorcycles. Cook Neilson on Ducati at Daytona, Mike Baldwin on Moto Guzzi at Charlotte, and Ron Pierce on BMW at Loudon. Kawasaki hadn't a win, but had taken several podium places, including two seconds. Sears Point was up next.

Superbike Pioneer - Cook Neilson

Cook Neilson has class. Cook was a top Superbike contender in 1976 and 1977, racing a 1974 Ducati 750SS he and Phil Schilling had bored to 883cc and developed to a very high state of tune. They learned a lot about how to make horsepower from that motor in the process. This knowledge gave Cook an advantage on the track, but he and Phil were always ready to share tuning information with anyone. They spent many hours and dollars learning these bits of knowledge, then gave them away for free. A class act.

Cook is also a superb wordsmith. His writing and editing were two of the reasons *Cycle* became the motorcycle magazine with the highest readership in the *world* in the 1970s. As an example of his writing, in the

Cook Neilson in 1977.

August 1977 issue, Cook was lamenting the fact that really fun motorcycle roads can be spoiled by overpopularity. Then he describes a road he and some of his pals found:

> Its length is just over 30 miles, draped through the San Gabriel Mountains by road engineers who must have been the most unregenerate motorcycle enthusiasts ever to hold steady jobs with the state. It comes from nowhere in particular, and goes its lyrical way with no discernible destination in mind. ... There was no oil, no centerline divider, and no evidence that the road's builders were prone to setting traps for sinners like us. The road climbed and dipped and danced in delight, and had nothing in store for the attentive except reward. The traction was exceptional, the scenery magnificent, the police somewhere else. ... If Leonardo had built a road, it would have been like this one.
>
> And now you're wondering where this road is. I'll tell you. Some other time.

In some ways Cook was my mentor. He showed me a way forward in racing, helping me on more than one occasion, and I consider it an honor to have competed with and against him. He was then, and is still, my friend.

Oh, yes. That road he described in the August 1977 issue of *Cycle*? He never did tell the magazine's readers where it was. Bastard.

Superbike Pioneer – Phil Schilling

Like Cook Neilson, Phil was well known in the industry as *Cycle's* executive editor before his efforts with the Superbikes. He was also known in a smaller circle as one of the best sources of go-fast knowledge of single-cylinder Ducatis made prior to 1974. Schilling was a Ducatisti from way back, having raced and tuned the singles in the 1960s.

Phil was a great resource to people racing Ducati singles, and he became a great resource for Ducati twins as well. He, like Cook, was always willing to share his information with anyone.

Phil was one of a small number of people who had the patience and skill to tear apart a Ducati bevel-drive engine, replace hunks of its insides, and put it back together correctly. The motor, with its vertically split crankcases, was full of shims of various thicknesses that were used to set the clearances of shafts and gears to precise tolerances. Assembling that

Phil Schilling in 1977, working on Old Blue.

motor correctly requires watch-maker talent and patience. I learned lots of stuff from Phil, both single- and twin-related. He and I became good pals.

When Cook resigned as editor of *Cycle*, Phil was promoted to that position and he had ability there as well. *Cycle* continued to set the standard for the world. He also authored a beautiful book titled *The Motorcycle World*. These days he is retired but keeps his hand in by occasionally writing a magazine article. He also maintains a registry of all the Ducati 750SS models ever imported into the U.S.

When I think of Phil back in the day, my image is him late at night in the shop, up to his elbows in the Ducati's crankcase, juggling shims and gears and rocker arms and desmo camshafts, and loving every minute of it.

There is a Neville Shute novel entitled *Round the Bend*. One of the themes in the story is the formation of a quasi-religious movement among aircraft engine mechanics who show their reverence to the Almighty by doing flawless work on the engines. I believe Phil would be an easy convert.

The AFM Pre-National Race

The AFM had a race at Sears Point two weeks before the scheduled July 16-17 AMA National and AMA Superbike contenders Cook Neilson and Reg Pridmore, winner of Daytona and class champion, respectively, came to the race to get some track time. At the AFM races the Superbike-spec bikes raced in the Open GP class and were allowed to compete in the Superstreet class even though, strictly speaking, they weren't Superstreet legal. As I recall, we raced in that class but did not earn class points.

Dale had been bringing the Superbike along carefully since its track debut in August 1976. He had done some additional work since then. He had installed the oil cooler that came with the Ducati race kit and the external oil lines that delivered cooled oil to the cams and rocker arms. Dale did only a small cleanup on the intake and exhaust ports, keeping the standard valves. He did make one important change to the heads—he installed the Imola desmo camshafts available from Ducati and re-jetted the carburetors. The rest of the motor was stock Ducati Super Sport: pistons, rods, crankshaft, gearbox, etc.

A pattern developed during the Open GP race between Cook and me. His bike, Old Blue, had more top speed, but Dale's bike had more acceleration and I knew the track better. His speed superiority was nullified somewhat by the tight nature of the Sears Point track, but there were a couple of places where Cook used it to his advantage. He would pass me going through the start/finish area. I would follow him through the hill section, then pass him back in the Carousel (turn 6). He would run me down on the short straight between 6 and 7 and squeeze past me on the brakes going into turn 7. I'd pass him back through the esses or in turn 10, then he'd zip by me near the start/finish line. This went on for several laps in a row. I finally pulled out enough of a lead to keep him from overtaking at turn 7 and stretched it out a little in the esses (turns 8–10) to take the win. It was great fun.

Reggie was having trouble with the Kawasaki. The Sears Point bumps were more than a match for the Kawasaki chassis. He pitted during the Open GP race to change the shocks and went back out, without much improvement. During the Superstreet race, he bottomed the suspension in turn 11, the slow hairpin near the pits, producing a low-side crash when the front end washed out.

For Cook and me, the Superstreet race was nearly a carbon copy of the Open GP tussle. After swapping places a few times in the first four laps, I had again stretched it out to keep the lead for a full lap on the penultimate lap. On the last lap there was a waving yellow flag at turn 2. Turn 2 is one of the several blind turns at Sears and I got this image of a bike and rider lying in the middle of the track as we crested the hill, and I slowed big time. It turned out all the crash debris was off the track and wasn't a problem, but I had lost momentum and Cook passed me going into turn 3. I re-passed in the Carousel but didn't have enough of a lead to hold him off at turn 7 and he took the win by a couple of bike lengths.

The score: Dale and I won one, Cook and Phil won the other. My fastest lap of the day was a new personal best of 1 minute 55 seconds. Cook's fastest was in the low 1:56 range, which was darn quick for his first time on the track. I was pretty excited about not only bettering my lap times, but proving I could compete head-to-head with a couple of the best Superbike racers in the country.

The Sears Point AMA National

Anticipation for the National was high after the good showing at the club race two weeks earlier. My sponsor, Dale Newton, brought the bike to the track with the fairing and fenders installed, as required by the AMA Superbike rules. The nice reverse-cone megaphones that he had originally put on the bike were replaced by the stock Conti muffler shells with the interior baffling removed, also per AMA rules. The Conti silencers were nearly the shape of a reverse-cone megaphone anyway.

Dale hadn't made any drastic changes to the intake and exhaust ports, which was a contrast to what Cook and Phil had done with Old Blue. As a result, Dale's bike was strong in the mid-range, with lots of torque but not much top end speed. Cook's bike would make good power up to 9,500 rpm while our bike ran out of breath at 7,800 rpm. At Sears Point, however, a healthy mid-range and strong acceleration were good things, because there weren't many places where a top-speed bike could show its stuff. With its relatively low top speed, keeping a high corner speed was essential, which was one of my strong points. Fortunately for me the Sears Point layout had lots of corners and few straights.

Saturday practice went well. The bike was running nicely as long as we didn't try to over-rev it, and I was riding well, lowering my lap times another second to just under 1:54. People were noticing. At lunch a club racer pal of mine came up and told me a member of the Yoshimura team was timing me.

"It's funny," he told me. "He hits the stopwatch as you pass the timing line, looks at it, and just shakes his head. Ha!"

I never started out with the idea of becoming a competitive American Superbike racer. It just seemed to be the logical direction things flowed. I discovered I loved riding, and then I realized I liked riding fast in the curves. I moved to road racing for the relative safety of the track as compared to the street. As time went on, my skills improved, and when I started racing a competitive motorcycle, I started winning. I won a club championship and earned a sponsored ride, which fell into my lap when Dale Newton asked me to ride his bikes.

I kept getting faster at club races on Dale's Ducati Superbike, culminating in the AFM's warm-up race, when I raced Cook Neilson head-to-head and we both left Reg Pridmore in our dust. That was pretty cool, but it was still just a club race.

So with no real planning on my part, I was about to race in an AMA National road race, as a rookie, with a legitimate chance of winning. Sure, Superbikes was a support class and I wasn't going to try to keep up with Kenny Roberts or Gary Nixon, but it was a National race and some very talented expert riders were entered. At Saturday lunch I thought about what was about to happen, and I got a case of the jitters that stayed with me all the way to the start of the heat race that afternoon. Gulp.

―――――――

The Saturday Heat Race

What am I doing here? I thought. I was in the middle of the starting grid at Sears Point raceway on a Ducati 900SS Superbike. The first row had some of the best road racers in North America: class champion Reg Pridmore, Daytona-winner Cook Neilson, the veteran Ron Pierce who won the

It was a race between pals. We learned a lot from Cook and Phil. Myself, Cook, and Dale discussing conditions at the 1977 National at Sears Point.

Loudon National earlier in the year. Just behind them on row two were Steve McLaughlin and three other expert-ranked fast racers, all on 1,000cc Kawasaki Z1 Superbikes. I was reading Ron Pierce's name in the motorcycle magazines before I was even riding. I would be racing the gods.

The third and fourth rows had the rookies, me, and the other racers who were competing in their first professional road race. I was in the middle of the third row, surrounded by snarling Superbikes on all four sides. We were gridded up for Saturday's five-lap heat race that would establish the starting positions for the next day's 16-lap Superbike final.

As the one-minute sign turned sideways and the revs rose around me, I thought, *I don't belong here. I'm a computer geek from a non-motorcycling family. Who am I trying to kid?* I snicked the bike into first gear, held the clutch lever against the bar, and leaned forward, eyes focused unblinking on the starter and the green flag in his hand. Like everyone around me, I opened the throttle until the motor was screaming, near red-line. The starter waved the flag and I released the clutch as quickly as possible while still keeping the front wheel on the pavement. We all roared off toward the first turn like a pack of greyhounds chasing a mechanical rabbit only we could see. By the time I got to turn 2, the adrenaline had kicked in and my thought was: *Now I remember what I'm doing here.* There were eight guys in front of me. Time to get to work.

Cook Neilson took the initial lead on his Daytona-winning Ducati. I moved up quickly, passing a few racers in the hill section and another two going through the Carousel, to get into fourth halfway through lap one. Just ahead of me were Reg Pridmore and Steve McLaughlin fighting for second. I slipped past them both at the bottom of the esses to take over second place as we completed lap one. I could see Cook a little bit ahead and wanted to catch him quickly. Exiting right hand turn 2 at the beginning of the second lap I was a little too, um, generous with the throttle while still leaned over and things suddenly got *very* exciting.

Too much throttle while still leaned over caused the rear tire to spin, lose traction and slide to the left. When that happened, my instinctive reaction was to close the throttle. Error. The rear tire caught grip again and the bike snapped violently upright. I was thrown into the air but managed to hang on to the handlebars; imagine me above the bike, with a death grip on the bars and my feet over my head. When I came back down, my chest hit the fairing windscreen and it shattered into several pieces, my stomach landed on the fuel tank. The Ducati straightened itself out and I was able to slide back into the saddle.

All these gymnastics widened the bike's line and it ran off the track on the outside of the turn. Somehow I managed to stay upright, bumping along through the tall trackside grass until I could get back onto the pavement. McLaughlin and Pridmore went past while I was busy grass tracking. McLaughlin later told me that as he passed he thought to himself, *We won't have to worry about Ritter anymore.*

He was mistaken.

Once I was back on the pavement, something magic happened … the extra shot of adrenaline from the near-crash…. It's difficult to describe, but it felt like time slowed down, all my senses expanded, and I could feel every tiny detail of what was going on between the motorcycle and the track. Once I realized I was back on the pavement, the only thoughts in my mind were *Go! Win!* I turned three of my fastest laps ever, caught Steve and Reg on the third lap and passed Cook in the Carousel on the final lap, and *won* the heat race.

Oh my God, oh my God, oh my God! What the hell happened? Did I just win a five-lap sprint race after running off the track? There is no one in front of me. Looking back I saw Cook close behind, giving me a thumbs up. I'll be damned, I did it.

I finished the cool-off lap in a daze, waving to the cheering spectators, and then rolled back into the pits. Dale came trotting up to take the bike, a big smile on his face. Then he noticed the fairing screen was completely gone and the smile turned to a look of puzzlement. I just laughed and said, "Don't worry, I'll explain later." I hadn't come down from the adrenaline high yet and I was nearly dancing with excitement. Lots of people were coming by to offer congratulations.

When things calmed down, I told Dale about the near crash that shattered the windscreen, the off-road excursion, and the magic results that came from it. He just smiled and shook his head. He then showed me the lap times he recorded, which made my jaw drop. Lap two was pretty slow, but laps 3-4-5 were stunning. My fastest lap was 1:51.4. That was a good two seconds per lap faster than I had ever managed before.

The Sunday Final

Take the jitters I had before the heat race and double them. That's what I had in my stomach for Sunday's 16-lap final. By Saturday evening the rush of winning the heat race had faded and there was time to think about it. I realized I had *no idea* how I had managed to go so fast without crashing. Dropping two seconds a lap is a lot.

Sunday practice went well. I was turning times in the high 1:52s. In spite of having the pole position, I got a poor start: sixth into the second turn. I blame the jitters. McLaughlin got the hole shot and led until Cook out-braked him into the turn 7 hairpin on lap one.

Just like in the heat race, the jitters disappeared and I got to work, getting past other racers. By the time I had worked my way into second place, Cook had built up a four second lead, which I couldn't seem to close. We were both running consistent lap times between 1:52 and 1:53. As the laps when on, I was beginning to wonder if I could catch Cook.

I could barely see the top of Cook's helmet just over the crest of turn 3 for several laps in a row. Around lap 10, I realized I could see his entire helmet; on lap 11 I could read his name across the top of his shoulders. I was gaining on him!

I can do this! I thought. The effect on me was dramatic–I got another shot of adrenalin and turned another couple of 1:51s on laps 13 and 14 and caught Cook, then passed him in the Carousel with a lap and a half to go.

He did not pass me back at turn 7 and I really poured it on through the esses, trying to build up some cushion. I felt something hard touch the track in the left-hand turn 9, and the bike slid a few inches sideways but it didn't otherwise get upset, so I made a mental note and just kept the gas on.

I caught up to Cook entering the downhill turn 4 and passed him two turns later in the Carousel on the penultimate lap to take and hold the lead.

I stretched my lead to about a second at the checkered flag. Third went to Ron Pierce on the BMW (about 20 seconds back), who had just edged out Reg Pridmore's Kawasaki after a race-long duel. Steve McLaughlin retired with a mechanical failure; local riders Leroy Gerke and Vance Breese took 5th and 6th on a pair of Moto Guzzis. Erik Buell was 7th on a Ducati.

I only vaguely remember the winner's circle ceremony. I was over the moon with joy and happiness. I got interviewed and said all the right things, thanking my sponsors, I think. I also remember Cook saying, during his interview, "… and he passed me in the Carousel for about the millionth time." I got a 3-foot tall trophy, a bottle of good California sparkling wine, and $360 for the win, half of which went to Dale.

That hard part that touched the pavement in turn 9? Just before we packed the bike up for the trip back to Chico, I looked under the bike's left side and was stunned to see a fresh scrape mark on the oil sump. I had touched the crankcase to the track! After that I started hanging my weight off the inside more.

Why I Raced

My non-motorcycling friends sometimes asked why I did something as dangerous as race motorcycles. Even my racing buddies would sometimes wonder what it was that made us race, even after seeing friends and acquaintances get seriously hurt and even killed.

A friend and fellow club racer claimed we were adrenaline junkies and said, "It would be so much cheaper and less dangerous to just go to the clinic once or twice a month and get a shot."

What was this need for some of us to scare ourselves silly every so often? Many years after I stopped racing, I saw the April 1998 issue of *Men's Journal* and the cover article was "The Lure of Danger: Confessions of an Adrenaline Junkie" by S. Junger. It was about war correspondents who put themselves in the line of fire during battle, but a small part of it really resonated with me and explained better than anything else I've ever read why I raced motorcycles. After what happened to me during the near crash in the heat race, I believe this is the best place for it.

A friend of mine once found himself cowering in an obliterated apartment building during heavy street fighting in West Beirut. A sniper was raking his hiding place with gunfire, and my friend just lay there, wired out of his mind. "I was on the floor, aware of everything," he told me. "I could sense things I couldn't see. I could hear people breathing 100 feet away. I was"–he searched for the words–"completely amped. The feeling was like a drug."

In fact, it was a drug. A lot was going on in my friend's brain at that moment, chemically speaking. Fear causes a neurotransmitter section of the brain that governs the senses. Neurotransmitters move nerve impulses across synapses; the more impulses there are, the more active the brain is. When someone is scared, norepinephrine cranks all five senses–sight, hearing, smell, taste, touch–right off the chart. The body is taking in so much information at once that time seems to pass very slowly. In addition, the sympathetic nervous system slams the body into a state of high alert, the heart rate is sped up, and blood is diverted from the skin and organs to the major muscle groups, where it's needed for fighting or running. Finally, intense exertion floods the body with natural opiates, or endorphins, which dull pain and allow you to focus on the crises at hand. That's what makes fear pleasurable, what keeps people returning to it again and again. Dopamine, the chemical byproduct left over in the brain after a terrifying situation, can stimulate the body for hours. Dopamine, which rouses the pleasure centers of the brain, is produced during a slew of behaviors–foraging, exploring, biting, feeding–that are integral to survival. Attaching a chemical reward to these actions is probably the body's way of making sure they get done. Dopamine is also released during sex.

There's fairly good evidence that some people need that "amped" feeling more than others do.... In our insulated society, there are precious few situations that can trigger a high-performance response. And so, like good dopamine enthusiasts, we go out and create them.

Other racers may have different reasons for why they do it, but Junger's description makes sense to me and my experience with racing. This is the feeling I would have while running downhill through the left-hand Carousel turn at Sears Point, motor roaring, ever so slowly rolling on the throttle, feeling the tires grip, slip a little, then grip again, the G forces pushing me into the saddle. My pulse and respiration rates would be elevated and adrenaline coursing through my veins. Today, 35 years later and 15 years since riding, I can still feel it.

I'm also willing to bet that the really good racers, national and world-class front-runners, can bring up this amped feeling on demand. They don't need a near crash to get into this state. All it takes is the wave of a green flag, or the starting lights going out, and they are there.

Pocono, Pennsylvania

Dale and I did not travel to this late-August event. Class champion Reg Pridmore took the win. Reggie's win was doubly notable because he started from the back of the grid, and it was the first win of an AMA Superbike race on a Japanese-built motorcycle. I was rooting for Cook on the *Cycle* Ducati, of course. Cook finished third in the heat race, but the drive chain broke on the warm-up lap of the final and there was no time to repair it.

Pocono was the fifth AMA Superbike race in 1977 and so far there had been five different winners on four different brands of motorcycle. In order the winners were Cook Neilson/Ducati, Mike Baldwin/Moto Guzzi, Ron Pierce/BMW, Paul Ritter/Ducati, and now Reg Pridmore/Kawasaki. The Superbike class was fulfilling its promise of bringing different brands of motorcycles into the winner's circle. It was also bringing more fans to the track, fans who could hope to see a win by their favorite brand.

Laguna Seca

The National road race at Laguna Seca was the Champion Spark Plug 200 that had been running at Laguna since the early 1970s. In 1977 the main event was an International Formula 750 race and European racers were there. A full program was scheduled, with a 250cc race, Superbikes, and Sidecars as support races.

The Laguna Seca track in the late 1970s was different than today's track. It was shorter, only 1.9 miles long. The track ran from turn 2 directly to what is now turn 5, which was, of course, called turn 3 then. The rest of the track is the same as now and included the famous Corkscrew. It was almost a circle track. Except for turn 8 and the second half of the Corkscrew, it was all left-hand turns. Laguna was deceptively fast with only two slower turns, the Corkscrew and the tight left before the start-finish straight.

During the second practice I was mixing it up with Ron Pierce on his fairly quick BMW. Ron, a former member of the Suzuki factory race team, knew the track well, so I followed him for a bit. I was amazed at how late he braked for turn 4. I started using his brake marker and improved my lap times. He was also out-braking me at the entrance to the

Corkscrew, but that is a scary turn and I couldn't force myself to wait as late as Ron before braking. I did pick up better lines in a couple of spots.

I frankly don't remember where I finished the heat race, probably fifth or sixth behind McLaughlin, Pridmore, Neilson, and Cooley, and perhaps Pierce.

At the start of the Superbike final, McLaughlin got off first with the new Yoshimura Suzuki, a GS750 bored out to 944cc, and opened up a decent lead in the first two laps, but after Neilson's Ducati got past Wes Cooley's Kawasaki, he was able to catch McLaughlin. Pridmore was slowed with ignition problems caused by bad coils and couldn't make it a trio at the front, but was holding third place ahead of Cooley who had opened up some space on Ron Pierce's BMW and my Ducati. Neilson placed himself on McLaughlin's rear wheel and started measuring him up, planning his end-game move.

Cook never had a chance to make his play. Steve had been grounding the Suzuki's alternator cover in seven of the eight left-hand turns and, as Cook put it, "He finally struck oil." Oil from the hole in the engine cover coated the left side of the Suzuki and Neilson's face-shield and fairing screen. Vision impaired, Cook had to slow and was nearly caught by Pridmore on the last lap, but he held on to capture second place.

I finished fourth, shaking off the early challenge by Pierce on the BMW, getting faster each lap as I got more familiar with the track. I was

During practice eventual race winner Steve McLaughlin (83, Suz) drifts wide while Cook Neilson (31, Duc) leads me (276, Duc); we finished 2nd and 4th, respectively. Mike Baldwin (186, Moto Guzzi) follows. *Felix Adamo*

delighted to have finished in fourth place. Wes Cooley had the Yoshimura Kawasaki in the fourth spot for a while but stopped with a mechanical failure. Pierce was fifth and Dave Emde brought a Suzuki home in sixth.

Superbike Pioneer - Steve McLaughlin

Steve rode different Superbikes at different times–a BMW in 1976, Kawasakis and Suzukis for Yoshimura, and a Racecrafters Kawasaki. He was also a strong racer on Yamaha TZ250s and TZ750s in the expert ranks–fast enough to be included in one of the American teams that traveled to England for the Anglo-American Match Races.

Steve was a natural born promoter. He tried to get more people interested in motorcycle racing, and he promoted road racing, Superbikes in particular, as well as himself. His self-promotion irritated some people, but I didn't mind as long as it brought in more fans. Although he certainly earned more purse money in the 750cc class, Steve genuinely liked Superbikes. The 1978 Laguna Seca round was a really close race between three riders right up to the checkered flag. During his victory circle interview, Steve said, in a voice that reverberated across the entire site, "Once again, the Superbike race was the best race of the weekend."

Steve was a major player in the establishment of the World Superbike race series in 1988; some would say he was *the* major player. The book *World Superbikes–The First 20 Years* by Julian Ryder and Kel Edge says, "The creation of the World Superbike Championship is down to the vision of one man, former racer turned promoter, Steve McLaughlin." WSBK rules were based largely on a modified set of the AMA Superbike rules.

Steve McLaughlin (83) on the 944cc Suzuki GS750 and the Yoshumura team. Photo from an ND spark plug ad in 1977.

Through the years there has been some great racing in the WSBK I've enjoyed watching. Thanks, Steve.

Riverside Raceway

The final AMA road race of the 1977 season was at Riverside International Raceway in Southern California on October 1-2. It was a track I knew well from club racing, a fast, flowing course that rewarded good horsepower and top speed, but also required decent handling. Even though we would be at a disadvantage with our relatively low top speed, Riverside was a fun track and we enjoyed racing on it.

Because it was the last Superbike race of the season, the championship points battle was on many people's mind. Reg Pridmore on a Kawasaki Z1 had the season point lead, but both Mike Baldwin's Moto Guzzi 850 Le Mans and the *Cycle* Ducati ridden by Cook Neilson had mathematical chances to take the championship.

Steve McLaughlin and the Yoshimura Suzuki won Saturday's five-lap heat race to get the pole position for Sunday's final. Cook's Ducati started making funny noises and he pulled in with a blown engine—the big-end bearing had expired. Pridmore's bike had something wrong in the front end and it was wobbling badly. Reg backed off to settle for a safe fourth place rather than risk a crash. I was battling with Wes Cooley's Z1—he would pass me on the start-finish straight and I'd pass him back in the twisty esses leading into turn 6. He would pass me on the back straight, but I could get though turn 9 better. As I recall, I slipped underneath him in that last turn, the wide sweeping horseshoe, and screwed it on just enough to beat him to the flag. I was a surprise second place in the five-lap heat after winning the handling vs. horsepower battle with Wes.

The short Sunday morning warm-up showed that Phil Schilling had the *Cycle* Ducati running strong again, but Cook would be starting from the back of the grid. Pridmore's crew had fixed the front-end problem and Reg was back to his normal fast speed.

Sunday's warm-up was not so successful for us. In the previous practice someone spilled some oil in turn 6, the tightest turn on the track, and I crashed there. It would have been no big deal except I tried to stand up before I had stopped sliding. Not a good idea. I fell down again as I couldn't keep my feet underneath me, and this time I wacked the back of my helmet hard against the pavement. It didn't hurt, but I felt dizzy and slightly nauseous. These are not good signs, usually indicating a slight concussion. There was no more practice for Superbikes, so I went into a

Wes Cooley (33 Kawasaki) and I (276 Ducati) battled for second place in the heat race, and I just edged him out. I couldn't keep up with him in the final.

corner of the garage and tried to figure out whether I should race or not. I wasn't sure I could ride safely. I told Dale what had happened and he told everyone to leave me alone.

About 15 minutes before the call to grid, I realized, *Hey, it was time to go racing!* A small jolt of adrenaline shot into my blood and I suddenly recovered. My vision cleared and the nausea disappeared. I remember getting up and saying, "Let's get ready," and we did.

At the start of the main event, the two Yoshimura bikes, McLaughlin's Suzuki and Cooley's Kawasaki, shot into the lead. I grabbed third with Pridmore right behind. Pridmore's bike got only as far as turn 2 when it lost all spark. Near the end of the lap McLaughlin dropped out with a burnt clutch, leaving Cooley alone in the lead. I was in second for a short time, with Mike Baldwin close behind, but it wasn't long before Cook came past us both. I tried to hook on in hopes of getting a tow, but Cook's bike was too fast. I watched as he moved ahead to join Wes Cooley at the front and the two of them slowly moved away from me.

Near the end of the race, Mike Baldwin missed a shift and broke his gearbox, coasting to a stop near the finish line. Pridmore's crew had found and fixed a broken battery wire and Reg was back in the race but several laps behind.

Neilson and Cooley were doing the same thing Wes and I did during the heat race. They dueled for the lead, with the Ducati having a handling advantage while the Kawasaki had better top speed. They fought back and forth all the way to the end, when Wes won the dash to the checkered flag by one bike length ahead of Cook. I finished a lonely third place, ahead of two BMWs.

With only 17 starters, Reg Pridmore finished in 15th place, which was out of the points. Baldwin pushed his bike across the finish line after the checkered flag waved, and was listed in 14th place, earning a single point. Neilson earned 16 points for his second place. Did that give him enough to overtake Reggie?

I was delighted to finish on the podium in third place, and was also pleased with the Ducati two-three finish. After the winner's circle celebration, Wes, Cook, and I were put in the back of a small pickup truck for a victory lap of the track. We were waving and acknowledging the applause of the spectators when the driver swerved off the pavement just before turn 7. What the ... ? A stream of snarling race bikes came past. The Novice 250cc race was scheduled after the Superbike race, and race control had released the bikes for their warm-up lap before we had finished our parade lap. We all had a pretty good chuckle about that, once we were safely in the pits.

Superbike Pioneer - Wes Cooley

Wes Cooley was Yoshimura's lead rider in those early Superbike years, initially on a Kawasaki Z1 and later with the Suzuki GS750 and GS1000. He was one of the toughest competitors in the field in 1978, when he either won (twice) or broke. He had more success in 1979. By then the Yoshimura bikes had become reliable as well as fast, and Wes finished on the podium in every Superbike race.

Wes had the amazing ability to go top speed at the drop of the green flag–Wes's best laps always seemed to be his early ones. Tough as nails on the track, he was a good sport whether he won or not.

Wes had a near-fatal crash in 1985 that put him in a hospital for a stay. He recovered and returned to racing and had some success, but never regained his pre-accident speed.

He was so impressed with the people who cared for him after the 1985 accident that, after retiring from racing, he went back to school and

Wes Cooley at Laguna Seca in 1981.

Bill Mullins

became a registered nurse. The last I heard he was working in the medical profession somewhere in Idaho.

1977 Superbike Season Summary– That Marvelous Second Year

The second year of AMA Superbikes turned out to be the sort of racing series promoters dream about and spectators love. The seven Superbike races had produced seven separate winners on five different brands of motorcycles. These days it's hard to imagine going to an AMA Superbike race and having *no idea* who is going to win and on what brand of motorcycle. In addition to the five winning brands, there were top-10 finishes for Laverda, Honda, Yamaha, Norton, and Triumph. In chronological order the victors were:

Venue	Winner	Brand
Daytona	Cook Neilson	Ducati
Charlotte	Mike Baldwin	Moto Guzzi
Loudon	Ron Pierce	BMW
Sears Point	Paul Ritter	Ducati
Pocono	Reg Pridmore	Kawasaki
Laguna Seca	Steve McLaughlin	Suzuki
Riverside	Wes Cooley	Kawasaki

It was a great year for Superbikes. Entries were up compared to 1976, more sponsors were getting involved, and payouts, though still small, had increased. Most of the time the racing was close and there was very good brand representation, which led to high spectator enthusiasm.

Reg Pridmore was the 1977 Superbike champion, the top rider for the second year in a row by virtue of one win and several top-five finishes. The top 10 in the championship standings were:

	Rider	Bike	Points
1.	Reg Pridmore	Racecrafters Kawasaki[1]	71
2.	Cook Neilson	*Cycle* Magazine Ducati	68
3.	Mike Baldwin	Reno Leoni Moto Guzzi	56
4.	Ron Pierce	Johnny of Bakersfield BMW	53
5.	Kurt Liebmann	Reno Leoni Moto Guzzi	50
6.	Wes Cooley	Yoshimura Kawasaki	47
7.	Paul Ritter	Aero-Union Ducati	44
8.	Kurt Lenz	Ducati	27
9.(t)	Keith Code	Kawasaki	25
9.(t)	David Emde	Kawasaki	25
9.(t)	John Fuchs	Honda	25

Here's how the top five earned their points:

Rider	Daytona	Charlotte	Loudon	Sears	Pocono	Laguna	Riverside
1. Reg Pridmore	4th	–	2nd	4th	1st	3rd	–
2. Cook Neilson	1st	–	–	2nd	–	2nd	2nd
3. Mike Baldwin	5th	1st	6th	–	2nd	–	14th
4. Ron Pierce	–	–	1st	3rd	–	5th	5th
5. Kurt Liebmann	7th	2nd	3rd	–	3rd	–	–

Of the top five Reg Pridmore was the most consistent, earning points in five of the seven races. Only three points separated first and second place. Cook Neilson is best known for his 1977 Daytona win, but he was more than a one-track phenomenon. The difference between first and second place is 4 points, and Cook finished in second place three times: Sears Point, Laguna Seca, and Riverside. If he had beaten Wes Cooley at that last race at Riverside, Cook would have been the 1977

---

1 Reg got 11 points while on a BMW with his 4th-place finish at Daytona. All his other points came on the Kawasaki.

Superbike champion on a Ducati. If the chain hadn't broken at Pocono ... if McLaughlin's bike hadn't leaked oil at Laguna ... but that's just racing. Sometimes Lady Luck is on your side and sometimes she smacks you down.

Cheating? Who, Me?

I've been asked how much cheating went on in the early days of Superbike racing and if Dale's Ducati was strictly legal. I typically answered, "Yes."

For this book I wanted to give a more complete answer, so I dug out copies of the 1977 and 1978 AMA Professional Road Race Competition Rule Book. According to the 1977 rules, a Superbike must have begun life as a standard production road model with full lights and instrumentation, and with engine capacity from 355cc up to 1,000cc, At least 200 models must have been available for sale in the U.S.

The motor: A Superbike had to use the manufacturer's castings for crankcase, gear case, cylinder(s), and head(s). The stock stroke was required, but it could be over-bored up to the 1,000cc limit. The stock carburetors were required, but the throat size could be changed and re-jetting was permitted. There is no mention in the 1977 rules of cams, pistons, crankshaft, con rods, gearbox internals, and so forth. Apparently all engine internals could be altered, except for stroke.

There were several sections about chassis changes. Cast wheels were allowed. The frame had to be the stock frame, but gussets could be added and brackets could be removed. Center-stands and side-stands had to be removed. Handlebars could be changed, but they had to use the stock mounts. The stock swingarm was required, but it could be reinforced, shortened, or lengthened. The stock forks were required, but the internals could be changed. Rear shocks could be changed, but the standard shock configuration (dual- or mono-shock) was required.

Body work had to *look* like the stock bike's. The stock fuel tank and seat were required, as were the fenders, but fenders could be moved to adapt to different wheel sizes and tire widths. Fairings were not allowed unless fitted on the as-sold model. The chain guard could be moved or removed to allow for different sprockets or wider tires. Air cleaner, toolbox, and license plate brackets could be removed. The stock exhaust system was required, but it could be relocated for ground clearance and the muffler could be modified as long as it retained the stock muffler shell. There was a noise limit, but it was well beyond what was legal on the street.

True road race tires were required; no D.O.T. tires. Lighting equipment and instruments, including generator, alternator or magneto, etc., had to be operational at technical inspection and at the start of the event. Head and taillights had to be taped, with a small gap left for inspection.

Were these rules violated or bent? Sure. Did it make a difference in the finishing order? Maybe. Some infractions I knew of for certain, while others were suspected. No names will be mentioned in this recounting.

There was at least one bike that had two tachometers, the standard cable-operated one and an electronic one. The electronic one was removed when the bike went through tech inspection and sound check. The sound test was made at half redline rpm, and the stock tachometer read high. The tach would say 5,000 rpm when the engine was actually turning maybe 4,700 or 4,600 rpm. Did anyone care? Not really. What are a few decibels one way or another?

During the process of building their race bike one team discovered the headstock of their Kawasaki Z1 frame was welded just slightly off-center, a situation that worked OK at normal street speeds but could produce rather creative handling at high speeds. They cut off the headstock and re-welded it on the centerline. Was this adding gussets or removing brackets? Not really, but nobody was going to force racers to use frames that were unsafe.

Frame modifications that bent the rules included changing the motor mounts. The BMWs and the four-cylinder bikes had very wide engines that had ground-clearance problems in the corners. Some teams altered their bike's frame to mount the engine higher from the ground. Was that considered gusseting?

Another area where violations were suspected was in the use of the bike's alternator or generator. The 1977 rules required the standard charging system be functional at race start, yet it was known some teams were running total-loss ignition systems. Why would they do that if their charging system worked? The generator or alternator typically added some flywheel weight to the crank. This is good if you want the bike to idle smoothly and run well at low rpm, but not so good if you want light weight and to gain revs quickly. Some teams probably removed their alternator and depended on a fully-charged battery to provide enough juice to finish the race.

Also, part of the four-cylinder engine's width was due to the alternator, positioned on the end of the crank. With the alternator gone the side cover could be shaved to narrow the engine. You couldn't take off much without becoming obvious, but even ¼ inch would give several more degrees of lean before any of the hard parts touched pavement.

In 1977 there would be, from time to time, some grumbling about missing alternators and creative frame gusseting, but there were no protests filed. Some felt a protest shouldn't have been necessary. The AMA, as the sanctioning organization, should check for alternators on all of the podium motorcycles as standard post-race procedure.

The Superbike rules were completely reworked in 1978. Here are the major differences.

- Maximum displacement was 1,025cc, up from 1,000cc. I believe this was to accommodate the new Kawasaki KZ1000, which had an actual displacement of 1,015cc. Bore *and* stroke could be altered up to the 1,025cc limit.

- Exhaust system could be original equipment with muffler shells *or* a catalogued aftermarket system. The noise limit wasn't changed.

- The section on lighting, instrumentation and ignition was quite different. Total-loss systems were specifically permitted; headlights didn't need to work and using only the shell was allowed. The engine ignition system could be changed, the speedometer had to be mounted, but it didn't need to have an operating cable, and the rules no longer required the motor to have a working alternator or generator.

These changes didn't really help the twin-cylinder European motorcycles. The Ducatis were already pretty narrow and the alternator for the Moto Guzzis and BMWs didn't impact ground clearance. The four-cylinder bikes benefited greatly, however. It wasn't long before the wide four-cylinder motors showed up with an angled slice taken out of the bottom of the side cover, replaced by a welded-in plate.

Cycle, in their 1978 Daytona coverage, put it this way: "Traditionally unwilling (or unable) to enforce the rules, the AMA simply changed them. ...As a result the twin-cylinder fanciers found themselves with a sharply reduced number of individual advantages."

Dale objected to these changes by keeping our 1978 bikes legal under the more restrictive 1977 rules. We got two podium finishes that year and Dale made sure the post-race AMA tech-inspector saw that his bike had an installed and functioning alternator.

To my knowledge there was only one protest ever filed during the first four years of AMA Superbikes, at Pocono in 1978, described in the next chapter.

A Sad Parting

It was time—probably past time, actually. As much as Virginia and I cared for each other, there was one very fundamental difference. I wanted to have children someday and Virginia did not. I didn't blame her for it. She didn't want to be a mother because she didn't think she would be a very good one, so she *chose* not to have children. I admired her for it. There are many people who know they will be bad parents but have children anyway. Fewer bad parents would mean fewer screwed up people in the world, I figure.

It didn't matter that I understood it; it was still a deal breaker. We knew it from early on in our relationship, and I pushed it into the back of my mind for as long as I could. But in 1978 I would be turning 30, and it was time to make the decision. I moved out of the house in Oakland during early 1978. It saddened me to leave, and it broke my heart to see her so unhappy, but I couldn't stay and still become a father.

Males have a biological clock too, although it's different from females. I wanted to be able to get down on the floor and roughhouse with my kids, the same way my dad did with me and my brother Phil. My father had some health problems in his mid-40s and roughhousing became difficult for him. I was eight and getting too old for the game, but my younger siblings missed out, and I'm sure Dad missed playing the game with them as well. I didn't want that to happen to me.

Virginia and I were together for over six years, but the children/no children issue made me hold back a little part of my heart. I don't think I ever told her I loved her, but I'm sure, now, that I did. No one stays that long with someone they just "like a lot."

She and her husband now live in Seattle, and we see each other now and then. VA, in fact, gave me copies of many of the early racing photos and encouraged me to finish this book.

CHAPTER EIGHT

Chasing the Championship

After the good results of the 1977 season, I no longer wondered what I was doing racing at the top level of Superbikes. I had proved to myself, and to my competitors, that the win at Sears Point wasn't a fluke. Perhaps more importantly, I had proved to myself that I didn't need to be a follower. To discover something that I truly loved doing, and that I was really good at doing, was deeply satisfying–especially for someone with Close Second Child Syndrome.

So far in this journey, every time I had some success, I was looking for the next level. I think Dale had the same attitude as well. At this time the next level was to run the full Superbike series. We believed we had a legitimate shot at the class title.

———

In 1978 there were six AMA road races at five tracks, only one less race than 1977, but two fewer venues. The road race schedule for the 1978 season was:

Date	Track
Mar. 5-12	Daytona, FL
Apr. 15/16	Sears Point, CA
June 17/18	Loudon, NH
Aug. 12/13	Pocono, PA
Sep. 2/3	Loudon, NH
Sep. 9/10	Laguna Seca, CA

Dale and I made plans. The 1977 results in the three races we entered were good for seventh place in the class, encouraging enough that we decided to run the full 1978 season and take a stab at the title. We cut back on the club racing schedule, choosing to contest only selected AFM races that would help us prepare the bikes for the Nationals and to keep my riding skills fresh.

Here's the motorcycle lineup we had. First was the 1977 Sears Point-winning bike, a lightly modified 900SS engine in a quality chassis. We called this bike the Stocker; it had really good torque and mid-range power. It pulled strongly out of corners and handled superbly, but with the stock valve sizes and only slightly modified ports, its top speed was poor compared to other bikes in the class.

The second bike we called Cook's bike, although in fact it was one of Dale's chassis with the Neilson/Schilling motor. Cook had retired from racing after 1977 and Dale bought his bike and all his Ducati spares. Old Blue was originally a 750SS that had been bored to 883cc and was highly modified with lots of special parts and extensive porting to the heads. Compared to the Stocker, it had less low-end and mid-range power, but came on strong on top, continuing to make usable power past 9,000 rpm. It was a fast bike for high-speed tracks.

There was a third bike that Dale had starting building during the winter, and he hoped to have it ready in time for Pocono. It had a couple of special cylinder heads and matching pistons the Ducati factory had gifted Cook and Phil after their win at Daytona in 1977. When Dale bought Old Blue, he also got all the spare parts, and these special heads and pistons were included. The diameter of the pistons that came with the heads gave the motor 905cc capacity so it ended up being called simply the nine-oh-five.

Road Trip! Daytona, Florida

Our first race in 1978 was Daytona, March 6-12. The Superbike heat race was scheduled for Thursday with the final on Friday the 10th. I took a couple weeks of vacation from work and drove up to Chico in late February.

"Do you know how to get there?" I asked Dale.

"Yeah, it's easy, just go to Los Angeles and turn right."

I brought up an image of the U.S. in my head. "Wouldn't that put us in the Pacific Ocean?" I asked.

Dale thought for a minute, "Oh yeah. I mean turn *left* at L.A." My faith in my sponsor's navigational skills restored, Dale, his wife Iola, and I piled into the race van and started south. In the trailer towed behind us were two Ducati Superbikes and a whole bunch of other stuff: gas, oil, tools, spares, tires, etc. We drove straight through, eight-hour shifts with one person sleeping on the cot in the back of the van, one person driving, and one person making sure the driver stayed awake.

Monday morning we went out to the track. I still remember my first impressions at the time: Daytona is *big*! It made even Ontario Motor Speedway seem average. The accommodations were as plush as Ontario and better than any other track I'd seen. The paddock area was paved and there were covered pit areas. Security was so good we could leave the bikes, gear, and even tools at the track without fear of them being stolen, so we didn't have to pack it up every night and unload every morning.

The course itself wasn't very difficult. It was the classic Daytona course consisting of an infield section with basically three horseshoe turns of various radii, one dogleg left-hander and one left elbow corner. There was a left-right-left chicane just before the second banked turn, designed to slow the faster bikes down. All the rest of it was full throttle speedway track, including the two famous 30-degree banked turns. It was long–3.87 miles per lap.

It took me about three tries to figure out how to ride the banked turns. As soon as I got on the banking, I kept dropping off onto the flat apron on the inside of the track. I would haul the bike back up onto the banking and try to continue around this left turn only to drop back down to the flat apron. *What's going on?* I thought.

I got around the first banking and headed down the straight toward the chicane. Right after the chicane there was the other banked turn, and darned if I didn't drive off the banking and onto the apron again. Midway through this banked turn, I figured it out: with our Superbike, the banked turns weren't really turns. If I rode them like a straight, with the wheel pointed dead ahead and equal pressure on the bars, full tuck out of the wind, the 30-degree banking swept me right around. Ride it as if it's a left turn, with pressure on the left handlebar, and I rode off the track on the inside. *Holy smokes*, I thought, *You don't have to turn for the turns!*

My other problem was turn 1. Nothing in my previous racing experience had prepared me for hauling the bike down from full throttle to the speed needed to get through the moderately tight turn 1. Things are zooming by *so fast* it's hard to pick out brake markers. People who have been here before are flying by me going into this turn. I never did get comfortable with turn 1.

By Wednesday I had gotten more comfortable with the track, except for turn 1, and we started pushing the bike a bit. To our surprise and dismay, it didn't respond. We couldn't get it to pull the gearing that Cook used last year, and the top speed was down nearly 10 mph. We added a couple of teeth to the rear sprocket. That helped, but I *still* couldn't get it to pull 9,000 rpm in top gear. Something was wrong. The fastest time through the speed trap was 142 mph, 8 mph down on the 1977 speed and a bunch down on the fast four-cylinder bikes. The bike was running clean, with no misfiring or hesitation, but it was clearly down on power from 1977. We considered running the Stocker, but even down on power, Cook's engine was faster than the Stocker.

Wednesday night Dale and I loaded the race bike into the van and took it back to the hotel. After dinner I watched an amazing thing. Dale, with me helping a little, took the bike into the parking garage beneath the building, found an empty slot just beneath a light, and did a teardown. In less than an hour he had the engine *completely* apart on the concrete. I had never seen anyone work so fast with such precision. And I mean apart–the heads were off the motor with the rocker arms and cams exposed. The cylinders were off, the pistons off their rods, and the crankcase was split.

Everything that could be checked was checked, but Dale found nothing wrong, so we put things back together. After we muscled the reassembled engine back into the frame and connected the wiring, exhausts, and carbs, I realized that in about three-and-a-half hours Dale

Me (96 Ducati) and Harry Klinzmann (87 BMW) in turn 4 during practice. The gray "wall" in the background is the high banking of the track. *Sally Garoutte*

had completely stripped, inspected, and reassembled the engine, in a parking space, without power tools. Dale was truly a master mechanic. I never saw better.

The bike was no better after the teardown and inspection, but no worse either. We were not competitive and we knew it, but we would run as well as we could and pick up as many points as possible.

Friday was Superbike race day, with heat races scheduled on Thursday. For the first time in Superbikes, there were enough entries to require *two* heats to set the grid. Reg Pridmore won the first heat. Heat two, the faster of the two heats, was won by Wes Cooley, giving him the pole position for the Friday final. As for myself, I frankly don't remember where I finished in the heat race. It must have been so-so. If it was really good or really bad, I would remember it.

Wes Cooley took full advantage of his pole position and grabbed the lead at the start. I got an average start, and after a couple of laps settled into sixth place, pretty much by myself.

On lap three or four I was at full throttle in the straight between turns 1 and 2 when the engine stumbled for just a fraction of a second, then picked up again. *What was that?* I thought. Just as I completed the thought the rear wheel locked up solid. *Wow!* I whipped in the clutch lever, and the bike started coasting. Just to check I let the clutch out gradually to see if it would restart the engine. Nope. It just skidded the rear tire. I parked the bike at the side of the track and walked back to the pits.

Steve McLaughlin took the win on the Yoshimura Suzuki followed by the Racecrafters Kawasaki of Reg Pridmore barely ahead of John Long on one of the ex-Butler & Smith BMWs. Mike Baldwin brought the Leoni-tuned Moto Guzzi home in fourth. Four different brands in the top four spots, nice.

Our post-mortem: crankshaft failure. The big-end had heated up enough to weld itself into a fairly solid mass. We knew running near 9,000 rpm was hard on the Ducati crankshafts and big-end bearings, but not *that* hard. The crank was brand-new at the start of the week. Dale sent the remains of the crank and a new crank he had bought at the same time to Jeff Bratten of Rennsport Werke. Jeff, an expert on roller bearing cranks, found corrosion in the big end of the unused crank. The Daytona crank was too messed up to tell for sure, but Jeff suspected corrosion there too. I guess a shipment of Ducati parts had sat a bit too long at some dock, soaking up the Mediterranean sun and salty sea air. It's a poor way to start a championship challenge, with a DNF and no points.

Superbike Pioneer - Dale Newton

Dale Newton had been a motorcyclist in his youth, but stepped away from the sport when he started a family and his own business. With his kids mostly grown and his business on solid footing, he got back into bikes, racing a Ducati 750 Sport in the AFM club races in 1976. We got acquainted then since we raced the same model.

He was not built to be a road racer; Dale was a big guy, well over 6 feet tall and probably over 200 pounds when I met him—not chubby but not thin either. After the 1976 season he hung up his racing leathers and became a sponsor/tuner/mechanic. I was the lucky guy who got to race his motorcycles.

Mechanically, Dale was a perfectionist. His equipment was always well prepared and beautifully turned out. He not only got the big picture but understood attention to detail was important. His business involved maintaining airplanes, where you don't just roll to a stop at the side of the road when the engine quits. If we had a mechanical problem of any kind, he would analyze it and make a change. We never had a repeat failure during two racing seasons and dozens of races, a credit to his tuning and wrenching skills.

Dale was a straight-up guy; his handshake was as good as a contract. He was remarkably calm-natured and I rarely saw him get angry. Dale

Dale at Sears Point 1977.

was dedicated to his family. He had built up a pretty large collection of motorcycles, from old British singles to Yamaha TZ race bikes. He left all his bikes in trust, to be sold as needed to finance his grandchildren's college educations.

I lost touch with Dale when I drifted away from motorcycles for a few years. When I started riding again it saddened me to learn Dale had passed away from some sort of blood poisoning. He was too young. There are many questions I'd like to ask him. Besides I miss him.

Sears Point Gets Rained Out

The 1978 AMA National at Sears Point on April 15th and 16th was rained out. I woke up on Friday, the unofficial practice day of the AMA race weekend, to rainy weather. I expected a cancellation, but I drove to the track anyway. Sears Point had not yet opened the gates and there were many race vans and trailers parked in the approach area. We hung out there for a few hours, just shooting the breeze, before the official word filtered down: no race this weekend. It wasn't bad for me. I lived nearby, a 45-minute drive to the track. It took Dale less than three hours from Chico, still not too bad. I felt sorry for the riders and teams from the East Coast who had traveled for several days only to sit for a short time in a wet parking lot near Sonoma, then turn around and travel back home. The race was rescheduled for mid-July, basically the same time of year as the 1977 event.

A Visit to New England

After the rain-out in April at Sears Point, the next road race on the AMA's 1978 schedule was June 17-18 at Loudon, New Hampshire. Dale had repaired the motor that had self-destructed at Daytona, and we were back to having two Ducatis, the one with the Neilson/Schilling engine and the Stocker.

This was my first time at the Bryars Motorsport track, a configuration that doesn't exist today. During practice we tried both bikes and found there was no real difference in lap times. We chose to run the Stocker because it had always been pretty reliable. There was a heat race to set the Superbike grid, but nothing memorable happened since I don't remember it.

The fast bikes were the Yoshimura Suzukis of John Bettencourt, Wes Cooley, and Ron Pierce, and the BMWs of John Long and Harry Klinzmann. Other fast guys included Pridmore and Keith Code on Kawasaki KZ1000s and Mike Baldwin on his Moto Guzzi.

The main event was 25 laps. I got my usual mediocre start, but began slowly picking guys off. Cooley took the early lead, but was soon being harassed by Bettencourt, then a small gap to a battle for third between Klinzmann and Baldwin.

Attrition began to take its toll as Pierce's clutch failed, Baldwin crashed unhurt, and Cooley's engine packed up. Near the halfway point the pit signals told me I was in fifth, and I recognized the next rider ahead of me–it's Reggie. I moved up and began practically chewing on his rear tire, looking for a way around. This went on for about three laps until we hit some lapped traffic and Reg got a little separation from me. I tried to regain the space but couldn't–my shoulder, injured at a club race fall two weeks prior, started to hurt a lot and I had to slow.

A lap from the end, we were given a gift of racing luck. Harry Klinzmann, in a secure second place on the San Jose BMW, pulled into the pits with cracked engine cases. Harry is a good guy–he could have tried to finish the last lap, but choose to pull in rather than oil up the track.

Close racing in Loudon's turn 6 Bowl during practice. Reg Pridmore, Mike Baldwin, myself, Erik Buell, and Ron Pierce; Kawasaki, Moto Guzzi, Ducati, Ducati, and Suzuki. *Mary Grothe*

This moved me up to fourth place at the checkers. John Bettencourt won by a lot on his Suzuki, followed by John Long on the surviving BMW, Reg Pridmore's Kawasaki, and me on the Ducati. Local rider John Fuchs finished fifth on a Honda. Five different makes in the top-five places—pretty good brand representation, eh?

After the race I was really beat. My sore shoulder and the sheer physical exertion of racing in 90-degree heat with 90 percent humidity had really wiped me out. I was sitting in the van trying to cool off when one of the spectators came by, looked at my bike, and said, "I'm surprised to see the wheels still on it."

I was so exhausted his joke went right over my head. All I could manage was, "Huh?"

"I'm saying you rode the wheels off it," the guy explained.

"Oh. Uh, thanks," I replied.

We were pretty pleased with the results, however. I'd figured out most of the track, with only two turns—the banked-turn 7 and the hairpin with the elevation drop, turn 9—still giving me trouble. My lap times during the part of the race when I was catching up to Pridmore were competitive. And there was another race scheduled here in September. Yeah, a fourth place on a track I'd never seen before was pretty good work.

Superbike Pioneer - John Bettencourt

To his friends he was Johnny B. An East Coast racer, John Bettencourt had several top-10 Superbike finishes in 1977 and 1978, including the win at Loudon in 1978 on a Yoshimura East Suzuki. A very good-natured fellow, John was always smiling or laughing and clearly having a good time. He could have the worst things happen to him and he would just laugh and say, "That's racing."

At the 1979 Ontario six-hour endurance race, there was a two-bike pile-up on the main straight that caused a red flag race stoppage. It seems that John, riding one of the Yoshimura 1,000s, had gotten tangled up with a smaller bike. I didn't see the crash, but I saw John's bike afterward and the front end had been completely ripped off. The front wheel and fork were connected to the rest of the motorcycle only by the speedometer cable and brake lines.

I had a chance to talk to Johnny afterwards. He said he was drafting another liter-bike at top speed down the main straight, just a few feet off the other guy's back tire. Suddenly the lead bike did a quick flick of the bars and moved a couple of feet to the right. Directly ahead of John was a small Production bike going about 30 mph slower. He had no time to react and rear-ended the smaller bike. "Man, that must have been a bummer," I said. Johnny just laughed and said, "Hey, that's racing."

Back Home at Sears Point

A recap so far: two races under our belts, a DNF at Daytona (broken crank) in March, and a fourth at Loudon in June. We returned from New England tired and pretty happy about the finish, determined to do better at Sears Point, my home track. I had narrowly beaten Cook Neilson the previous year, so I was the defending Superbike champ.

We took the Stocker to the AFM's Golden Gate Challenge July 2 for practice, because the AMA race had been rescheduled for July 15-16. Racing in Open GP behind two TZ750 Yamahas, one of the stock pistons failed, coming apart in turn 9 with a clatter that could be heard in the pits. Ugh. Once again Dale had to delay development of the 905 to fix a broken bike. But fix it he did, and he showed up at the National with a fresh engine, bored out to 883cc from the stock 864cc and fitted with a pair of high-compression aftermarket pistons.

Practice showed three serious contenders. Wes Cooley had gotten the Yoshimura Suzuki going really well, and Mike Baldwin was riding the fast Moto Guzzi tuned by Reno Leoni. My lap times put me in contention as well.

In the Saturday heat race Wes Cooley got the holeshot on the Suzuki, with Mike Baldwin on the Guzzi in second. I got my usual average start, but moved up right behind Baldwin in the esses on lap one. I pulled alongside him exiting turn 10 when his motor backfired loudly and stopped. Mike pulled immediately into the pit lane and I put myself on Cooley's rear tire. I probed a bit, but Wes was riding well so I didn't push the issue.

I could go faster. I thought about nailing him in turn 10, but he was taking a rather early apex and a wide exit. *It's only the heat race, I've got a front row start, don't get stupid*, I told myself. Later Wes was quoted saying, "I could hear a big twin on my tail, and figured it was Ritter or Baldwin, so I blocked as best as I could." We were turning times in the high 1:51 to low 1:52 range, and it felt pretty easy. I was sure I could go faster and felt pretty confident, even rather cocky, about the main event. I was going to win.

I learned later that Baldwin's Guzzi was running a total-loss ignition system (legal under the revised 1978 rules), and someone on his crew had left a switch on after practice. He ran out of spark and would be starting the final from the rear of the grid, a break for the rest of us.

The Superbike race was set for 16 laps. I got a poor start, fifth into turn 1, while Cooley got the quick start. I got past Harry Klinzmann on the BMW in the Carousel on lap one, grabbed third from Dennis Smith (Suz) on lap two, then caught and passed Reg Pridmore's Kawasaki on the fifth go-around. It took some time to get past Reggie, as he was riding well.

Cooley had built up a lead of about 10 seconds while I was getting clear of other traffic. I was in second now and really pushing hard, expecting to close the gap on Wes.

Five more laps went by, and I still couldn't see him. Damn! The bike was sliding both wheels through the Carousel–I was yelling in my helmet, "Stick, damn it, stick!" I was going as fast as I could, and still no Wes. What's happening? I should be able to catch him. The starter signaled five more laps to go and Wes was still about seven seconds ahead. *This wasn't the script I wrote*, I thought.

On lap 13 I saw him in turn 7. He was slowing, coasting to a stop! He was looking down at his bike's drive chain. I passed and took the lead! I took a quick look back–nobody in sight. Whew! I backed off a click. Coming around through turn 11, I saw Dale running out to the pit wall, his index finger high in the air. I gave him a little wave to show I was

My knee nearly touches down while trying to catch Cooley in 1978 at Sears Point. This is turn 10, which was one of the fastest turns on the track.

aware of the situation. Dale's helper Tom was holding his arms wide with his palms parallel, the racer signal for "you have a big lead." I was grinning ear-to-ear inside my helmet. When I got to turn 7, I saw Wes with his bike parked and his helmet off. He grinned and gave me a big salute. He had stopped because the power of the Yoshimura engine had sheared off all the bolts holding the rear sprocket to the wheel, and the sprocket was just freewheeling on the axle.

Dale's bike ran flawlessly the last three laps and I finished 12 seconds ahead of Reg's Kawasaki. Klinzmann brought a BMW home in third, and Keith Code finished fourth on another Kawasaki. Mike Baldwin made a good run, starting from the rear of the grid, to get up to fourth, but his Guzzi's engine broke.

It was a joyous but sobering win. I turned faster lap times than the previous year, and I did *more* fast laps than in 1977. But Wes was even faster. He set a new lap record, and would have won if his rear sprocket bolts hadn't broken. Yoshimura had finally managed to build a big four with power *and* good handling. It was an early warning to those of us campaigning European twins—we had been competitive because our bikes had a good balance between power and handling. There was no way the current crop of Ducatis, Moto Guzzis, and BMWs could match the in-line-fours in power, and if the fours could be made to handle, we would all be in real trouble.

No Honeymoon at Mt. Pocono

Long Pond was a pretty little town nestled in the Pocono Mountains of eastern Pennsylvania, not far from the cities of Philadelphia and New York. It was a popular honeymoon spot, judging from the number of motels and cabins with names such as Honeymoon Haven and Newlywed Retreat. It is also the home of Pocono International Raceway, and Dale and I were there for a different sort of excitement.

In spite of the DNF at Daytona, a fourth at Loudon and a win at Sears Point had put me back into the championship race. Reg Pridmore was in the lead with two seconds and a third in the three races, but nobody else was as consistent as him and my two good finishes nearly made up for the one DNF.

We took two bikes to Pocono. Dale finally had the 905 running, but it failed during early practice and was a non-issue for the weekend. That left us with the bike with Cook's engine, which had been reborn. After the disappointment at Daytona where the bike was slower than it had been in

1977, Dale had gotten it running at top speed again and we were seeing an honest 150 mph at 9,000 rpm in top gear.

Pocono was a speedway track, like Daytona or Ontario, but with three turns instead of four. The motorcycles used a large portion of the huge NASCAR/Indy triangle, with a rinky-dink, flat infield part and a chicane. Turn 1 to turn 2 was particularly treacherous. Turn 1 was a wide right sweeper coming off the long front straight, while turn 2 was a tight left hairpin. Imagine a funnel starting six-bikes wide, wedging down to one-bike-width. There were a few more turns, a short infield straight, a left horseshoe, then a tight right hander back onto the speedway part of the track. My friend Mark Homchick describes racing there: "Imagine going down the freeway, exiting to do a quick lap through the 7-11 parking lot, and then getting back on the freeway."

I didn't much like Pocono. Too much straight, not enough curve.

There was one interesting development. Reno Leoni had switched from Moto Guzzi and his two riders were on Ducatis. The bike Mike Baldwin was riding was a full-on NCR-modified 900SS Leoni had brought into the U.S. from Italy, while Kurt Liebmann had a more standard 900SS in Superbike tune. Baldwin was going quite quickly on the NCR bike. (NCR is a specialty Italian speed shop that each year makes a few very fast, highly modified Ducati-engined specials.)

In Saturday's heat race, the funnel into the hairpin worked as feared, and Erik Buell (also racing a Ducati 900SS) and I hooked bikes as we got mooshed together. We parted with an audible *snap!* I made it through the corner, but Eric took the escape road. Whooo! I survived the rest of the heat and, if I recall correctly, got a second-row start position, not bad. Have I mentioned I didn't like the track? Erik also finished the heat race but farther back than normal for him.

Clouds were threatening as we were called to the grid for the main event, but the track was dry and everyone was fitted with slicks. I got a decent start; the lap charts showed me in fourth place at the end of lap two. During lap three it started to rain on the far infield and the back straight. I lost traction and had a lowside crash in the right hander exiting the infield. Billy Addington, right behind me on a fast 1,000cc Kawasaki, ran over my bike and mashed the ignition that was hung on the end of the Kawasaki crank. I was unhurt, quickly up and pushing, trying to bump start the bike and rejoin the race, but the Ducati wouldn't fire. Bill's bike was dead, needing a new points plate. We sat and watched as the rain increased.

As the track got wetter, riders were dropping like crazy. In this one turn I watched four other riders slide out. That was six down at *this* turn. A corner worker told me other turns had similar problems and there were more bikes parked flat-side-down than still on wheels. Finally the race was red-flagged during lap four.

There was nothing wrong with the Ducati. After we got back to the pits, on the crash truck Dale flooded the carbs with the tickler and the bike fired right up.

"Don't you need to flood the carbs only when it's cold?" I asked.

"Nope, it's necessary any time you start it."

Sigh. I should have known. Billy and I had been credited with only two laps completed. Most of the others had completed three. We were a lap down.

It was still raining pretty hard, and Dale decided to mount the intermediate rain tires. The AMA outsmarted us and waited until the rain stopped completely and the track was nearly dry before restarting the race. Most of the others had kept their slick tires on. It was a gamble. The track was still damp, and if it started to rain again, we'd be in good shape. However, if it didn't rain, the track would soon be dry and we'd be at a big disadvantage.

Wes Cooley took the lead on the restart with Mike Baldwin keeping him honest, putting the NCR Ducati into second not far behind.

It didn't rain again, and after about three more laps, the track had dried completely and my tires weren't working. I had almost no traction and was losing positions to other riders. The race came to an end for me when the front end tucked in the turn 2 hairpin and I fell a second time, banging my shoulder hard. The bike was still able to race, but it seemed pointless, already a lap down and dropping farther behind. Another DNF. That's racing.

Some of the faster bikes were not able to make the restart, so some new names appeared in the top five. Longtime Honda faithful John Fuchs got on the podium in third place, behind Cooley and Baldwin. Liebmann was fourth and Rich Schlachter took fifth on the George Vincensi-tuned Ducati.

Mike Baldwin's second place on the NCR bike was protested and he was disqualified. NCR made some of their own engine castings, and because the bikes weren't sold in the U.S., they were not Superbike legal. Curiously, when Baldwin was disqualified, the AMA did not move the following riders up a place. John Fuchs, for example, is shown in the records as earning 13 points for third place even after the disqualification. Go figure.

The next race on the 1978 schedule was Loudon, New Hampshire, on Sept. 2-3, followed only one week later by the season finale at Laguna Seca.

Superbike Pioneer - Erik Buell

Erik Buell was at the 1977 Sears Point Superbike race, but I didn't actually meet him until the next year, when we ran into each other at the Pocono, Pennsylvania, AMA National in 1978. I mean that literally. As described above, Erik and I came together in the heat race, *bam*! We both stayed upright, but Erik had to take the escape road.

He found me later in the pits, coming up with a grin, talking rapidly about the heat race. He explained that the force of us pulling apart had rotated the clutch lever perch on his handlebar, and when he went to downshift, his fingers grabbed air. He got it straightened out and was able to rejoin the pack and finish the heat race, but well down from where he normally would have placed.

I would have been bummed out if it had happened to me, but Erik seemed quite happy about the whole thing. He was pleased just to be there having the experience, and we had a good laugh together about it. In those

Erik Buell on his way to seventh place in the 1977 AMA National at Pocono, Pennsylvania. *Erik Buell*

days he was racing a Ducati 900SS, probably a 1977 or '78 model. Perhaps that's where Erik developed his love for V-twin engines. We met again later that year at Laguna Seca, but not in such a dramatic fashion. We talked for a while in the pits, and he was the same cheerful, active guy I met at Pocono.

If Erik were a youth today, he would likely be diagnosed as having a hyperactivity disorder. He appeared to me to be a bundle of energy, dashing about and having a great time. I bet he is one of those people who would go nuts if he were forced to sit still and be quiet.

No Autumn Loudon for Us

We didn't go to the September AMA National at Loudon. It was a tough decision, because I had scored a fourth place there in the spring race. But there were some compelling reasons to skip the event. The AMA had scheduled the fall Loudon race on September 3, and then set the Champion 200 at Laguna Seca for the very next weekend, September 10. Madness. We would have had to drive 3000 miles, race in New England on Sunday, drive 3,000 miles back, and then get the bikes ready for Laguna Seca on Friday. That's four days! Dale needed time to fix the 905, and I had used up all my vacation time traveling to faraway races.

The DNF at Pocono had changed things. With two DNFs in four races, we figured we were out of the championship race for the year. The decision was made to skip Loudon and prepare for Laguna.

At the autumn Loudon race, Harry Klinzmann and his BMW got the win he had nearly taken in the spring. Dave Emde put the Yoshimura Suzuki into second, but after that it was controversial. John Long finished third on the second BMW, but was docked one lap for an infraction and ended up credited with 11th place. According to John, they had some trouble getting his bike started before the final, and when it finally fired, he moved through the other bikes to the grid position he earned in the heat race. The AMA said John was moving on the grid after the one-minute sign was displayed, which was a serious safety violation. John and tuner Udo Geitl appealed the ruling but were turned down. Instead of heading for Laguna with 13 more points in his kit, John was only able to collect four, and the racers who finished in 4th to 11th were moved up to positions 3rd–10th.

Apparently we weren't the only ones not attending the September Loudon. The AMA lists only 15 finishers for this race compared with 20 finishers in June.

Superbike Pioneers –
Harry Klinzmann and Dave Emde

I'm putting Harry and Dave together in a single vignette because in my mind they are a matched set. I met them racing in AFM club races. Both of them were young, tall for road racers, and lanky–long arms and legs and trim, fit bodies. They were both wickedly fast on Yamaha TZ250s. They teamed up at the Ontario six-hour endurance races, which makes it even harder to think about them separately. The pair won the Ontario six-hour in 1977, defeating a very strong Yoshimura team.

Harry rode the San Jose BMW Superbike in 1977 and 1978, scoring several top-five places and getting an outright win at the September Loudon AMA National in 1978. He and I shared a bottle of bubbly at Sears Point in 1978 with Reg Pridmore as the three of us made the podium. In 1979 he switched to Kawasaki and continued to score in the top five. He was a bit brash at times, full of energy and impulsive. At Daytona in 1978, Dale and I were in Dale's van, towing the trailer full of Superbikes on Monday morning, the very first day of Bike Week. From our hotel there was a short drive on the freeway to get to the track, and while we were on the on-ramp, Harry, driving a similar van and trailer combination, roared past us at full throttle using the on-ramp shoulder! It

Harry Klinzmann in the early years,
sponsored by Mr. Al's Restaurant.

made me laugh, and I thought, *The kid's got nerve!* When I saw him in the pits, I told him, "That was a bold move." He laughed and said, "I gotta do something to get the blood flowing in the morning."

Dave Emde was from a well-known racing family. Dave's father had won the Daytona 200 in his youth, and Dave's older brother Don won the Daytona 200 in 1972. Dave raced Superbikes as the third member of the Yoshimura team, initially racing a Kawasaki Z1 and later a Suzuki GS1000. At Loudon in 1978 when his pal Klinzmann won the AMA Superbike race, Emde took second. Dave never won a Superbike race, but he came mighty close, with two seconds and a third in the '77-'79 seasons.

Both Harry and Dave also raced Yamahas in the 250cc and 750cc class, usually scoring well. Dave was especially good on his 250, taking home the 1977 AMA 250cc Expert class title after battling against such strong opponents as Gary Nixon, Randy Mamola, Skip Aksland, and Mike Baldwin. Dave continued to work in the motorcycle industry after active competition. Sadly, he was killed in 2003 in a street motorcycle accident. He was elected posthumously to the AMA's Motorcycle Hall of Fame in 2010.

Dave Emde in his BMW leathers. This is probably from the early 1980s.
Don Emde Collection

The Newton 905 Ducati

I've mentioned that the cylinder heads and pistons of the 905 were given to Cook and Phil during their 1977 visit to the Ducati factory. What was special about the 905's cylinder heads? They were machined to have their valves at an included angle of 60 degrees instead of the normal 80 degrees. All other things being equal, a narrower included valve angle allows higher compression with an improved combustion chamber shape. When the two valves are nearly at right angles to each other, high compression requires a high-dome piston and the combustion chamber resembles a deflated tennis ball with one side pushed in. The spark plug is offset so the spark fires off to the side when the piston is some degrees before top dead center, 38 degrees BTDC in the case of the Ducati, and the flame front has to travel over the top of the piston and down the other side to achieve full combustion.

If the included valve angle is decreased, the piston dome doesn't need to be as tall to get high compression, the flame front's path is not so convoluted, and the ignition doesn't need to be so advanced. All these are good things.

Dale started on the 905 early in 1978. Having the heads and pistons was nice, but it was merely a starting point; this was no simple bolt-on kit. The rocker arms and camshafts made for the 80-degree heads wouldn't work. New or modified rocker arms needed to be fabricated, and new cams were necessary. Dale had to grind new desmo camshafts for the 905. This was no simple matter for a privateer in 1978–no computer-aided manufacturing (CAM) back then.

The 905 took the development Cook and Phil started with the 750SS one step further. Was the 905 an improvement over Old Blue? There were several indications the 905 was a step forward. In 1978 I rode three different Superbike Ducatis: a bike fitted with Old Blue's motor, Dale's original Sears Point winner, and the new 905. The contrast between the

With valves at a 60° included angle (left), the combustion chamber is less concave than with the valves at an 80° included angle (right).

three was striking. The Sears Point bike had noticeably more torque and mid-range power than Old Blue, but ran out of breath around 7,800 rpm. Old Blue was softer on the bottom, but kept developing power past 9,000 rpm and had a considerable top-speed advantage over the Sears Point bike. The 905 had *both* the mid-range torque *and* the top speed. It was a combination of the best features of the other two bikes, and it showed its merits at the 1978 season-ending round of the AMA Superbike series at Laguna Seca.

Corkscrewing at Laguna Seca

Instead of racing at Loudon, we took the 905 to an AFM event at Sears Point on September 3. When I met Dale at the track, he was all smiles: "I figured out the problem we had at Pocono. It's running good now."

He wasn't kidding. The bike ran flawlessly and I won the Open GP race, turning easy 1:51 laps on an oily track. We were ready for Laguna.

I figured with only two scores in five races I was out of the championship chase, but I was wrong. After the second Loudon race, the top five were:

Rider	Points
Reg Pridmore	45
John Long	43
Harry Klinzmann	36
John Bettencourt	33
Paul Ritter	31

With 20 points for a win, all five of us had a mathematical chance to become the 1978 AMA Superbike champion. Back in 1978 I had no idea I was that close.

Saturday morning practice went well. The 905 was running great and I was getting some very decent lap times with it. There was the usual five-lap heat race on Saturday afternoon to set the grid. To my surprise, I got a *great* start and was second into turn 1 just behind John Bettencourt on the Yoshimura East Suzuki. I followed him closely through 2 and 3, and then he got into 4 a little hot and drifted toward the barrier on the exit. He had to back off and I slipped inside him and scooted up the hill toward the Corkscrew. I remember thinking, *Hey, I'm leading! Cool. Don't look back, just go! Watch out for that first right in the Corkscrew.* I ran hard for two laps, expecting someone to eventually come past, but no one did, so I slowed down just a little to see who would catch up first. At the end of lap three,

Wes Cooley came past on his Pocono-winning Suzuki GS and I tucked into his draft. We both started braking for turn 2 at the same time, but as I released the brakes and started banking into the turn, I was surprised to see Wes was *still braking hard!* I had to sit up and get back on the binders quickly to keep from smacking his rear wheel.

I spent the last two laps probing. The 905 was faster through the first half of the track, in turn 7 and the following banked right-hander. Wes had the advantage at the entry to the Corkscrew and in the final turn, and he could out-accelerate the 905 up the start/finish straight. The 905 finished the heat race in second place, giving us a front row start. I was thinking, *This might be a good race.*

It wasn't a good race. It was a *great* race! Back to my old habits, I blew the start. The lap sheets showed me fifth at the end of lap one. Cooley took off like a shot with John Bettencourt's Suzuki and the Kawasakis of Steven McLaughlin and Hurley Wilvert in pursuit. Wes built up a good lead in the early laps, but McLaughlin caught up and began pestering him. I finally got around Wilvert on lap six and moved up behind Johnny B, who did me a favor by slowing with mechanical problems that eventually caused him to drop out. On lap seven of the 20-lap race, I moved into third, with Cooley and McLaughlin 10 seconds ahead of me. I thought, *No traffic in front of me at last, let's see if I can catch those guys.*

It only took four laps. I caught up on the 12th lap, just as we were starting to lap slower traffic. Once there was clear track, I was able to run a string of sub-1:12 laps and joined the front running pair. During this run, the 905's best lap was 1:11.4, which was a new Superbike lap record, topping Cooley's best lap of 1:11.8, set earlier in the race. The three of us spent the rest of the race no more than a second apart, and mostly nose to tail.

Wes maintained the lead throughout. Steve and I swapped places once in turn 8 amongst lapped traffic, but he immediately regained second on the start/finish straight. Fourth place, being contested by Reg Pridmore's Kawasaki and the BMWs of John Long and Harry Klinzmann, was 30 seconds back by the 12th lap.

Catching them was one thing, getting past them was another! The old Laguna course was a fast, narrow track. There were two slow turns, the Corkscrew and the final hairpin, but everything else was fast–a 1:12 lap time was an average of 95 mph. The 905 could go quite a bit faster than the two big fours in the turn 2-3-4 stretch. In fact I needed to get on the brakes hard a couple of times to avoid running into Steve as he slowed for

Close racing coming onto the start-finish straight. Wes Cooley,
Steve McLaughlin, and myself. We ran like this for seven or eight laps.
Felix Adamo / Cycle News

those turns. But the racing line was narrow there and wandering off the line greatly increased the chance of running off the track. I could pass on brakes going into the slow turn 9, but I'd just be passed back going up the hill to the finish line. I needed to pass earlier in the lap and build up enough lead by turn 9 to keep from getting re-passed on the main straight. All this strategy was developing, mind you, as we were going at each other hammer and tongs.

After several laps of nose-to-tail racing, Wes started getting a bit of a gap on Steve and me. On lap 19 Steve left a little bit of an inside opening going into turn 4. I didn't know it was lap 19, but I knew if he did the same thing on the next lap, I could pass him there. It was on lap 20, the last lap, (but none of us knew it) that I out-braked Steve going into turn 4 and passed him, and made it stick going up the hill to the Corkscrew. I thought, *Whew! I'm through. If I can open up some room on Steve in turns 7 and 8, and keep him behind me until turn 2, he'll never catch me, and I can pick off Wes the same way on the next lap.* In turns 7 and 8 I closed the gap to Wes so I was right on his rear tire as we rounded turn 9. *Just wait for turn 4 and I'll get you*, I thought.

Exiting the corkscrew on the final lap. Cooley, myself, McLaughlin. Wes had built up a small gap, but I was able to close it by turn 9. *Bob Ocano*

It never happened. As we rushed up to the finish line–Wes, me, and Steve–the starter waved the checkered flag at us. Huh? For a second we kept racing, thinking it was an error–maybe I mistook the white for the checkered? But Wes sat up and looked at me, shrugged his shoulders. I glanced back at Steve, who held both arms out, palms up, in the classic "Don't ask me" posture. I realized two things: damn, the race is over, and *wow* I got second place! What a race! I was really jazzed, and was bouncing up and down during the winner's circle celebration. I gave both Wes and Steve big hugs.

Fourth went to John Long and fifth to Klinzmann as the BMWs did well. Reggie took sixth and Keith Code's Kawasaki finished in seventh.

I had mixed feelings after the race. Second was a really good result, and being able to put the Ducati up there with those horsepower-rich 1,000cc four-cylinder bikes was very cool. The 905 was down a bit on peak power but had handling superiority and was faster on three-quarters of the track. It was a really fun race to be in and a *great* race to watch. However, we were disappointed that we didn't win. The 905 was certainly up to the task. If only I had passed McLaughlin a lap sooner, if only I had gotten a good start, if only … there were a lot of "if onlys." But hey, that's racing.

Some post-race information of note:

- During the victory circle interviews, Steve said he never knew I was on his tail and was just waiting for the white flag to pounce on Wes. He also pointed out, "Once again the Superbike race was the best race of the weekend."

- Cooley's bike was having front brake problems. When the Yoshimura mechanic started to push it to tech inspection, it wouldn't budge. The front brakes weren't totally locked up, but the discs weren't free either. It took two people to push it.

- At the post-race tech inspection, Dale took off the right engine-side cover, exposing the 905's complete working alternator charging system, and pointedly let the AMA tech inspector know what he thought of the new more liberal rules.

- The AMA said there was no white flag because the race was an FIM-sanctioned Formula 750 event and the FIM doesn't use the white flag to signal one more lap. We weren't very happy about that. Superbikes weren't an FIM class.

1978 Superbike Season Summary

There was a little less variety this year than there had been in 1977. Instead of seven winners in seven races on five different brands, there were five winners in six races on three different brands. It was still a pretty good mix. In chronological order:

Track	Winner	Brand
Daytona	Steve McLaughlin	Suzuki
Loudon	John Bettencourt	Suzuki
Sears Point	Paul Ritter	Ducati
Pocono	Wes Cooley	Suzuki
Loudon	Harry Klinzmann	BMW
Laguna	Wes Cooley	Suzuki

It looked like a Suzuki-dominated season if you just considered the winner at each event, but that didn't tell the whole story. Looking at the individual points table, the highest placing Suzuki rider was Wes Cooley in *fifth* place. Wes also gained the distinction of being the only rider in 1978 to win two races. However, that's all he scored, two wins to earn 40 points. He suffered from some mechanical failures during the year.

The championship ended in a tie, with Reg Pridmore (Vetter Kawasaki) and John Long (Longevity/Geitl BMW) each earning 54 points. The top five in the championship were:

Pos.	Rider	Motorcycle	Pts.
1.	Reg Pridmore	Vetter Kawasaki	54
2.	John Long	Longevity BMW	54
3.	Paul Ritter	AeroUnion Ducati	47
4.	Harry Klinzmann	San Jose BMW	46
5.	Wes Cooley	Yoshimura Suzuki	40

Here's how the top five earned their points:

Rider	Daytona	Loudon 1	Sears	Pocono	Loudon 2	Laguna
1. Reg Pridmore	2nd	3rd	2nd	-	-	6th
2. John Long	3rd	2nd	5th	-	11th	4th
3. Paul Ritter	-	4th	1st	-	-	2nd
4. H. Klinzmann	-	12th	3rd	-	1st	5th
5. Wes Cooley	-	-	-	1st	-	1st

As you can see by the large number of dashes, none of the top five had a very consistent year. John Long was most reliable, earning points in five of the six races. Neither Pridmore nor Long had a win, but Reggie had two second places to John's one and Pridmore was declared the 1978 champion, his third Superbike crown in three years.

That one-lap penalty John Long was assessed at Loudon in September really came back to bite him. If he hadn't been penalized, or if the penalty had been less severe, John would have had more than 54 points and would have been the 1978 Superbike champ on a BMW.

I was third with 47 points, coming from placing first, second, and fourth in the three races I finished. I needed seven points to have tied Reg and John, and I would have been the AMA Superbike champion because of my win at Sears Point. What's seven points? It's an eighth place finish. If we had a good crank at Daytona ... if we had gone to Loudon on September 3rd ... if it hadn't rained at Pocono ... if I had known to flood the carbs to restart the bike.

Hey, that's racing. Sometimes the luck's with you, sometimes it's not. It was a great year and Dale and I had loads of fun, and we finally got the 905 running right. People were pretty amazed at the speed of that bike. I have no regrets about 1978, though sometimes I like to imagine how my life might have differed if I had scored those seven points.

CHAPTER NINE

My Final Superbike Season

It was a shock and completely unexpected. After the end of the 1978 season, with the excitement of the Laguna success of the 905 still fresh, Dale told me he would not be able to compete in 1979. When Dale and I decided to race the full 1978 season, he hired a person to do his job at his company so he could concentrate on developing and maintaining the Ducati Superbikes. Dale's replacement had not done a very good job.

Aero-Union was Dale's company. He didn't just work there; he owned it. It was the source of all the funds we had to go racing. Aero-Union maintained a fleet of piston-engine bombers that dumped fire retardant chemicals on the wildfires that are a part of summer in California. The company got some income from doing custom machining, but the backbone of Aero-Union was government contracts from federal and state agencies such as the U.S. Forest Service and California Dept. of Forestry. The company had been nearly shut out in the last round of contract bids and offers. Dale had to stop racing, at least for a while, and take care of his company.

I went looking for a ride and got two solid offers. One was to ride an experimental hub-center-steered motorcycle as a development rider. It wasn't a Superbike and I wanted to stay in that class rather than go back to mostly club racing. The other offer was from San Jose BMW to ride the ex-Butler & Smith BMW Harry Klinzmann rode in 1978. This was more interesting. Harry had some success with the bike, and John Long had finished second in the class in 1978 on a similar BMW. I didn't figure on being a title contender, but I thought I could have some success, and some fun, with the bike.

I met the owner and the mechanic, Chris, at Sears Point for a track day in the early spring of 1979. There were two potential riders, myself and another AFM racer, and we took turns riding the bike on the track. The motorcycle made decent power, handled OK at first, and had *really* good brakes. The feedback from the front end under braking was quite amazing to me–I did my first stoppie going into the turn 11 hairpin when the rear wheel lifted right off the ground as I put on the binders. The feedback was so good I felt completely in control when it happened. I recall calmly thinking, *The rear brake isn't going to help much here.*

The other test rider, whose name I can't remember, decided it wasn't for him, thanked the owner for the chance to ride the bike, and left.

I got more used to the bike and started upping the speed. At full throttle the bike hit a set of bumps between turns 2 and 3 and went into a massive tank-slapper. The bars waved madly back and forth, increasing in amplitude as long as the throttle was fully open. I could barely hold on, and the only way to stop it was to close the throttle. It was a completely new and scary experience. I continued the lap and started pressing again when it did the same thing after turn 11, the final hairpin. I was on full throttle when I hit the ripples near the end of the pit wall. Another vicious tank-slapper started and I had to shut off or crash. I aborted the lap and returned to the pits.

I told Chris about the tank-slappers. He had seen the one that happened near the pit wall and was startled by it. The bike had a hydraulic steering damper and we tightened that up to see if it would help. No improvement. We tried different weight fork oils, different fork spring pre-load settings, different weight fork springs, and anything else we

Season Four Schedule

At the beginning of 1979, the fourth year of AMA Superbikes, the AMA National schedule listed six road race events. The schedule looked like this:

Date	Venue
March 9	Daytona, FL
June 17	Loudon, NH
July 15	Sears Point, CA
Aug. 5	Laguna Seca, CA
Aug. 12	Pocono, PA
Sept. 2	Loudon, NH

could think of. Nothing helped. If I had the throttle fully open and hit some bumps, the bike would tank-slap itself silly. We worked the rest of the day trying to fix it without success. I finally had to call it a day. It was getting late and my thumbs were really sore from holding on to the bars as they whipped back and forth.

We never did solve the problem. I had to race the bike without being able to use full throttle at several points during a lap at Sears Point. The bike was better behaved at smoother tracks, Loudon for example, but I lacked confidence in it, worried that it would happen again at any time. Honestly, the bike scared me. It's a shame we never found a solution. It would have been a decent ride.

The San Jose BMW guys and I decided to skip Daytona as the bike wasn't likely to be competitive there and it was the most expensive race to attend because it was a full week long. We were planning on going to the other five races. My thinking was if we could get the bike working enough for me to use full throttle I would be able to do well at Sears Point, Laguna Seca and the two Loudon races. I didn't think we would be very competitive at Pocono, but we ought to have been able to pick up some points.

Unfortunately the proposed schedule didn't happen. Sometime during the year both the Pocono race and the second Loudon race were canceled, leaving only four AMA road races that year, and only three for us because we skipped Daytona. It was the leanest season for Superbikes since the first year, 1976.

Daytona Superbike Developments

Even though I wasn't at Daytona in 1979, there were some very interesting changes in the normal Superbike schedule. The race was lengthened from 62 miles to 100 miles, 26 laps instead of 16, in response to the urging of track owner Bill France. There was talk of having the Daytona 200 as a Superbike event sometime in the future and the 100-mile race was an investigation into that possibility. The extra distance meant dead-engine fuel stops for most of the field.

There were a whopping 85 entries for the race, although attrition during practice and the two heat races would trim that to 54 who made the final grid. Not only were entries up, sponsorship had increased as well. It was the Bell Superbike 100, with Bell Helmets kicking in enough money to raise the winner's payout to $2,000 with a total purse of $11,500, not counting contingencies—a quite respectable sum in 1979.

Kawasaki was up to something. With factory backing, they had hired Mike Baldwin and provided him with a Formula 750 race bike based on the three-cylinder motor from the H-2 Mach 4, and a couple of KZ1000s for Superbikes. No one knows how Baldwin might have done in the 100 mile Superbike race because Mike crashed his F750 bike in Thursday practice and was not fit for the Friday Superbike race. The race was dominated by the Yoshimura Suzuki team, taking all three podium spots: Ron Pierce, Wes Cooley, and Dave Emde in that order. John Long took fourth on a BMW.

A Hot Time in New Hampshire

It was nearly 100 degrees in New Hampshire with humidity to match on June 16, Saturday of the race weekend. The heat affected tires, engines, and riders in negative ways, and it was literally making people sick.

The Daytona-dominating Yoshimura Suzukis were having problems. The best tires available would be good for about five or six fast laps, after which the power from the motor and the heat combined to soften the tires. At that point they offered almost no grip. The short times of the early laps became longer and longer as the riders started to concentrate not on racing but on keeping their bike on the pavement.

We weren't having such problems with the BMW. It's lighter weight and relatively mild horsepower did not destroy the tires in spite of the heat. Ditto John Long's Beemer and Ducatis ridden by Freddie Spencer and local ace Rich Schlachter. Our problem was mostly with the rider. We had not figured out what caused the wild tank-slappers when the bike hit bumps on full throttle. Loudon was a smooth track compared to Sears Point, but it had a couple of bumps, and every time I hit them, I backed off. Basically, the bike still scared me.

There were enough Superbike entries in 1979 to require two heat races on Saturday. Mike Baldwin on his factory-sponsored Kawasaki won the first heat ahead of Harry Klinzmann's Kawasaki and Rich Schlachter on the George Vincensi-built Ducati. The second heat was a Wes Cooley run-away. Freddie Spencer took second on the Reno Leoni NCR Ducati, which had been modified just enough to satisfy the AMA rules.

We didn't finish our heat race. On the second lap the bolt holding the ignition rotor came loose, the rotor started spinning freely on its shaft, the spark plugs started sparking randomly, and the bike coasted to a halt. I would be starting at the rear of the grid, a serious disadvantage at this tight track. I was totally bummed about this, because Loudon was one of the tracks where BMWs went well.

Saturday night we took the bike to the workspace of Udo Geitl. I got to meet Udo and Todd Schuster and some other members of his crew. They were working on John Long's BMW and gave us room to re-set the timing on our BMW.

Sunday felt no cooler than Saturday. At the start of the 25-lap (40-mile) final, Wes Cooley (Yoshimura Suzuki) jetted off into the lead with the Kawasakis of Steve McLaughlin, Mike Baldwin, and Harry Klinzmann on his heels. The Ducatis of Spencer and Schlachter followed in fifth and sixth. Rich said later he wasn't worried; he was just waiting for the heat to get to the big four-cylinder bike's tires. I was slowly working my way up from the rear, as finding places to pass was difficult. I was getting past only one or two per lap and that wasn't enough to get near the front.

Toward the end of the race Schlachter had moved up to fight with Mike Baldwin for the lead. It was a good battle. Schlachter and Baldwin started swapping the lead as they lapped slower traffic. They lapped me about lap 18 or 19, going around me on the outside in turn 6, the banked hairpin. I remember thinking, *So that's how this turn should be taken.* They moved away from me pretty quickly so I didn't get to learn much from them.

With approximately five laps to go, a red flag, came out and stopped the race. There were enough crashes with injuries to use up the ambulances so the race had to be stopped. There was some discussion about doing a re-start and finishing the last four or five laps, but the AMA decided to call it a completed race. When a race is stopped by a red flag the scoring reverts to the previous lap, and Schlachter was the winner over Baldwin by a single bike-length.

Wes Cooley had kept the Suzuki on pavement to grab third just ahead of Spencer's Ducati. I'm sure I finished the race, but for some reason my name doesn't appear in the AMA's official list, so I can't tell you exactly where I finished. I recently exchanged some e-mail with Malcolme Tunstall and he remembers finishing just in front of me. Malcolme is listed in 15th place. I must have finished in 16th or 17th, out of the points, but up from my 30-something starting spot.

Superbike Pioneers - Udo Geitl and Todd Schuster

I met Udo Geitl and Todd Schuster at Loudon in 1979 when Udo invited us to share his shop space to fix the timing on our BMW. While Chris re-timed the San Jose bike, I watched Udo's crew take John Long's BMW motor completely apart, inspect everything, and reassemble it. It was very similar to what Dale did with our Ducati at Daytona in 1978.

Udo started with BMW in 1976 when Butler & Smith funded the effort and the BMW team dominated the AMA Superbike series that year. Butler & Smith dropped their race support after the 1977 Daytona event, but Udo had kept his hand in. He and Todd put together a plan: Udo would do the engine work, Todd would do the chassis, and eventually they found racing veteran John Long to ride it. It worked. In 1978 John tied Reg Pridmore in the points chase, and a tie-breaking formula was necessary to decide the class championship.

It was pretty amazing what had been done to the BMW. Kevin Cameron wrote an article on the bike that was published in the March 1979 issue of *Cycle*. Cameron needed over *three pages* of text to describe all the modifications to the engine and chassis. And that does *not* count the photographs or ads. Udo was a real wizard with the engine modifications. The list of changes Cameron described was long and complex. Just one example: the inlet ports were welded up and re-bored at a different angle to improve airflow.

Schuster was a big man with big skills. He did some amazing things, such as installing a Chrysler hemi engine (his favorite motor) in his Ford van simply for the fun of doing it. The anti-dive mechanism he installed on the BMW front wheel was ingenious.

Udo's and Todd's modifications added up to dozens of changes from small to large, and it kept the pushrod-twin motorcycle competitive with the overhead-cam fours far longer than anyone expected.

Home Again at Sears Point

The third AMA road race in 1979 was back at my home track, Sears Point, in the middle of July. We still had not solved the handling problem with the San Jose BMW and I was feeling glum. I could not use wide-open throttle in the bumpy sections without the bike trying to throw me off. And Sears had several bumpy sections.

The race was notable for another reason. It was the first Superbike win by the future World Champion, Louisiana-based Freddie Spencer. Freddie did not win on the Ducati he raced at Loudon, however. Both Spencer and Rich Schlachter had jumped from their Ducatis and taken rides on the Kawasaki KZ1000s that had been built for Mike Baldwin. Baldwin wasn't racing at Sears Point. After nearly winning the Loudon Superbike race, Mike crashed during the Loudon Formula 750 race, getting a season-ending broken leg, and his two fast KZ1000s were now available.

On the BMW at 1979 AMA National at Sears Point. *Ken Mullins*

From practice times the racers who looked like they could win included Spencer, the Yoshimura Suzukis of Wes Cooley and Ron Pierce, and Kawasakis ridden by Schlachter and McLaughlin. My times on the BMW were not competitive.

There were two heat races. Spencer won the faster one and Ron Pierce the other. Cooley, after challenging Pierce for the lead in heat two, had a flat tire and would be starting from the rear of the grid. When Cooley dropped out, I moved up to fourth in the heat, garnerning a third-row start in the final. The BMW's motor was running fine and the bike steered well, but it still wouldn't work on full throttle over the bumps.

The Superbike race had been shortened to 10 laps because of a long delay caused by a multi-bike pile-up in the earlier Novice 250cc race. When it was finally flagged off, Freddie Spencer led flag to flag, turning lap times in the 1:47-1:49 range. During the second lap of the race, Wes Cooley came past me in the short straight between turns 6 and 7 as Wes was moving forward from his back row start. I latched onto him and was able to keep up through the esses, but when we got to the exit of turn 11, I didn't have the nerve to hold the throttle full open and he moved away quickly, eventually passing all but Spencer and Ron Pierce to grab third.

Around mid-race I found myself behind Roberto Pietri on a Suzuki, a rider I could normally outdistance on Dale's Ducati. Pietri was slowing me up through the hill section of the track and in the esses, but I just couldn't force myself to hold the throttle fully open to get around him. I finished a disappointing 11th, the first European bike behind five Kawasakis and five Suzukis. It was a very depressing result. Racing, which had for years been one of the high points of my life, was now a bummer. I missed the Ducati a lot.

Frustration at Laguna Seca

I was actually looking forward to the August Laguna Seca race. I had done really well there the previous year and since it was a smooth track, I expected to be able to use full throttle. The bike *was* better behaved than at Sears Point on the less bumpy track, but other problems popped up.

During the first practice session on Saturday, the bike blew a cylinder base gasket on one side, coating the right foot-peg and my boot with oil. Back in the pits I recall Chris saying the gasket was an experiment–usually they didn't use one, just O-ring seals. The bike was repaired in time for the second practice session, during which it blew the *other* cylinder's base gasket, putting oil on the left foot-peg and boot. Back to the pits again for repairs.

On Saturday afternoon Ron Pierce's Yoshimura Suzuki won the faster of the two heat races just ahead of Freddie Spencer on the factory-backed KZ1000 Kawasaki. Pierce, a wily veteran racer, was using the so-called Bakersfield Line, named after Ron's hometown. He made a tight approach to the corners so the only way past him was around the outside, a move that seldom worked. Spencer claimed he could drop his lap times by two seconds if he hadn't been blocked.

Wes Cooley won the second heat easily from Rich Schlachter, who was riding the other ex-Baldwin KZ1000. In my heat race the BMW ignition rotor came loose and the bike stopped between turns 2 and 3. I would be starting at the back of the grid again. Damn. It was the second time for this particular failure, as the same thing had happened at Loudon.

Then I made a mistake. I felt I wasn't getting out of turn 9 quick enough and I asked the team to replace the four-speed transmission with the five-speed gearbox. San Jose was only about an hour's drive away and I knew the swap could be done back at the home shop. The team owner warned me that the five-speed transmission was "a bit delicate," but I insisted it was necessary.

Chris had the bike ready on Sunday morning with the five-speed installed, but I discovered it didn't really help. It wasn't worse–it just wasn't any better. The four-speed would have worked just as well. Other than that, practice went fine—no mechanical failures this time.

In Sunday's Superbike final, Spencer got off the line in front. Pierce tried to squeeze past in the first turn, but Spencer was having none of it and cut Pierce off sharply. The little set-to was just enough for Cooley to jump past Pierce and the final podium order of Spencer, Cooley, and Pierce was set before the first lap was even half over. The interesting battle was for fourth place, contested by the Kawasakis of Harry Klinzmann, Steve McLaughlin, Schlachter, and Chuck Parme.

My race was over quickly. Between the start and the Corkscrew, I passed quite a few slower riders. As we approached the Corkscrew, I was setting up to go around the outside of a rider as he braked for the initial left-hand part of the turn. He surprised me by braking as deep into the corner as I did. He then surprised me even more by *not* turning left but going straight and crashing in the dirt on the outside of the turn. I had to get on the brakes really hard to avoid him, and the rear wheel locked up and the back end started hopping up and down. I managed to avoid the crash and continued, but when I downshifted to first at turn 9 and tried to accelerate, the engine just revved—there was no forward drive. I upshifted to second gear and got forward motion, but the motor was making alarming noises—it rattled like a box of rocks. At the end of the second lap, I went into the pits, got off the bike, and found a good sized crack in the rear of the engine case. Oil was already starting to leak out. The shock from the locked-up rear tire as it bounced against the pavement in the Corkscrew broke the gearbox. My race weekend was finished.

The finishing order at Laguna Seca in August was Spencer, Cooley, Pierce, and Schlachter. The race for the top three positions turned into a follow-the-guy-ahead affair, quite a contrast from the previous year.

According to *Cycle World* magazine, Kawasaki gave Spencer a $10,000 bonus for winning at Laguna, in addition to the $5,000 bonus for winning at Sears Point. If there was any doubt about how serious Kawasaki was about the Superbike class at the start of the year, this settled the question. $15,000 was a lot of money in 1979. The U.S. Census Bureau statistics says that the median family income in 1979 was $16,461. Not bad for a 17-year-old kid, eh?

Laguna Seca was the last AMA National road race of 1979 because the August Pocono and September Loudon races had been canceled for some reason. Because we had chosen to skip Daytona, that meant the San

Jose folks and I had exactly three AMA National races together. After the disappointing Laguna results, I had a chat with the San Jose guys and told them I didn't think things had worked out. I thanked them for giving me the chance to ride their bike, but I didn't want to do it anymore. They understood and we parted company on good terms, I think.

Superbike Pioneers – the Others

I've written about many of the early Superbike riders and tuners, the ones I knew personally. There were a few I never did have a chance to talk to so I didn't know them personally, but I would be remiss in not mentioning them.

Reno Leoni, Mike Baldwin, and Kurt Liebmann

These three were on the same team from 1976 through 1978, tuner Reno Leoni and riders Mike Baldwin and Kurt Liebmann. The three of them were responsible for putting the Moto Guzzi 850 Le Mans at or near the top of the finishing list. I did talk to Reno once, at Pocono in 1978, but not enough to get to know the man. He was from Italy and came to the U.S. to help the Berliners, the U.S. importers, with the Ducati and Moto Guzzi lines. He had a lot of knowledge about the Guzzi motors and made the fastest Moto Guzzis in the country. However, the Guzzis were a bit fragile when pushed to the limit and the team switched to Ducatis midway through the 1978 season. Reno's Ducatis were also fast. (A bit of trivia: Reno Leoni's first name was actually Rino, which is pronounced ree-no in Italy. After moving to the U.S., he got so tired of Americans calling him rhy-no that he changed the spelling to Reno. In Italy Reno would be pronounced ray-no.)

I never talked to Baldwin or Liebmann. This may have been an incorrect assumption, but Mike always seemed to be angry, so I avoided him. As for Kurt, I didn't avoid him, but our paths simply never crossed.

Ron Pierce

A pioneer Superbike racer worth mentioning is Ron Pierce. Ron won Superbike races for BMW and Yoshimura in the first four years. Ron and I had a good dice at the 1977 Laguna Seca National, but I never chatted with him in the pits. Ron was a veteran racer who had been at the front for many years, an ex-factory racer, and I was a bit in awe of him. I was reading his name in motorcycle magazines long before I started racing.

John Long

John Long would have taken the 1978 Superbike title from Reg Pridmore if he hadn't been given a one-lap penalty at the autumn Loudon race. At 6'2" he fit his name. He was tall for a road racer, but he was good at it. John was surprisingly fast on the BMW in Superbikes and rode competitively on 250cc and 750cc Yamahas in the other AMA classes. He had a reputation of being a very cool and calm character for someone so busy on race weekends. For example, at Sears Point in 1978 the AMA schedule had John racing in two heat races and three finals, all on Sunday. That's Endurance.

John Fuchs

John Fuchs was an East Coast racer I never met. I liked the fact he almost single-handedly kept the Honda name in the top-10 lists in the early Superbike years, until Honda got serious and hired Freddie Spencer for the 1980 season. Fuchs' best finish was a podium third place at Pocono in 1978, and when Mike Baldwin's bike was disqualified, he should have been moved up to second. I hope the AMA gave him the second place purse even if they didn't award John the points. Fuchs was tied for sixth in the championship that year.

1979 Superbike Season Summary

The AMA road race season ended prematurely, as the last two races of the original schedule were canceled; this left only four races for the year. With four races, it's difficult to get much diversity, but the class did about as well as possible. There were only three winners but on three different brands:

Track	Winner	Brand
Daytona	Ron Pierce	Suzuki
Loudon	Rich Schlachter	Ducati
Sears Point	Freddie Spencer	Kawasaki
Laguna	Freddie Spencer	Kawasaki

The young phenom and future world champion Freddie Spencer won half the races, but he did not win the championship. A DNF at Daytona probably cost him the title. Yoshimura rider Wes Cooley had the most points and his teammate Ron Pierce was second, as once again consistency paid off in the championship race. The race at the top was pretty close, with only seven points separating first through third places, the points earned with an eighth-place finish. The final totals were:

Pos.	Rider	Motorcycle	Pts.
1.	Wes Cooley	Suzuki	58
2.	Ron Pierce	Suzuki	55
3.	Freddie Spencer	Ducati/Kawasaki	51
4.	Rich Schlachter	Ducati/Kawasaki	45
5.(t)	Harry Klinzmann	Kawasaki	30
5.(t)	Chuck Parme	Kawasaki	30

There are several interesting things here. Both Spencer and Rich Schlachter earned points riding a Ducati and a Kawasaki, so it's hard to pin a single brand on them. Spencer earned 40 points with the Kawasaki and 11 with the Ducati, while Schlachter's points were almost evenly split, 23 from Ducati and 22 from Kawasaki.

The other item of interest is the fading of the European bikes. They were dominant in the first two years of AMA Superbikes and strong in year three, but except for Schlachter's win on a Ducati at Loudon and fourth place finishes by Long (BMW) and Spencer (Ducati), at Daytona and Loudon, respectively, the European bikes didn't have much impact. In the last two races of the year, they were shut out of the top 10.

Here's how the top five earned their points:

Pos.	Rider	Daytona	Loudon	Sears Point	Laguna
1.	Wes Cooley	2nd	3rd	3rd	2nd
2.	Ron Pierce	1st	9th	2nd	3rd
3.	Freddie Spencer	–	4th	1st	1st
4.	Rich Schlachter	12th	1st	4th	4th
5.	Harry Klinzmann	5th	–	5th	5th

One of the most notable things here was the relative lack of dashes compared to the same charts from 1976-1978. The Superbikes were becoming more reliable. The Yoshimura bikes in particular impressed. They took eight of the 15 available podium spots, including the sweep at Daytona. The Yosh bikes were always fast. In 1978 they started to handle decently and in 1979 they finished races.

The Superbike Class Moves On and Up

In 1980 everything about the Superbike class changed. There were some hints of what was coming in 1979 when Kawasaki got involved with AMA Superbike, hiring Mike Baldwin as a rider and preparing two KZ1000

Superbikes for him to race. That effort also included an F-750 racer for Baldwin, so the Kawasaki effort could be seen as an attempt to challenge Yamaha's hegemony in Formula 750 racing with the Superbikes as a side effort, or vice versa.

There was no mistaking Honda's intent in 1980. In 1979 Honda introduced a new CB750 model with an all-new engine. The original CB750 was an air-cooled, single-overhead-cam, inline-four with two valves per cylinder and 736cc displacement. The new bike, called the CB750F Super Sport, also was an air-cooled inline-four, but it had *two* overhead cams, *four* valves per cylinder, and a displacement of 749cc. Another interesting fact—serial numbers of the older CB750s always began with CB750. The new bike's serial number started with RC04. In the past Honda had always reserved the RC label for pure race bikes, such as the 250cc six-cylinder RC166 raced by Mike Hailwood in 1966.

Honda hired Freddie Spencer on a non-exclusive contract to ride in Superbikes. Spencer still raced Yamahas in the 250cc and 750cc races, which probably caused some grinding of teeth in the Honda camp. Honda also paid Steve McLaughlin to be team manager and hired the Udo Geitl/ Todd Schuster pairing to prepare and maintain the new motorcycles. The Superbike Freddie rode was a bored-out CB750F with an actual displacement somewhere above 900cc. Kawasaki countered by hiring Eddie Lawson to ride the KZ1000. Suzuki already had a top talent in the series with class champion Wes Cooley on the Yoshimura-prepared GS1000.

There were *10* AMA road races in the 1980 season, a big improvement from 1979. The year started with New Zealander Graeme Crosby winning Daytona, but after that it was a fierce battle between the three factory hired guns. Of the remaining nine races, Spencer won three, Cooley won three, and Lawson won three. That was the season—10 races, four different winners on three different brands of motorcycles. The final points standings were Wes Cooley 128, Eddie Lawson 121, Freddie Spencer 111. Cooley was the Superbike champion for the second year in a row, beating two future world champions.

The three-way battle continued in 1981 when there were eight Superbike races on the schedule. Cooley won the Daytona opener, but the next seven events went Spencer, Lawson, Lawson, Lawson, Spencer, Lawson, Spencer. That year Eddie Lawson took the title with 125 points, Spencer was a close second with 121, and Cooley third with 91 points.

Some consider 1980-1981 the Golden Era of Superbike racing. It was a special time for sure, but in my opinion it's the *second* Golden Era of Superbikes. The first special time for Superbikes was 1977-1978. Those two years, with many different winners on several different brands of motorcycles, set the groundwork for the class.

The next several key dates for Superbikes were:

- 1983–Superbike rules were changed to limit the four-cylinder bikes to 750cc while twins could stay at 1,000. It didn't help the twins; they were still outclassed. The AMA created the Battle of the Twins (BOTT) class to give them a place to race.

- 1985–The Daytona 200 became a Superbike race. In 1984 Bill France, the owner of the Daytona racetrack, told the AMA the 1985 Daytona 200 would be a Superbike race. The AMA said, "No, Superbike is a support class. The main event has to be Formula 1." France said, in effect, "You boys don't understand. I'm not asking for permission." The 1985 Daytona 200 was won by Freddie Spencer on a Honda Interceptor VF750, the first Daytona 200 win for Honda since Dick Mann in 1970.

- 1987–Superbikes became the premier racing class in the U.S. with 250 GP and Pro Twins (formerly BOTT) as support classes. Other classes, such as sidecars or Formula 1, were optional.

- 1988–Mainly through the efforts of Steve McLaughlin, the World Superbike Series began, using rules largely based on the current AMA Superbike rules. The first World Superbike champion was Californian Fred Merkel on a Honda.

And the rest, as they say, is history.

My Racing Career Winds Down

The 1979 season for me was a complete failure, to put it mildly. The year had not been fun, but I wasn't ready to quit racing. The Superbike series had completed with the August 5th event at Laguna Seca, but there were two months left in the club racing season and I thought maybe I could get some of the magic back if I returned to racing a Ducati. Dale was still working at getting his company back on solid footing and wasn't available, so I dusted off my 1974 Ducati 750 Sport and prepared it for an AFM race at Sears Point in October.

Preparing the Sport for racing was not much fun. In 1976, when I raced the Sport for the full club race series, I enjoyed that part of the racing effort, but this time it was more like work. I had gotten spoiled during the years riding for Dale, when he did the all the maintenance work, and I didn't enjoy the hours in the garage the way I used to. But I got it ready in time and finished second to class leader John Williams on a current-model 650cc Kawasaki (bored to 750cc I believe). We had a race-long dice. He passed me in the final turn on the last lap, making a desperate late dive inside me and beat me to the flag. It was a fun race and my best times were below 2:00, the fastest I'd ever been on the Sport. Fun racing, but not so much fun wrenching.

I had all winter to get the bike ready for the 1980 club season. The first race was in late March; it was a beautiful spring day, sunny and pleasantly warm. The countryside around the Sears Point track is really pretty this time of year–everything is green. Later in the year it's hot and the hillside grass has all turned brown. I won the 750 Production class race that day, but there was no serious competition.

I wasn't looking forward to preparing the bike for the May race, but drug myself out to the garage. I checked the valve clearances, checked the timing, and mounted my last Goodyear 1170 rear racing slick. It was three years old but had only been used in one practice session.

This second race of the 1980 season wasn't successful. Halfway through the race I was well behind a good young rider on one of the new Honda CB750F bikes when I felt a little vagueness in the handling coming out of the last turn. Normally my Ducati is rock steady in this stretch. By the time I got to turn 1, there was definitely something wrong–the bike was starting to waggle its rear end. I pulled off the track, dismounted, and looked at the back of the bike. The rear tire was noticeably soft, apparently from a slow leak. A few days later I inspected the inner tube and found two tiny holes that looked like a snakebite, a clear sign I had pinched the tube during installation. It was discouraging–a rookie mistake. Not only did I not enjoy working on the bike, but apparently I wasn't very good at it. I decided racing and preparing my own five-year old Ducati wasn't going to bring back the joy I was looking for.

Then I got a phone call from Dale. One of the rival companies that had out-bid Aero-Union had defaulted and Dale was able to pick up the contract on very favorable terms. He wanted to race again, and we went to Sears Point with the 883cc Superbike. I was really excited, looking forward to the event.

There was some serious competition this time. My pal Vance Breese was racing a bike he called the Aluminum Steamroller, his special race bike with a highly modified Harley-Davidson 1,200cc motor. It simply drove past my Ducati through the start-finish area and in the straight stretch between turn 6 and 7. My bike was faster in the turns, especially in the esses coming down the hill from turn 7, but he had a good 5 to 10-mph advantage in top speed. I had to work hard, but I finally got far enough ahead of Vance to keep him from catching me at the start line or on the way into turn 7.

I got the white flag indicating one more lap and I screwed up. It's embarrassing to crash on the last lap when you're in the lead, so I slowed a little. I thought I had gotten far enough ahead, but no. Vance passed me going into turn 7. Damn! I followed him through turn 7 and the little left-right wiggle just before turn 8, planning to pass him through turn 9 and try to beat him to the flag. At the apex of turn 8A, leaned over nearly to the maximum, I grabbed a big handful of throttle, and the rear tire lost traction and I crashed.

Normally in a crash like this I would separate from the bike and slide to a stop, but this time I hit the pavement right near the top of a downhill section. The bike and I parted company, but I started spinning instead of just sliding. It was sky-ground, sky-ground, sky-ground, *bam!* sky-ground, sky-ground, sky-ground, *thwack!* as I bounced and tumbled down the hill.

I was spinning sideways like a barrel rolling and bouncing downhill, not going head-over-heels, thank goodness. I had pulled my arms into my chest, but my legs were still slightly spread out. I tried to pull them together so they wouldn't get bent or broken, but I couldn't. The centrifugal force generated by my spinning was so strong my muscles couldn't overcome it.

I came to rest beneath a bunch of old tires on the outside of the track near the apex of turn 9. I lay there for a while, assessing my condition. When I realized I was basically unhurt, just battered and bruised, I started pushing tires away. The turn workers showed up and helped me get out of the tires and on my feet. I felt slightly dizzy. That may have been the sign of a slight concussion or simply the aftermath of my spinning.

I was truly bummed out. The crash had been entirely my fault; I knew better than to slam on the throttle when still leaned over. It was simply a rider error. Poor Dale! He was away for 15 or 16 months, and on his first time back, I trash one of his motorcycles. I apologized to Dale, then sat in my van to think about things.

Something had changed, in a fundamental way. I wasn't enjoying the racing. If I was going to literally risk my life, there needed to be some major payback and I wasn't getting it. I got out of the van and went and talked to Dale, and told him it was time for me to quit racing. He seemed to understand.

What does a racer do when racing is over? Good question. How do full-on adrenaline junkies get their fix? It's tough to quit cold turkey. The answer of course varies depending on the person and the circumstances. If I had to stop racing after the end of the 1978 season, when I came close to winning the championship title and the 905 showed so much promise, I probably would have taken up some other high-risk sport. Skydiving and hang-gliding come to mind, two sports I was always interested in, but never had time to try.

————

I didn't stop racing at the end of 1978, but continued to race and suffered through that miserable year with the BMW. I think that year gave time for the adrenaline addiction to subside a bit, and when I did stop racing, the extreme need was no longer there. It wasn't gone completely and I started backpacking in the Sierra Nevada Mountains in the summer, camping at or above the 10,000-foot elevation and scrambling to the tops of 14,000-foot-plus high mountains. The Sierra is pretty impressive above timberline, and I think the thin air and lack of oxygen to my brain gave me a bit of a euphoric feeling slightly similar to an adrenaline high. In the winter I took up downhill skiing. I had been a cross-country skier before racing, and still went on an occasional X-C ski trip, but the thrill from hurtling at high speed on the downhill slopes on the edge of control provided some of the adrenaline rush I craved. I got to be a good intermediate-level skier, but went down the expert runs for the added scare factor.

My Life Takes a Turn

I continued to follow the races for a while, but slowly I drifted away. In 1982 I had a chance to buy a house and sold all but one of my motorcycles and racing parts to get enough money together. I kept my Ducati 750 Sport, converted back to a street bike once more. I wasn't riding very much, though. The Sport wasn't running right and I just couldn't generate the energy to do the needed overhaul. At one point I was planning on buying a plain reliable street bike to ride while fixing the Ducati, but termites were discovered in the garage and *poof* the money for a second motorcycle was gone.

I was in my mid-30s and was concentrating on my engineering career and racing no longer had the draw it once had. I was also riding on the street less and less. I got married in 1985 and moved to Oregon in 1987 with plans to start a family. I intended to fix the Ducati someday, but events kept me busy. A son came along in 1990 and, wanting to be a responsible husband and father, I gave up the idea of riding. The Ducati sat in the corner of the garage under a cover, neglected for eight long years.

I wasn't done with motorcycles though, or perhaps I should say motorcycles weren't done with me.

PART II

MOTORCYCLE TO WHEELCHAIR LIFE

CHAPTER TEN

Back in the Saddle

When I moved to Oregon in 1987, I stopped riding. I had been riding very little even before the move because the Ducati Sport, by then my only motorcycle, wasn't running well. In Oregon I was too busy with other stuff: a bride, a new job, a new house with no landscaping. I was busy. Motorcycling just wasn't a very high priority then. Things can change, though, in response to circumstances.

———

It was my soon-to-be ex-wife who got me riding motorcycles again. By late 1995 my role as father of a now 5-year-old boy was going well, I think, but the husband-wife relationship had gone slowly off track. After some meaningless argument, she said, "When you get all stressed, why don't you go jogging, or take a motorcycle ride or something, instead of getting into a fight with me?"

The question brought me up short. Why *didn't* I take a motorcycle ride? The risk of injury from an easy ride through the local hills would be low, so I could ride and still be a responsible parent. I started looking for a bike, something reliable and practical while I did the long overdue restoration of my Ducati.

Motorcycling had changed, so it took some time to figure out what to buy. Instead of nice general-purpose bikes the owner could modify for his own purpose, the factories were making niche bikes: sport bikes, cruisers, touring, sport-touring, adventure bikes, etc. I didn't want a niche bike. The Ducati Sport was niche-ish enough.

The many motorcycle-related Internet groups helped me with my investigation. After weeks of research I decided to get a Honda Hawk GT, a mid-size V-twin that was not a niche bike, but one described as a good all-arounder. They were hard to find because Honda imported them to the U.S. for only four years, 1988-1991. I located one near Chicago, a low-mileage unmodified 1988 model offered by a seller who was highly respected on the Hawk GT website.

Between the time I started looking and the time I finally found the Hawk GT, my wife and I had separated. She and our son had moved to an apartment in town and I was very depressed about the whole situation. When the crate arrived, there was only myself in the house, no one to share in the excitement, no one I could tell, "It's here, come see!"

I uncrated the bike, added all the necessary fluids, installed a new battery, and it started right up. I wanted to see how it rode, so I decided to ride it up and down my dead-end street. I dug out my old gloves and helmet, checked inside for spiders, put them on, and pulled out of the driveway and down the street.

Oh. My. God. I can't correctly describe the rush of feelings I had during that slow ride, but one phrase kept popping into my head: *this is Correct.* It felt so good, so *right.* This is where I needed to be–in the saddle. I must have ridden that bike for an hour back and forth in the two blocks from the corner to the cul-de-sac. The end of the street had a circular turn-around and I would first circle left, then right, and then do a figure eight. I could feel my world, which had been running quite out of balance of late, starting to correct itself. It was an epiphany.

It was a shame I stopped riding all those years. I shouldn't have let it happen. Then again, perhaps the break and the rebirth were necessary to allow me to understand I was not just a guy who had ridden bikes in his youth, but I was, in fact, *a motorcyclist.*

Old Habits Don't Die, They Hibernate

Once the Hawk GT was registered and licensed in Oregon, some of my not-used-for-years habits returned. I started putting miles on it, riding it to work, to the store, to visit friends, etc. My parents had retired and lived in Portland, and my younger brother and his family lived just west of the city, so I would ride there to visit them. I searched out non-freeway routes from home to Portland or Beaverton that were prettier or curvier and made the trips longer.

I studied maps and found weekend and lunchtime rides. The Oregon Coast Range, sitting between the Willamette Valley and the Pacific Ocean, has many nice twisty roads; East of the valley are the Cascade Mountains and there are additional fine rides in the Cascade foothills.

During the summer of 1996 I took the Hawk GT on many of these rides and got more familiar with it. It was a very good motorcycle, but not perfect. It handled well in smooth turns, but bumpy pavement upset it a bit and the stock tank's range was painfully short. I kept hitting reserve after 105 miles, even though the mileage was decent, in the 40-mpg range. The exhaust system was quiet but also very heavy. The seat slanted down and I kept sliding forward, bumping my crotch on the fuel tank

By this time the Hawk GT had gained an almost cult-bike status, and there was an active on-line discussion group dedicated to the model. There were well-known solutions to the suspension weaknesses, things that had been tried and well tested. I made plans to add these adaptations once the rains started in the fall. Several aftermarket companies made replacement exhaust systems that were recommended.

I still needed to figure out something about the tank. Stopping every 110 miles or so to fill up was a pain. Trips into rural areas where towns were spread out had to be planned with fuel range in mind. I grew to really dislike the situation.

The only aftermarket option available at that time was an expensive carbon fiber tank that was wider than the stock tank and pushed the rider's legs outward. I still needed to figure out why the range was so short. The tank looked big enough but somehow it wasn't doing the job.

Separation and Renewal

The failure of my marriage hit me hard. At first I hoped there was a chance the problems could be resolved, but it was soon clear reconciliation wasn't going to happen. It was over except for the legal aspects.

One evening I went for a walk in the neighborhood, a path my wife, son, and I would often take on summer evenings. We would feed grass to the horses pastured in the field around the corner, or pick and eat some wild blackberries if they were in season. When the house came into view as I returned home, I was engulfed with an intense feeling of sorrow and burst into tears.

The house was full of good and bad memories. The good ones would be sorely missed and the bad ones would be painful. I couldn't stay there and be mentally healthy, so at that moment I realized the house must be sold. After the sale I was able, with my share of the equity and a bit of a financial stretch, to buy another place on the other side of town. It was not new and had a rather odd floor plan, but it had a view of the Three Sisters

Cascade volcanoes, a splendid deck that wrapped around three sides of the house, and a four-car garage.

It was the garage that sold me on it. It wasn't a conventional four-car setup with four bays lined up side by side; they were arranged in a square. Think of it as a two-car garage with double-deep bays. It had been designed to allow for a large RV or travel trailer, as one of the two garage doors was 10-feet tall. The garage ceiling itself was almost 12-feet high. For a while I had a basketball hoop installed in one corner and on rainy days my son Steven and I could shoot hoops inside with his junior-size basketball. The setup allowed me to have one bay for the Hawk GT with space for storage, one bay for the minivan, a bay for the workshop and one for the mini-basketball court.

Garage Therapy

I have three ways to work through problems that seriously depress me. Two are conventional—I seek professional help from a therapist, and sometimes anti-depression medicine. The third is to hole up somewhere away from people, work on something using my hands while my mind works in the background to resolve problems. I had questions such as: What exactly happened? What was my part in it? Can it be avoided in the future? Kind of like a wounded animal taking refuge in a cave, nursing his wounds until he is ready to face life again.

In the case of the divorce, I did it all: medicine, weekly sessions with a therapist, and daily sessions in the workshop.

Modifications to the Hawk GT

I bought a Hawk GT I found in Puyallup, Washington, that already had the improved suspension modifications and a stainless steel exhaust system much lighter than the stock exhaust. After a little work in the garage, I had a low-mileage Hawk GT that handled better, took the bumps in stride, and weighed less. I also had a slightly higher mileage unmodified Hawk GT. A completely stock Hawk GT was rather rare and I was able to sell the now-stock Puyallup bike for the same price I paid for it, which meant I got the upgrades for the cost of a few hours of therapy work in the garage, a pretty good trade.

To fix the sloping seat I got a used seat base, made some drawings, and sent it off to Sargent Seats. I had them convert the slanted seat into a stepped seat with level rider and passenger sections. The result looked good, was just as comfortable as the stock seat, and there was no more problem with sliding forward into the fuel tank.

The next thing to tackle was the Hawk GT's lack of range. I went to the local bike salvage yard and bought a used Hawk GT tank. I wanted to see why the tank held so little fuel without disabling my own bike. Upon examination of the salvage tank, the answer was pretty obvious. There were three problems. The main problem was the underside of the tank had a very large cutout space to make room for the airbox. In effect the tank wrapped around the airbox, leaving a space on top, a space between the airbox and the seat, and two wings that went down along the sides of the airbox.

The tank had a recessed filler cap so it could be filled only to the bottom of the recess, not to the top of the tank, leaving about 1 inch of space empty.

The third problem was that the exit pipe, the pipe the petcock screwed onto, did not exit the tank at the lowest spot. There were two small pockets at the bottom of each side wing that still held gas even if the tank was drained bone dry through the petcock.

I decided to make a larger tank. I didn't want to re-jet the carburetors so I needed to keep the airbox as is, but I tackled the other problems. Extra tubes were brazed in to allow fuel to flow from the two side pockets to the petcock. I cut out the recessed fuel cap and replaced it with a raised filler cap. Lastly, I cut the tank into top and bottom halves, raised the top one inch in front and 0.5 inch in back, and then welded in extra sheet steel to fill the gap. When I started filling it with water to test the capacity, it leaked from practically every joint. My welding skills were, um, let's say they were below average.

I wrapped the tank in several layers of fiberglass and resin to make it leakproof. The end result was really ugly and very heavy, but it held a full five gallons. I primed it and painted it blue and put it on my bike. I got several runs of right around 200 miles before hitting reserve, and one of 206. The frustration of stopping so often for fuel was gone. It was still ugly, though.

When I do fabrication work like this, the first one is usually a throwaway. I learn all the things not to do on the first one, and the second is the one to keep.

I'm not forgetting the therapy part. Some of the tank creation required careful thought and some of it was more mindless, such as wet-sanding the coats of paint. During these latter stretches I pondered what had happened to my marriage and my role in the events. I was beginning to understand the what and why.

With the experience from the first tank, I made a much better second one. I decided to retain the recessed filler cap even though it limited capacity a bit. The cap looked good and leaving it in saved a big chunk of time. My welding improved with practice, and although I wasn't able to weld a completely leak-proof tank, I was able to use a lot less plastic filler and fiberglass to make it hold fuel, and look good. It measured out at 4.8 gallons and gave me a range of 180 miles before reserve when ridden sensibly. It wasn't 200 miles, but it was good enough.

I continued what I'd come to think of as the Therapy Project by making a few more tanks and selling them to other Hawk owners who disliked the short range as much as I did. I made eight jumbo tanks in all. Their price was low for a couple of reasons. Firstly, they were short of the quality one would expect from a true commercial product, and I made sure my customers were fully aware of that fact. Secondly, working as my own boss allowed me to pay myself really crappy wages.

But it worked. I spent about a year being asocial, doing my day job, a weekly hour with the therapist, time in the garage, and not much else. Then I emerged into the light of day, gave up the anti-depression meds, and started dating again.

Social Networking

There is something about motorcycle people. I enjoy interacting with them more than with a randomly selected group of the general populace. I was trying to figure out why this is when it came to me—shared passion. I could have strong political or religious differences with other people, but if they liked motorcycles, we could enjoy each other's company.

I'm sure this shared passion isn't restricted to motorcycles. There are no doubt groups that are passionate about model trains, chemistry, skeet shooting, different sports, certain TV shows, etc. But my passion, and the passion of most of the members of the e-mail lists I took part in, was motorcycles.

At this point in my life I was living alone in the house with the four-car garage, and life was fairly solitary. I had friends at work, but most people went home to their families at the end of the workday. My social activities became web-centered. I joined a number of motorcycle-related e-mail lists, and eventually I stayed active on three lists.

The Hawk GT list was for owners of Honda's Hawk GT motorcycle. It was a national list with members in many different states, and the list knowledge of that model was immense. If you wanted to know something about the Hawk GT, you could ask the list and you would get an answer or three, or more. There were no list-wide organized get-togethers, but I did meet a few when one of my visits to my siblings in the San Francisco Bay Area coincided with a Hawk GT ride in the hills west of San Mateo. I met a few others, including the man who sold me my first Hawk GT, when I rode to Sears Point in 1997, the 20th anniversary of my first AMA Superbike race win. He had moved from Chicago to Novato, California, only 10 miles from the racetrack, and he let me crash in his house.

There was a list called Bevelheads that covered all Ducati models that featured bevel-driven overhead cams. There were many bevel-drive models, single-cylinder and twin-cylinder, ranging in size from 250cc to 1,000cc and in vintage from the 1950s to 1985. My 1974 Sport featured a bevel-driven overhead cam so it was a natural fit. The Bevelheads list is international, although most members live in the U.S. Many of the group would get together every year in Monterey, California, during the Laguna Seca World Superbike races and I got to meet a few of them face-to-face.

The third and most active list was WetLeather, a non-brand, non-model-specific group that was geographic in nature. Most of the members lived in Oregon, Washington, and Idaho. This group had four annual events when they would get together in real life, and a fifth was added in 1998. I got to know several members well and made many good friends from that list. In fact I met my new girlfriend, a woman with the nickname ToTB, on the WetLeather list. When we got together in the spring of 1998, it marked the end of recovery from my divorce. Life was far from perfect, as ToTB lived in San Jose, 600 miles from me, and my son Steven lived 400 miles away, but it was pretty darn good.

CHAPTER ELEVEN

The Track Lures Me Back

After not racing for so many years, I figured I was over my adrenaline addiction. I was wrong. In the summer of 1997, I took a ride with a small group of people in the Cascade foothills. Part of the ride was this tight, twisty, technical 60 miles of road. My pal Squido and I attacked that rode, leaving the others behind.

Oh my, the feelings! Knowing I was with a group let me cut loose more than I would have if I were solo riding, and the adrenaline started flowing, endorphines were swirling around in my body. It's like being an alcoholic, no matter how long to stay on the wagon it only takes one drink to knock you off. After the group rendezvoused, I told the ride leader, "I'm feeling things I haven't felt in nearly twenty years." I felt happy the entire rest of the day.

————

The American Historic Racing Motorcycle Association (AHRMA) program had classes for old bikes, from 20 years old back all the way to the 19-teens. They also provided a few classes for more modern motorcycles. It sounded like fun, but my vintage race bike, the 1974 Ducati Sport, wasn't running. Not to worry, my WetLeather pals said. Some calls were made, word was put out, and, presto, I was loaned a 1967 Ducati 250cc single-cylinder race bike. It came complete with a race van and a few boxes of spares. It was in Carson City, Nevada. I had to get to Nevada, drive the race van with bike to Steamboat Springs, Colorado, race, drive back to Nevada, drop off the van, and then go home, a round trip of just under 3,000 miles. A piece of cake; I'm in.

I rendezvoused with ToTB in Carson City, where we left our vehicles and picked up the race van and bike and headed east on U.S. Highway 50, the historic route of the Pony Express. Two days later we were in Steamboat Springs.

The Magic of Muscle Memory

There were two Saturday morning practice sessions for bikes in the Vintage 250cc class. The track wasn't too difficult and the first session went OK until I came in at the end. I coasted into the pits and jumped off the bike to push it back to my pit spot. The bike wouldn't push, because the rear brake was locked up. I got it loose enough by jiggling the brake lever, got the bike back to our pit and on the stand, and watched in amazement as my hands took over.

I had raced and maintained a Ducati single for three years when I first started racing, but switched to racing a twin in 1976. I had once been very familiar with the singles, but I hadn't done any actual wrenching on one since 1975. That was 23 years earlier, yet my hands knew exactly what to do, a fraction of a second *before* my mind had fully grasped it. I didn't need any mental search to try to remember how to pull the rear wheel out, for example—all the knowledge about the Ducati singles I learned from 1973-1975 was suddenly there, in my hands.

The rear wheel was off in a few minutes and the brake hub out of it. It was hot! I had to use rags as hot pads to handle it. The return springs that were supposed to pull the brake shoes away from the drum when the brake lever was released looked wrong—too weak. As the hub continued to cool, I rummaged through the boxes of spares and found a pair of springs that looked right. The brake shoes were popped off, the stronger springs installed, all the moving parts given a coat of grease, and the rear wheel reinstalled in time for the second practice session.

The second session went better. The bike was quite a bit faster when the rear brake wasn't constantly trying to slow it down. There was one corner I hadn't quite figured out because the camber changed right in the middle of the turn, but the rest of the track wasn't complicated.

It was time to relax, have some lunch, and watch some of the early races. My race was scheduled for 2:30 Saturday afternoon while most of our group would race on Sunday.

I don't remember the accident, which is probably a good thing. I remember morning practice, having a banana at lunch, and watching one race for pre-1920s bikes. I had been knocked out twice before and I remembered everything right up to the blow that turned the lights out, but this time was different. I don't remember the start of my race or the two laps that ran before the accident, and many, many days after the accident are missing. Some of my story from this time is from my memory, but much of it has been pieced together from what I've been told by other people.

———

I was a newbie at this track and new to AHRMA, so I was gridded well back in the pack. As lap one concluded, I was told, I had moved up quite a bit. I later asked ToTB, who was watching from the pit area near the start line, if I was passing other racers and she said yes. I didn't come around to complete lap two and shortly after that the red flags came out to stop the race.

The Investigation

The accident happened on a part of the track that was slightly curved and somewhat downhill, a full-throttle, top-gear section. There was nothing tricky about that part of the track, and barring a seized motor or tire blowout, an accident would have been unlikely. Speeds would have been around or slightly above 100 mph for the 250cc bikes. I'm told someone in front of me had a problem that resulted in a crash. He was thrown up in the air, came down just as I arrived, and peeled me off my bike. The bike continued on for a good distance before glancing off the fence and falling over. While on the pavement, I was hit by a following rider, which would have been when most of the damage happened. I never did find out what caused the initial problem.

Injury List

I'll start with the list of injuries, least to most serious. I had a cut in my forehead from my glasses (that were never found) and a broken index finger on my left hand. Yes, I'm left-handed, thanks for asking. There was a brachial plexus injury at my left shoulder from having my arm twisted up and back behind my head. It gave my lower left arm and hand an odd tingly feeling. There was a hard hit to the helmet that gave me a severe concussion. I donated that helmet, which had a nasty gash on one side, to the Team Oregon group that teaches the New Rider Class. They use it to show how a helmet absorbs and spreads the shock to minimize the blow to the head, making the point that the rider *did* survive the accident that destroyed the helmet.

The broken back with a spinal cord injury (SCI) was pretty serious, and the SCI was permanent, leaving me paralyzed from mid-chest down.

If that wasn't enough, the most life-threatening injury was a torn aorta, the big artery that leads out of the heart.

I'm told that when the track safety worker got to me I said, "I can't feel my legs," so they knew it was serious. I was taken on a backboard to the Steamboat Springs Medical Center. It seems I was talking to the staff, but when they started to cut my leathers off so they could examine me, my blood pressure went to zero and I passed out. The doctor suspected a torn aorta in addition to the back injury, because a really hard blow to that particular area of the back or chest can cause an aorta tear. They left the rest of my leathers on, wrapped me back up with Ace bandages, and put me on a medical transport plane to Denver, over 100 air miles away.

The statistics weren't promising. Nine out of 10 people with a torn aorta die. Some expire quickly, bleeding out in minutes. Some take a bit longer, and a few die even *after* they get to the hospital. When the plane left Steamboat Springs, I was breathing, but nobody could say for sure if I would still be alive when the plane landed. I was truly racing the gods during this plane ride.

ToTB wasn't allowed to take the plane ride with me, so she had to drive the race van the 150 or so road miles from Steamboat to Denver. She didn't necessarily keep to the speed limits, she admitted to me later. When she finally arrived at Denver Health Hospital, they wouldn't tell her if I was there because she wasn't immediate family.

She demanded to know, saying, "If he isn't here, he's in the morgue and I'm the one who will have to tell his immediate family he's dead!" Eventually she broke down the petty bureaucratic walls and they let her into the Intensive Care Unit and started treating her as a family member. I must have been quite a scary sight. ToTB said I had hoses coming out of many parts of my body and the only clear area was my forehead, so she stroked my forehead and talked to me as I lay unconscious in the bed.

Memories (or Not) of Intensive Care

Consciousness following the crash returned in dribs and drabs, a little here and a little there—the process was very disconnected. I was drifting in and out, so at times I appeared aware of what was going on, and I remember some of those interludes, but not all of them. I don't know if it was due to the severity of the concussion or from the massive amounts of pain killing drugs I received, or a combination of both.

I was alive but not really living. It was very disorienting and frustrating not being able to rely on my mind. I became passive, letting things happen to me, trusting that the doctors would do the right thing.

———

At Denver Health Hospital I was put straight into the Intensive Care Unit, where I stayed for three weeks. The medical folks didn't waste any time with the aorta tear; it was fixed that very night. I've wondered how that was done–did they stop my heart while doing the suturing then re-start it? I've been afraid to ask. Some things are better not known.

I'm told the heart surgeon was a good-looking blonde woman. You'd think I'd remember that but, alas, no. ToTB asked the surgeon how I managed to survive the aorta tear. The doctor thought it was due to some soft tissue swelling plus the snug-fitting racing leathers. She also thought my being in good shape helped. She was surprised to learn I was one month shy of 50 years old.

I was unconscious for three days. ToTB told me our first post-injury conversation went like this:

"There's a spaghetti dinner tonight," I said.

"No, that was Saturday. It's Tuesday now," she replied.

"Oh." I paused to let that to sink in. Drat. I was looking forward to that dinner, "How did our friends do in their races?"

"Not very well. Everyone was worried about you."

"Well, *that's* a convenient excuse."

I honestly don't remember this conversation. I'm sure I meant it as humor, not snarkyness. Anyway I was on drugs.

The ICU room was small. In front of me was a window that must have looked into a hallway–I remember people looking at me through the window. It might have been a window in the door to my room. To my right was a bare wall, and on the left was an opening to the nurses' station. Behind me were machines; I couldn't see them, but I could hear them hissing and whirring and clicking, and sometimes I could see their lights reflected in the window.

ToTB contacted my family. At first they weren't too concerned. "Paul's crashed before; he knows how to handle it."

"You don't understand. They need a next of kin who can make decisions or sign stuff."

Those three words, "next of kin," made them realize this crash was different. My younger brother, Russ, could get away most quickly and he came to Denver. I'm told he was stunned when he saw me in the ICU, but he recovered quickly and started taking care of things.

There were many, many phone calls to be made. Family and co-workers needed to be kept up-to-date, the human resources department where I worked needed to be contacted, and my health insurance company was told of the situation. Things got complicated and more calls had to be made, to state representatives, the Oregon insurance commissioner's office, and congressmen. ToTB mentioned to WetLeather that it was difficult keeping up with only one or two cell phones and suddenly she had a handful. WetLeather rocks.

Apparently I wasn't a very good patient in the ICU. There was a feeding tube through my nose into my stomach and I pulled it out three times. I only remember it once in a vague, hazy sort of way. Something was hurting my nose, but I couldn't figure out what it was. I kept pulling on this *thing* that seemed to be causing the pain. When I felt the end of the tube pass through my throat and out my nose, I remember thinking, *I probably shouldn't have done that.* The nurses thought I was willful, but I didn't mean to misbehave. It was just that the narcotic fog in my brain left me unaware of many of my actions. I remember when the fourth tube was inserted they fastened it down with a huge wad of tape on my nose. I complained that it hurt, but got a stony silence.

I remember this incident: my breathing was very shallow because I couldn't use my lower torso muscles to totally fill my lungs, and I was being given auxiliary oxygen. When the oxygen bottle ran low, I had trouble breathing; I'd press the button for help and someone would swap in a fresh bottle.

After installing the fourth feeding tube, the nurses put a leash on my hands at night. I could still move my arms, but not enough to reach my nose. No one noticed I also couldn't reach the call button. I woke that night short of breath and couldn't call for help. I pulled as hard as I could on the strap, but it held. I finally gave up and I recall thinking, as I lost consciousness, *I'm in a hospital, what bad can happen?* Dumb question, I know, but I was drugged.

I opened my eyes again in only a few minutes—I could breathe easily, all the lights were on, and there were several people in hospital garb looking at me. I remember asking, "Are we having a party?" I know it sounds silly, but I was on drugs.

A guy looked at me, smiled, and said, "Um, yeah, it's a party."

A few weeks later, after some of the drugs had worn off, I wondered about this incident. Did I pass out after not reaching the call button or did I just fall back to sleep? Did my blood oxygen level drop and cause alarms to go off at the nursing station? Had I been in any real danger?

I remember the smell of roasting turkey. I have no idea where that came from, as there was no kitchen anywhere near the ICU. They must have been good drugs. I vaguely remember my sister, Ardath, came to visit. She's a registered nurse so I should have paid attention to her. She later said she found me very lost in thought and uncommunicative. Part of it was the narcotics, but I was also trying to figure out how to stay in my house—where to put elevators, stair lifts—at the time.

After a few days I stabilized from the aorta repair and it was time to do something about my back. The back surgeon and the X-ray tech got into a pissing contest. The surgeon wanted images that were in better focus; the X-ray tech claimed they were as good as he could make them. The problem was that one of my vertebrae was so shattered it looked fuzzy no matter what. In the meantime I was lying on my back, unable to cough hard enough to clear my lungs and fluid began to collect. I had to have a tracheotomy tube installed so my lungs could be cleared. This meant there was no air going past my vocal chords so I couldn't talk. Finally a more senior doctor intervened, told the back surgeon to stop whining and get to work. Bone from my pelvis was taken to help rebuild the damaged vertebrae, and titanium rods and wires were installed to hold the bones in place while they knitted together.

During the recovery from the back operation, my older brother and sister-in-law came to see me. I remember it was a frustrating visit. It was nice to see them, but I couldn't talk because of the trach tube, I couldn't write with my broken left finger, and I couldn't write legibly using my right hand (I tried). I was given a letter board to communicate by spelling out words letter by letter. It was very slow, and by the time I'd finished spelling the third or fourth word, I had forgotten what I wanted to say.

When I stabilized from the back operation, I was put into an upper-body cast that prevented me from twisting my torso. It ran from my hips to my shoulders, with an extension to my chin so I couldn't turn my head. It was in this condition that I was transferred to Craig Hospital for rehabilitation work, somewhere around the first part of October 1998.

CHAPTER TWELVE

Rehabilitation

It must be quite a shock to have a friend, a family member, or a doctor tell you you'll never walk again. I've misplaced that experience. I know at some point somebody told me the paralysis was permanent, but it was one of the many events I lost in the painkiller fog of the early days. When I got to Craig Hospital, they started weaning me from the pain medicine, and as my mind started clearing, there was no shock, no sudden realization I would be using a wheelchair for the rest of my life. It was something I just knew as the narcotic haze faded away and I started remembering things such as what I had for lunch or who had visited that week.

Soon after the accident my family and friends started looking for a good rehabilitation place, led mainly by ToTB and my younger brother Russ. They learned of a highly rated one in Seattle and another in Santa Clara, California, but the obvious choice was in Colorado, Craig Hospital in Englewood, a suburb of Denver. Craig was highly rated, top five nationally, as I recall. It specializes in rehabilitation from spinal cord injuries and traumatic brain injuries, and treats around 100 SCI patients per year.

The move from Denver Health Hospital to Craig Hospital was a difficult transition. I was still getting lots of pain meds so I was rather loopy, and I couldn't talk because of the trach tube. I'm told the first time they tried to move me I became quite agitated because I didn't understand what was happening. I have no memory of that episode. They tried again the next day and it worked, so I transferred to Craig in October 1998. I don't remember the actual ambulance ride, but I knew I was in a different place.

Craig had an intercom system between the beds and the nursing station. When I needed help, I would push the call button and the bed would say, "Can I help you?" I couldn't answer with words so I made a clicking noise with my tongue against the roof of my mouth. I didn't need air for that–it's just meat slapping meat. The bed replied, "I'll send someone in." A few minutes later an aide or nurse would appear and we would play charades as I tried to explain what I needed. The people at the nursing station knew which bed had called in, and they all knew I couldn't talk, but we had to go through the same, "Can I help you?"–"Click, click" dialog every single time. Sheesh.

The trach tube was installed in my throat while I was in the ICU to allow my lungs to clear of the fluid that had collected during the days on my back, not being able to cough. I don't remember how it was used in the ICU, but I have vivid memories of the process at Craig. As I breathed through the tube, the fluid in my lungs would begin to collect near the opening and my breathing would get all raspy. An aide would take a small vacuum device and vacuum the junk out through the trach tube. It was one of the most unpleasant and painful procedures I've ever had to endure, and I was overjoyed when my lungs cleared enough to make the trach tube unnecessary. Not only did I no longer need to have my lungs vacuumed out, I could talk again.

Since the accident I've read some biographies of people who have received similar paralyzing injuries–motorcycle road racing champion Wayne Rainey, movie actor Christopher Reeve, author/cartoonist John Callahan, and others–and there seems to be a common progression people go through. It's similar to the five stages of grief people go through after losing a loved one. It is a loss after all.

The first stage is denial. "This can't be happening," or, "It will heal after awhile."

Stage two is anger, which is pretty common if the accident was caused by someone's negligence, such as a drunk driver. People can also be angry with themselves or with God: "Lord why did you let this happen? I didn't deserve it."

Bargaining is the third stage. In the case of grief over a loss, it's described as something that is done before the loss (death, divorce, etc.) occurs. In this case there's no advance knowledge of the SCI, but still there can be promises to go to church every week if things turn out OK.

Depression usually happens next, sometimes suicidal. Many people, especially the younger ones, figure life will no longer be worth living and wish they had died. This phase of grief is not the same as the long-term bouts with depression, but instead refers to the immediate post-injury emotional state.

Lastly, there is acceptance, and the hard work of building a new life begins.

While still in the ICU, I went through the denial phase. After all I had a partially paralyzed arm in 1972 and recovered from that. At one point I recall, vaguely, feeling my legs were splayed out and I pulled them together. I recall thinking, *See, it will be all right,* but I never even opened my eyes to check, I was so doped up.

I skipped the anger phase. It's something racers accept. You can get hurt and it's nobody's fault. If you can't accept that, you shouldn't go racing. For me, there was nobody to be mad at.

I also skipped the bargaining and the initial depression/suicidal phases. In the 1970s one of my co-workers, Andrew, had a spinal cord injury from Vietnam and got around in a wheelchair. The members of the small research group where I worked were not just co-workers, but also friends and I had gone to parties at Andy's house. My life was going to be different, for sure, and probably more difficult, but from Andy's example I knew there *was* life after paralysis. He had a meaningful job, good friends, professional respect, and what appeared to be a satisfying life in spite of being in a chair. Thanks to Andy's example, once I realized my injury meant permanent paralysis, I was able to skip straight to acceptance, and as soon as recovery from my injuries allowed, I jumped into learning what I needed to know to live in this new way.

Although I avoided the initial depression, it did appear later, and it has been a struggle to avoid the blues during certain phases of my post-SCI life, as you will see.

Lessons from Craig Hospital

The odds were against me. At my age recovering enough to become independent from the injuries I suffered was going to be very, very difficult. But I had beaten long odds before; motorcycling had taught me to at least try. What are the odds of a rookie winning his first Superbike race? Also I had already beaten the 9:1 odds against surviving a torn aorta.

I approached the problem the way I had tackled racing, or learning to ride a bicycle for that matter, by breaking what looked like an overwhelming task into smaller, more manageable pieces and working on them one by one. Each time I had a success I would move on to the next step. I was perhaps a bit cocky about it, but I figured I could beat this.

I was determined to return to work, to learn to drive with hand controls, and to live on my own again, just like before except I'd be in a wheelchair.

My former workmate Andy was my shining example; he showed me that it was possible.

––––––––

New patients at Craig are assigned an occupational therapist and a physical therapist who stays with them for the entire time they are in rehab. I got two young women who did a great job. I was given range of motion and strengthening exercises, taught how to transfer out of my wheelchair using a slide board, chair to bed and vice versa, chair to the workout table, and chair to automobile seat. I was shown how to do weight shifts to avoid getting pressure sores. I was introduced to all kinds of tools to help with normal activities: special knives and forks, a device to hold nail clippers, devices to help put on your socks, and all designed to make SCI life easier. One of the tools I found most useful was called a grabber, or a reacher, a reach extender that had pinchers on one end and a pistol-shape handle on the other. Squeezing the trigger caused the jaws of the pinchers to close, allowing me to pick up things up off the floor or reach items over my head. I still use one. Ironically, it's the one item I drop most often.

I developed a love/hate relationship with my therapists. They were tough on me and pushed me not only to improve in body, but also in attitude. When I was faced with some sort of problem, the therapists would ask questions that would lead me to a solution as opposed to just telling me what to do. Early on in the rehab process, I was so overwhelmed with the sheer volume of new information I needed to learn I would resist and say, "Just tell me how I can get past this." One example was when I was able to finally sit up in a shower chair and take an actual shower. Boy, did that first shower feel good. I dropped the scrub brush halfway through and couldn't wash my back or lower legs. "I dropped the brush," I said to my therapist, who was waiting just outside the shower curtain.

"I see. How might you solve that problem?" she asked through the curtain.

I couldn't pick up the brush myself and I wanted her to do it. But I answered, "I could bring my reacher in with me."

"Maybe. But then you would have two things to drop."

"OK, would you please pick it up for me?" I asked.

"Not yet. Are you a skier?"

"Yes. Well, I used to be." *What has that got to do with it?* I thought.

"Did you ever drop a ski pole?"

"Rarely. They have this strap." I stopped in mid-sentence and looked down at the brush, stared at the pre-drilled hole in the handle. "I get it. I could put a strap on the brush."

"Bingo," she said and she picked up the brush and handed it to me through the curtain.

The attitude did sink in, and instead of looking to my therapist for a solution, I started thinking about how I could solve the problem myself. These days when I'm faced with an obstacle my first impulse is to look around my environment for something, anything, I can use as a tool to overcome whatever faces me instead of looking for someone else to help.

The Craig patients were divided into groups of about eight to 10 people who were at a similar stage of recovery, referred to as a class. In addition to the daily one-on-one work with my therapists, there was group work with the class. Weather permitting, we took daily outdoor wheelchair runs of several blocks in length. If the weather was nasty, we would use the gym.

We also attended actual classes. There were classes on hygiene, wheelchair maintenance, how the body adapts–they told us to expect changes for years, rapidly at first, then slowing as the years go on–up to and beyond five years post-accident. There was a class on how the body might misbehave post-SCI and the medicines that could control some of the negative reactions. The class on sexuality was well attended. Most of my classmates were young people and wanted to know everything. (Frankly, older members like me were just as interested.) There was a tutorial on the Americans with Disabilities Act (ADA) describing what sorts of legal issues we might end up facing in the future, and what remedies were available.

The recreational therapy department had a class on wheelchair sports and recreation. I liked the class, but with my injuries I still had a lot of healing to do and I had little extra energy. A game at the pool table was about the level of exertion I could put out at the time.

Downstairs from the rec therapy department, Craig had a practice room. There was a car passenger compartment–the side panels, the door, and the passenger seat. My therapists used it to teach me how to use an extra-long slide board to transfer from my wheelchair to the passenger seat of a typical car. They had a set of airline seats bolted to the floor and an airline aisle chair they used to demonstrate what would happen when I took a plane trip.

There was a person who did driver training. Craig had a modified van with a ramp and hand controls, and I was given two short, hands-on driving sessions. It was enough to know I would be able to drive again with the right adaptations.

During one of the rainy day wheelchair sessions, they tried to teach us to balance on two wheels. They had special anti-tipper bars that allowed the chair to go past the balance point but would prevent a tip-over, so we could practice balancing the wheelchair. I was surprised I couldn't do it. A couple of other guys were not only balancing, but were moving slowly around the gym—on two wheels. Back in the 1970s my co-worker Andrew sometimes transferred to the couch and let others try out his chair. I could balance it easily. It was actually quite stable once the balance point was found.

So what was the problem? Was it something about my chair? I asked the instructor about it and he wanted to know my level of injury. I told him T-3 complete.

"You can't use any of your torso muscles. You might not be able to do it. Not every para can," she said. I was crushed. If I could have balanced, I could have gone downstairs a few steps or off a curb. Moreover, it's a skill I used to have.

I had an appointment with a social worker who asked about my employer and what sort of medical and disability insurance I had. She contacted my employer's benefits department and made sure I got the coverage I was qualified for, made sure my ex-wife got the child support payments, and also started the process of applying for Social Security Disability Insurance. She took care of a lot of stuff I didn't have the energy or knowledge to handle myself, allowing me to concentrate on rehabilitation and healing.

There was a nutritionist who made sure my diet was optimal for healing. She told me the body needs extra protein to heal from the injuries I had sustained, and after reviewing the typical choices I made from the limited patient menu, she prescribed a protein shake I had to take with lunch every day. It wasn't bad, but it wasn't as good as a real milkshake.

Chats with Mickey Ginsberg

Mickey Ginsberg was the staff psychologist. He helped the newly injured make emotional adjustments to their new, traumatic circumstances. I remember Mickey being a rather quiet man, in his mid-to-late 40s. He was usually casually dressed in a long-sleeve shirt and slacks, sometimes a sweater. He smiled a lot and really seemed to enjoy talking to patients. His voice was low-pitched and nice to listen to. He was a very good listener and didn't try to direct the conversation, but let it flow in whatever natural direction it went.

Once I had gotten the tracheotomy tube out and could talk again, Mickey dropped by and asked how I was feeling. I told him that, compared to some of the young men and women in my group, I felt rather lucky.

"That's interesting," he said. "Why is that?"

I told him about the example set by co-worker Andrew, letting me know life in a chair isn't the end of the world. "The other reason," I continued, "is that I've had the chance to do things."

"What sort of things?" he asked.

"Race motorcycles, ride bicycles through the Napa County wine country, backpack at 10,000 feet in the Sierras, and scramble to the top of 14,000-foot mountain tops, playing tag with the waves at the beach, stuff like that. These young 18-20 year olds will never have the chance to do most of that stuff."

"I'm glad you've been able to avoid that initial my-life-is-over phase," he said, "but we have found that it's the older people who have the most long-term trouble adjusting to SCI."

This puzzled me at first, but as time has passed I've come to understand what he meant.

CHAPTER THIRTEEN

Is There Life in Assisted Living?

The folks at Craig Hospital didn't quite know what to do with me. I had completed the normal rehab they do for the newly injured, but that didn't mean I was ready to be on my own. I was still healing from the injuries sustained in the crash and hadn't recovered enough energy for solo living. Most of Craig's younger patients were released to the care of their parents, while most of the older patients had a spouse to help them. I had neither, and my girlfriend, ToTB, lived 600 miles from my hometown. I needed some sort of halfway house in the mid-Willamette Valley of Oregon. I still owned a house there and had a job to go back to when I was ready, so I didn't want to uproot and move somewhere else. I liked the area.

———

I needed an assisted living place. Assisted living is for people who, for one reason or another, can't live alone but don't need full-on nursing care. I wanted to find one with other people recovering from serious injuries, folks who needed more care than they could get at home, but who would eventually recover and leave. There weren't very many of those places in the area and there were no openings.

After a long search a nearly suitable placement was found and I left Colorado for Oregon in January 1999. ToTB flew with me and we had friends at each end help with luggage and chairs. I was bringing a powered wheelchair, a manual wheelchair, and a shower chair along with a few suitcases.

Conifer House

My new home was in Conifer House, an assisted living facility in Corvallis. I really didn't know what to expect. I had a two-room apartment. There was a full-time staff, most of whom had some first-aid training and they would provide meals. Beyond that I knew nothing.

We got there after dark and my arrival had some drama. There was a wide walkway from the street sidewalk to the covered front entry. The parking lot was on the left side of the building and there was a narrow sidewalk from the lot to the main walkway. After ToTB helped me out of the car and into my manual wheelchair, I rolled myself toward the front door as she and some Corvallis pals started unpacking my luggage. Just before the smaller sidewalk joined the main entry sidewalk was a bump. A tree root had forced one of the concrete slabs up and I had a one half inch high barrier to get over.

Because of my broken finger, I had been mostly using my powered wheelchair and I wasn't very practiced with the manual chair. When I hit the 0.5-inch step, I was stopped dead in my tracks. I tried rolling up to it slowly and pushing hard enough to get the small front wheels to lift up, but my arms were too weak. I tried using a bit more speed, but that only made the halt more abrupt. I was going to have to wheelie over the rise, so I backed up a little, moved toward the step, and gave the rear wheel's push rims a hard shove just as the front wheels neared the lip. The front wheels came up all right, and kept going up, and up, and *whack* the back of my head smacked against the sidewalk as the chair tipped over backwards.

The chair had some anti-tipper bars, but they had been removed to fit it into the rental car and I had forgotten to have them put back on. Ouch. A couple of youngsters were passing by and came up.

"Are you OK, mister?" one of them asked.

"I think so. Would you go around the corner to the parking lot and tell the people there I need some help?" I said. They did and I got picked up and put inside, and the anti-tipper bars were put back on the chair.

The house had an interesting floor plan. Left of the entry was the dining room with the kitchen directly behind and there was a large living room to the right. Across the main hallway from the kitchen was a TV room with some tables, a VCR, and a microwave oven. The room smelled of popcorn.

The main hallway formed a square, with rooms on either side. In the center of the building was an atrium, so each apartment had windows letting in natural light. Some of the outside apartments had doors that opened to a sidewalk and a small fenced-in lawn area that ran along two sides of the building. They weren't really apartments as there were no kitchens. They were more like motel rooms. I had a two-room unit on the inside of the square, one room for my bed and one for my desk and a couch. There was a private bathroom. The place seemed nice—my rooms and the common areas were clean and uncluttered. Because of the late arrival, I did not see any other residents.

There were about two dozen residents at Conifer House, all but one were elderly. The exception was a man in his 40s who was severely mentally handicapped and never talked. There was a wide variety of healthfulness among the residents, some in quite good shape, while others had problems of one kind or another.

There was one older couple where the husband was very sharp, but his wife was not. I had a few good conversations with him, but her short-term memory was completely shot. He had moved with her into the home when he could no longer take care of her by himself.

Tom, a widower, appeared to be a healthy older man, but he had suffered a stroke while he lived alone and his family was worried about him having another with no one there to help. He would tell stories about salmon fishing in Alaska, something he had done every year until his stroke. I liked him.

Howard had, I think, some kind of progressive disease. He had a shuffling walk and didn't get around very well, but there was nothing wrong with his mind. He managed OK when I first moved in, but some months later his body started a rapid decline. One day he was heading for his table in the dining room and he just stopped, stood very still for 10 or 20 seconds, then fell backward like a tree toppling. He went downhill from there. "I'm sure decrepitatin' fast," was how he put it. He was transferred to a nursing home as he needed more care than the assisted living home could provide. It was too bad—he was a nice guy.

Swede, another widower, used a small electric scooter to get from his room to the dining room. He could walk a little, but not very far, and got confused easily. He had a pretty strong Swedish accent and his stories didn't make much sense anyway. I seldom saw him except at mealtimes.

There were 18 or 19 elderly women, widows in their late 60s or 70s, some of them quite sharp and very active, while others were slipping into dementia. They never seemed to have much to say to me, nor I to them. I once tried talking to one, but all she wanted to do was complain about how under-cooked the vegetables were. I thought they were cooked just right, tender-crisp, but she apparently wanted them softer. Maybe they hurt her teeth?

I started out in good spirits because I didn't figure I would be there very long and I was glad to be back in Oregon. My social interactions were with the staff, frequent visits by ToTB and by my local pals, and with e-mail groups such as WetLeather and Bevelheads. I felt rather isolated in the place and emotionally it wasn't a good match for me. None of the other residents were expecting to get well and leave. They were in it for the long haul.

I had other plans, and soon after I settled in, I started working toward getting out. I was getting physical therapy to regain my strength and range of motion exercises to stay supple.

Getting the Ramp Van

Getting around was a problem. Conifer House had a small bus and would schedule activities, such as shopping trips, or movies, or to a park for a picnic, but it wasn't wheelchair-accessible so it didn't help me. The city buses had ramps, but they ran only once per hour and not very late into the evening. There was a senior/disabled mini-bus, called Dial-a-Ride. It worked well when it was available, but it was reserved in advance on a first-come, first-served basis and was sometimes not available when I needed it. It ran within Corvallis only and stopped service at 5 p.m. each day.

I had friends who were happy to take me places, but it always meant getting in and out of a vehicle that was not designed for wheelchair access. It was usually possible to figure out a way to do this, but it was never easy. There was an extra-long transfer board I would use to transfer from my wheelchair into the front passenger seat of the automobile. It took some muscle to pull my feet into position and I often bonked my head trying to duck past the roof.

When it became clear I would survive the accident at Steamboat, but with permanent paralysis, the informal WetLeather Benevolent Society swung into action. Even with good medical insurance, there are always uncovered expenses associated with such incidences. WetLeather set up a fund and contributions could be made with PayPal. The group held a T-shirt auction during one of the regular dinner get-togethers that brought in several hundred dollars. I wasn't there, but they sent me a video of the event.

There was a going-away party for Terry, a WetLeather member who was retiring and moving to Hawaii, hosted by Cardinal Shannon and Gary in their house in the hills above Newburg. It must have been sometime in February 1999 and was the first WetLeather get-together I attended after my accident. I was told there would be a check for me of donations from the group. When Cardinal Shannon presented me with a check for just over $10,000, I was speechless for a moment. Finally I mumbled out thanks, saying, "I'm very grateful, but also surprised that folks have been so generous."

The Cardinal just smiled at me and said, "You are loved."

Hearing that, I came *that close* to bursting into tears, but I think I managed to hold it down to just a couple of sobs. It's good to have friends who care that much.

With this money and some other funds, I was able to buy a used ramp van, a modified Dodge minivan. The wheelchair modifications are extensive and nearly double the price of the van. A new $20,000 van becomes a new $38,000 van when all the modifications are installed. The dealer's employee brought the van to Conifer House in April and he gave me a quick tutorial on the van's features. The middle seat was removed, leaving the two front bucket seats and the rear bench seat. It had a 10-inch-lowered floor where the center seat had been so I could sit inside in my wheelchair without slouching, and a ramp that extended out the side passenger door. Special air shocks in the rear of the van allowed it to kneel as the ramp extended, making the ramp less steep. A pair of toggle switches, one outside near the rear passenger-side taillight and one inside on the door pillar controlled the ramp. The door opened and the ramp extended by holding the toggle switch down, and the ramp was raised and door closed by holding the switch up.

The van had a special seat base for the driver's seat that allowed it to be moved back and rotated. I would back up the ramp into the van and line up my wheelchair next to the repositioned driver's seat, transfer from the wheelchair into the driver's seat, then swivel it to face front and move it forward, putting me in a normal driver's position. Transferring from my wheelchair into the driver's seat was difficult the first few times I tried it. While struggling to make the transfer during an early practice session, I felt a twinge of pain in my ribs and I thought I had tweaked some muscle. After a little practice, driving became an easy every-day activity.

The final two modifications were a hand control that was pushed for the brakes and pulled down for the accelerator, and a spinner knob on the steering wheel. I used my left hand for the controller while my right hand steered using the spinner knob.

I had done two sessions of driver training at Craig Hospital using a similar system, so I took the new van to an empty parking lot one weekend and practiced driving. It didn't take long to learn and in a few days I went to the DMV, passed their test, and got a new driver's license that certified me as qualified to drive with hand controls. They also took away my motorcycle endorsement. Rats.

It's hard to overestimate the positive impact that van made on my life. With the van I could meet friends at the theater to watch a movie, or drive to someone's home for a dinner party. I could decide to drive to Portland to visit my mom or to Eugene to see a stage play. I could, completely on a whim, decide to drive the hour to the coast to have a seafood dinner and watch the sun set over the Pacific Ocean.

Getting the van was a huge step forward in my struggle to rebuild a meaningful and satisfying life, and I am forever grateful to the WetLeather members and others who made it possible for me to buy that vehicle. Thank you one and all.

Thinning the Stable

After I moved into Conifer House, I needed to do something about my house and vehicles. I wasn't that fond of the house itself. It had a rather odd floor plan that didn't flow well, but it had a wonderful garage and a really nice deck that wrapped around three sides of the house, so I considered keeping it. But it was a two-story house sited near the top of a hill. Access was via a very steep driveway, too steep for me to negotiate in my wheelchair. I tried really hard to think of adaptations that might make the place accessible, but no matter where I planned to put ramps or install stair lifts or elevators, there were obstacles. Sadly I decided the house had to go and I put it on the market.

I had three motorcycles. My main rider was the Hawk GT, a bike I liked a lot. I also owned Thunder, a modified Ducati 750 GT I had purchased only a few weeks before the accident. I hadn't ridden it enough to become familiar with it. The Ducati 750 Sport was a different story. That bike and I shared a significant history. It is fair to say that while I really liked the Hawk GT, I *loved* the Ducati Sport.

I disliked selling the Hawk GT, but I hated the idea of it sitting around never ridden. I found a good home for it, a new owner who would ride it regularly. Thunder was easier. When I bought it, my WetLeather friend Rocket Science Racing had asked for first right of refusal if I ever sold it. I knew it too was going to a good home where it would be ridden.

I did *not* sell my Ducati 750 Sport. I still plan to finish the restoration and get it back on the road. Even if I can't ride it, I have friends who can and will. I don't think I will ever sell that motorcycle.

I owned a standard minivan before the accident and it was sold to help finance the purchase of the ramp van.

All these actions were progress toward building a post-paralysis life. Besides these steps I continued to gain strength, thanks to the physical therapy. My broken finger was healing and I was using the manual chair more often, which helped perk up my metabolism and increased the strength in my arms and shoulders. I was feeling good about my progress. Then everything got delayed.

Pain

Becoming paralyzed doesn't change a person's basic personality. The injured actor Christopher Reeve titled his autobiography Still Me *to emphasize that fact. ToTB, who of course knew me well both before and after the accident, jokingly wrote to her friends that she "hoped the blow to his head would knock some of the smart ass out of him but noooooo … " I was the same guy I was before the accident.*

Paralysis won't change one's basic personality, but constant, severe pain will. I was injured mid-September of 1998, but by the end of the year, the pains from that accident had faded away. The new pain started in April 1999, more than six months later. It wasn't bad at first, merely an annoying discomfort around my ribs, but it slowly and steadily grew worse. I had been making what I felt was good progress toward learning to live independently under my new circumstances. I was on track to leave the assisted living home by the end of 1999. The pain derailed that plan.

———

By summer of 1999 the pain was severe, a strong sensation around my torso right at the level of injury. The doctor asked me to describe the pain: "Was it a dull ache, electric, stabbing, or burning?" The closest I could come to was burning. Think of the Johnny Cash song "Ring of Fire." It burned, all the time and never stopped. On a scale of 1 to 10, it varied between 5 and 8. At its worse it sucked up most of my energy, and I had little left for practical issues or fun activities. Small efforts exhausted me. I stopped nearly all of my rehabilitation work and my sense of humor disappeared.

Hewlett-Packard required me to return to work within one year, so by September I was working again, but could only manage two hours per day.

The old HP was very understanding and gave me a small project to work on, one that was worthwhile but wasn't time-crucial. I would go into the site, ignore the pain long enough to put in my two hours of work, and visit a bit with my colleagues before going back to the home where I got back in bed and suffered. I would get up for my short workday, and for meals at Conifer House, but spent most of my time in bed.

Adding to the ring of fire was financial concern, as my house didn't sell. There wasn't a single offer in the 12 months it was on the market. Assisted living homes aren't nursing-home-expensive, but they are not cheap, and between the Conifer House fee and my home mortgage, I was losing about $1,000 per month. I remember it as a very depressing time in my life. What had begun with energy and direction had deteriorated into a time of quiet desperation. I wasn't a complete dud during this time. I did manage to ignore the pain to take part in some fun activities, such as going out to dinner or taking in a movie, and I went to the WetLeather Gather in both 1999 and 2000. But I was suffering, both physically and mentally.

Making matters worse was the situation in Conifer House. I didn't know when I would be able to leave, and things I could previously ignore were now getting to me. One day just after lunch I watched Mike, the younger man with the mental problems, empty his bladder in the dining area. He didn't seem to notice. I had to catch the attention of one of the staff. "Michael just had an accident," I told her. She looked at him, noticed the puddle beneath his chair, and took action.

Sometime during my second year there, I got a new next-door neighbor, an elderly woman who was suffering from Alzheimer's and incontinent. Every night at 2 a.m. a couple of staffers would come into her apartment and change her diaper. She apparently didn't understand what was going on and raised quite a ruckus about it, screaming and fighting. The soundproofing between the apartment walls wasn't good enough and it woke me up almost every time.

It was depressing and I was stuck there unless the pain issue got fixed.

The First Re-Evaluation

People with spinal cord injuries are advised to get yearly re-evaluations. There are a number of known problems with injuries such as mine that are difficult for the injured individual to detect. Things going on below the level of feeling can't be felt, of course, but can be detected during medical exams. For example, MRI, ultra-sound, and scoping can examine bladder and kidney health and function. Things such as weight, blood pressure, hand

and arm strength, and range of motion are measured. Any changes from the previous exam are checked to see if they need further investigation.

It made medical sense for me to return to Craig Hospital in Colorado, because they had all the info from the months of rehabilitation, but my medical insurance company wouldn't approve it. I ended up going to a small rehabilitation center in Eugene in the autumn of 1999. At that time I was having lots of problems with pain and I was very depressed about the lack of progress I was making in my effort to rebuild my life and get out of the assisted living home.

The rehab place in Eugene was good, as far as I know, but it was very small compared to Craig Hospital. At the time of my visit there were a couple of older people doing physical therapy to adjust to their new artificial hip joints, and a younger man getting therapy after a knee repair operation. The re-eval took two days as an outpatient. I drove there and back each day.

The therapist in charge of my re-eval admitted they didn't see many SCI patients, but he had consulted a text and also had talked to the doctors at Craig and thought he knew what needed to be done. On the first day he did an extensive interview asking questions about how much and what sort of help I received. Who did the shopping? Who cooked my meals? Could I feed myself? Could I take care of my hygiene? Day two included a number of exams and tests, including checking the bladder and kidneys, testing pinch and grip strength, checking arm and shoulder strength, and the like.

The conclusion: My spinal cord itself and all my internal organs seemed fine. I had very little pinch strength in my left hand because of the broken index finger. There was some arthritis in my right thumb joint that weakened the grip strength of my right hand. This arthritis didn't seem to be related to the injuries sustained in September 1998, but was more likely from an earlier injury. As for the pain, the problem giving me the most trouble, he didn't know what could be done about that.

All in all I wasn't very impressed with the job of the Eugene center. There wasn't anything wrong I could put my finger on; it was just their lack of experience with SCI patients didn't give me much confidence in their thoroughness.

Pain Management

My doctor was trying to solve the pain problem, talking with the Craig Hospital doctors to find a solution. It's called neurogenic pain and the docs at Craig explained it to me this way: the nerves near the level of injury are not getting normal communication from the brain and they freak out and start sending pain signals in an attempt to get the brain to reply. The brain, oddly enough, receives the signals as pain even though any messages it sends back don't get through. What used to be a two-way street had become one-way only.

This type of pain doesn't always happen and I wasn't emotionally prepared for it. None of the classes at Craig Hospital addressed it. "Everyone is different," they always said. Roger, a paraplegic I met back in Oregon who was injured at my same level, third thoracic or T-3, never had that sort of pain. He did, instead, have massive spasms in his legs. I have mild spasticity, which is well controlled by the anti-spasm medicine baclofen. Roger needed to take about eight times as much baclofen as I did, and it was damaging his stomach.

Things started to improve in the year 2000. In February I was able to rent my house for enough to cover the mortgage and taxes, so that financial worry was eliminated. The new tenant agreed to let me have a storage room built in the back of the garage where I could store my furniture and all the boxes of my old life that ToTB had been so kind to pack.

In the spring of 2000 the medicos found a blend of around six medicines that made my pain manageable. The primary ingredient was OxyContin, a strong time-release narcotic. The drug could be abused, so it was on the controlled list, which meant the prescription could not have refills, and the doctor couldn't fax it to the pharmacy. Each month I had to visit the doctor to get a piece of paper to take to the pharmacy to get a month's worth of pills. It was a nuisance, but it worked. I was able to increase my work hours to four per day, then six, and I was making progress again toward independent living. I took the medicine every six hours and the pain would fade away for about five of the six hours. I didn't need the clock to know when it was time for another dose—my body let me know.

Good things were happening again, finally, but there were some bad things as well. The months of pain-induced idleness and depression had taken their toll. My sense of humor had gone AWOL, for example. Eating the meals at Conifer House and being so inactive had the expected result –I gained weight. I ballooned up to more than 200 pounds, which was 30 pounds over my pre-injury weight, and I had to push that extra weight around with my arms.

My relationship with ToTB deteriorated. Her visits became less frequent and she wasn't enjoying them as much as in early 1999. I can't blame her. Long-distance relationships are hard to maintain under the best of circumstances and I was a pretty poor companion during those bad months. She stuck with me during the worst times, helped me in many different ways, and probably kept me alive in the time right after the accident. I owe her a great debt I will never be able to repay.

Time to Leave

Not long after the pain was managed, I felt ready to leave the assisted living home. In the fall of 2000 I started looking for an apartment to rent. My timing sucked as I started looking right *after* all the Oregon State University students had returned.

If there were any wheelchair-accessible apartments in town, I couldn't find them. I did look at one that wasn't intended for the handicapped, but it had a rare feature for a modern apartment: a bathroom large enough that a person in a wheelchair could actually turn around. Most of the recently built apartment complexes had a narrow bathroom that did not allow turning around. I could either back in if I wanted to go out frontward or back out if I went in frontward.

I looked at the demo for the complex that had the roomy bathroom, but when I said I was interested, they told me there were no vacancies.

A few days later I was checking out a newer complex that was right across the street from the roomy bathroom apartments. They had the typical narrow bathrooms and I complained that they didn't have the better bathrooms like the ones across the street. It turns out the two complexes were managed by the same company, and the lady in charge of the showings said, "I think there is going to be an opening there soon."

I had to wait until December, another three months in the assisted living home, but it was worth the wait. I moved in December, by which time I had lived 23 months in Conifer House.

CHAPTER FOURTEEN

Apartment Living

I figured I could take care of myself with just a little help, but I wanted to be able to call up someone if there was a problem with an appliance or the plumbing. Yard maintenance was also something I wasn't ready for. An apartment was suitable for me at that time; I wasn't yet ready to be a homeowner again.

———

The new apartment was a typical modern apartment, part of a newer complex consisting of several buildings with eight apartments in each, four upstairs and four on the ground floor. I got an end apartment that gave me windows on three sides. It was a two-bedroom unit with wall-to-wall carpet except for vinyl in the bathroom and kitchen. The front door opened into a small entryway, with the galley kitchen on the right and a hallway on the left. You could pass through the hallway or the kitchen to get to the living room and eating area at the rear of the unit. The bedrooms were off the hallway to the left, with the roomy bathroom between them.

The ground between the buildings was lawn, which meant I had no yard care duties. There was a reserved covered parking area for each apartment, not a garage, but at least the van was out of the rain and sun. There were coin-operated washers and dryers in the next building, accessible via my apartment key.

I felt I had lost a full year battling with the pain, and even though I was happy to be getting out of Conifer House, I was overall pretty depressed about my life. I didn't like being single and my social life was pretty poor. I had some good friends at work, but they mostly went home to their families after work while I went home to an empty apartment. I was glad to be in my own place, but it was a solitary existence. I couldn't even have a pet to welcome me home. It was a very low point in my life. I had sunk to the point where I didn't care if I lived or died. I wasn't suicidal–I had a 12-year-old son and a number of other people who would miss me, and some of them would be pretty pissed off if I took my own life. Let's just say if I had been hit by a bus or something like that I would not have cared.

Break a Leg, and Not in the Show Business Meaning

At first I tried doing the housework myself. Vacuuming the carpet was a struggle. It was hard to keep from running over the hose as I moved around. I used the power chair because I could move using the joystick with my right hand, leaving my left hand free to pull the vacuum around and push the nozzle back and forth.

One day I was pulling the vacuum out of my bedroom into the hallway. I went a little too far (controlling the power chair with the joystick requires a very delicate touch) and my right toe bumped the hallway wall. I was wearing some running-style shoes whose rubber soles curled up around the toe, and when I turned left toward the living room, the toe stuck against the wall. The bar for the chair's foot pedestal turned with the chair, pushing my heel to the left, twisting my entire foot outward. The power chair has a lot of torque and I wasn't very delicate with the joystick. I heard this strange *pop!* when the foot twisted. It didn't hurt, but it sounded weird.

Before the big accident at Steamboat I had never broken a bone, and I had no memory of that accident, so I had never heard a sound like that before. *Did I just break my leg?* It looked normal, but there was that odd noise. I had to think about what to do. If the leg wasn't broken, I could just go on with life. I'd twisted my limbs in different ways many times before with nothing more than a sprain at most. On the other hand, there was that odd *pop* sound. If the leg was broken, I could do additional damage when I transferred from my wheelchair into bed, into the driver's seat of the van, or onto the shower seat. Finally I decided to play it safe, not try to transfer into my van to drive to the hospital. I maneuvered my chair, carefully this time, over to the phone and dialed 911.

"911, what is the nature of your emergency?"

"I think I broke my leg."

There was a pause. "You *think* you broke your leg?" She sounded skeptical.

I explained that I was a paraplegic with no feeling below mid-chest. She understood and said she would send an ambulance. I asked if they had one that could accommodate a man in a wheelchair.

When the paramedics arrived, I calmly greeted them and invited them in. It was a team of three, two guys and a woman. "Where's the guy with the broken leg?" the team leader asked.

"Uh, that would be me," I said.

He looked at me, folded his arms across his chest, and said, "You don't look like a person who just broke their leg." Everyone's a skeptic today. I explained again about the paraplegia and lack of feeling.

"I guess we should take you to the hospital," he said. The ambulance had a lift so I didn't have to transfer out of my chair. They dropped me off at the rather busy emergency room at Good Samaritan Hospital.

After a medium wait, the doctor, a young man, came into my bay and asked what my problem was. I explained again about twisted foot and the weird pop sound, and why I didn't feel any pain. I watched as he gently felt the leg.

"I think we better X-ray it," he said.

"Sure," I replied. They took the X-rays and I waited back in the ER bay until the doctor breezed back in with a large envelope in his hand.

"You broke it all right," he said and showed me the X-ray images. One of the two lower leg bones was broken just below the knee and the other just above the ankle. It looked like a clean break to me, no splinters just a thin black line passing through the lighter bone, but I'm no doctor. He called it a spiral fracture and said they usually see them in downhill skiers.

"We'll need to schedule surgery to pin the bones together."

"Surgery? Um, why can't you just set it manually? It's not like I'm going to use it."

He thought for a moment and took another look at the X-rays. "I guess I could do that. It's a pretty painful procedure."

"I don't think that is a problem for me."

"Oh, right," he said, and blushed. "We're pretty busy and I was following the normal protocol, which doesn't really apply here." Did he just tell me I'm not normal? Well, I'm not. Paraplegics and quadriplegics need different protocols.

We pushed my sweatpants up past my knee and he did a little pushing and prodding on my leg while pulling on my foot. I felt nothing. "All right, let's get some plaster on that," he said. "Just sit quietly and I'll send in the cast guy."

It was my first time getting a cast, and things had changed since the last time I knew someone who had broken a bone. There was this woven strap-like tape the guy dipped in what appeared to be water, and he wrapped it around my leg where it hardened quickly. He even gave me a choice of colors. I picked purple.

The leg healed just like a normal one. There's a little bump near the ankle I can feel with my hand, but otherwise as far as I can tell, it's the same as the never-broken left leg.

Whenever I tell this story to someone and describe the twisted foot and the pop sound, they grimace as they imagine how much it must have hurt.

"No, really, I didn't feel a thing. There was no pain at all," I explain.

Life as a paraplegic isn't easy. I'll take any advantages I can get. Consider them small silver linings.

Oh yeah, after that incident, I hired a housecleaning service.

Traveling Solo

I had plenty of help getting from Denver back to Oregon, but I couldn't always depend on someone being with me. If I wanted to go places that were too far to drive, I would have to fly solo and get around using rental cars and staying in motels. Once I got into the apartment at the beginning of 2000, it was time to figure this out.

The rental car and motel experiences were tested locally. I called a car rental firm and asked for a car equipped with hand controls. I requested a coupe figuring the door of a two-door car would be wider than the door of a four-door sedan. That same day I rented a motel room in town, requesting a wheelchair-accessible room. A work friend was willing to be my backup–he would be on call any time of night if I ran into trouble.

The rental car was set up properly with hand controls that matched the ones in my van. Getting into the car was rather tricky. I used my long board, a longer than standard transfer board, to get into the driver's seat. Once inside the car, I took the wheelchair apart as much as possible. The chair's arms and splashguards came off and were placed on the floor behind the driver's seat. The seat cushion and backpack were taken off and put on the back seat. Both wheels came off and were stashed on the back seat behind the driver's seat. Lastly the back of my wheelchair was folded down. I lowered the back of the driver's seat as much as possible and then picked up the chair and passed it over myself and into the front passenger's seat. The stripped-down chair weighed about 25 pounds, so this step took a little muscle.

Once the wheelchair was tucked into the passenger seat, I raised the back of the driver's seat and drove to the motel. There the whole process was repeated in reverse to get me back into my wheelchair. The room was good, a single queen bed instead of two, so there was plenty of room to get the chair around the bed. The bed was right at the same level as the wheelchair seat so transferring into the bed was easy. I spent an uneventful night there, checked out in the morning, did the transfer into the car and drove back to the rental car office, got back into my chair and then into my van, and drove back to the apartment.

All in all it was a successful test. No serious problems, a bit of awkwardness getting in and out of the rental car, but nothing I couldn't handle at that time.

The next step was a plane ride. I decided to go to a WetLeather party in Coeur d'Alene, Idaho. It was within a day's drive, but I booked a round-trip airline ticket from Portland to Spokane, reserved a rental car at the Spokane airport, and reserved a motel room in Coeur d'Alene. I contacted my old racing teammate the Wizard, who lives in Spokane, and he agreed to meet me at the airport.

Air travel in a wheelchair takes a lot of extra time. The airlines want to board me early so I'm always one of the first on board and the last passenger off. Since no normal wheelchair fits in the aisle between the coach seats, I needed to transfer into a special, narrow aisle-chair. This isn't very easy and I got onto the chair slightly off-center. I didn't think it would matter that much, but I warned the boarding crew. They didn't seem too concerned either, so I let them strap me in place. My own chair was left to the mercy of the airline crew who placed the chair in the gate check area.

When the crew tried to move me to my seat, we discovered being off-center was a big problem. It made me too wide to go through the aisle. If my butt was centered in the aisle, the aisle chair was off to one side and wouldn't clear the seats. If they centered the chair in the aisle, my butt hit the seats on the other side. We had to make adjustments.

Once that was fixed, the trip went fine, the party was fun, the motel room was good, and the return flight was no problem. It was good to find out early it really does matter to be centered on the aisle chair.

Mickey Ginsberg's Warning

In chapter 12 I described some visits with Mickey Ginsberg, the psychologist on staff at Craig Hospital where I did my rehabilitation. At the time he warned me that people who get an SCI later in life tend to have more problems adjusting long-term than those who are injured when young. At the time I didn't understand what he meant, but as time passed and events unfolded, I realized he was right.

There are a couple of reasons. Firstly, you can't miss what you never had. For example, if you've never changed the oil in your own car, you won't know how easy it can be. But I remember how easy it was, and although I never thought it was fun, there was a certain satisfaction in being able to do my own routine auto maintenance. Now I have to pay somebody to do that, and it took me several years to be able to calmly accept this new reality. I've always disliked being done for; as in "Let me do that for you." I'd rather do it myself.

Another simple example is grocery shopping. I can't reach items on the upper shelves. There is seldom store staff around, so I have to ask a complete stranger for help. It took me three years, *three full years*, before I could make the request without resenting it. Sometimes I would go to the aisle where mops and brooms were sold, grab one, and use it to knock down and catch the item I wanted. People are always willing to help. I've never had anyone refuse to give me a hand, but the loss of independence was a bitter pill to swallow and difficult to digest.

Secondly, there are lots of things I can do while in a chair. My injury level was low enough that I did not lose hand and arm function, so there are many tasks and activities I can still handle by myself. However, virtually everything post-SCI is more difficult and/or takes more time than it did before. Consider taking the trash can to the curb so it can be picked up the next morning. I can do that in the chair, but it's a struggle to get the container down the driveway without tipping it over and spilling garbage all over the place. Our driveway is slightly downhill to the street, so I need my hands to control my speed. I can't hold onto the trash container, so I lean it over to put the handle on my knees. It can still get away from me and the handle can slip to my toes or all the way to the pavement, where the lid is prone to opening up. After that happened a couple of times, I started backing down the slope with the trash container on the uphill side. That made a runaway trash can less likely, but I couldn't clearly see where I was going. If I ever missed the driveway cutout and went over the curb, I would fall over backward.

This was such a simple chore before the SCI. If I had been injured at age 19 instead of 49, I may never have had to move the trash container to the curb and would not know how much easier it once was.

If all this sounds like I'm whining, I have a good explanation. I *am* whining. Mickey Ginsberg, in his own quiet way, warned me there were difficulties ahead as an older person getting an SCI. I always try to look on the brighter side and count the many blessings I have in my life, and remind myself I could easily be dead, but every now and then I'm allowed to lament my losses and howl at the moon.

My Second Re-Evaluation

I didn't have a re-evaluation in 2000. By the fall of that year, the pain problem was mostly under control with drugs and I was looking for an apartment and was pretty busy. I talked to the doctors at Craig and they said if there were no other problems it was OK to skip a year. In the meantime, during the open enrollment period at work, I changed my health insurance company. The new company had no objection to me going to Craig for my re-evaluation. They wouldn't cover travel expenses or living expenses while I was in Colorado, but the medical part would be covered, so I scheduled a re-evaluation at Craig in the fall of 2001.

———

About two weeks before it was time to fly to Denver, I had an extensive phone interview by a nurse at Craig, with lots of questions about my living situation and how much help I needed. At the end she asked me if I had any issues. I mentioned my left index finger still didn't work correctly. I couldn't completely curl it into a fist, nor could I straighten it completely. I told her my wheelchair had developed a pull to the left. I also mentioned I was fighting some serious depression issues left over by the months of chronic pain.

I contacted my Colorado pal Alan and he agreed to help get me from the airport to the apartment Craig had reserved for me. I flew in on Sunday because the re-eval began at 9 a.m. Monday morning. Flying was pretty surreal as it was less than a month after the terrorist attack on 9/11. There were armed military everywhere. If the re-evals at Craig hadn't required signing up six months in advance, I would have rescheduled, but I didn't want to wait another six months. Alan and his wife Jonna got me to the apartment and even did a grocery run and stocked up the little kitchenette with food for five days.

Intake Day

When I checked in to the outpatient clinic Monday morning, I was given a schedule that fully covered four of the five days. It was impressive. There were time slots for an intake interview, a physical, exams for the bladder and kidneys, and an MRI of the spine. It had multiple sessions with physical therapy and occupational therapy, a session with recreational therapy and the psychologist, an hour in the wheelchair clinic, and time to work on my left index finger. Friday of the week had been left open in case any of the earlier exams needed any follow-up time.

Monday was all intake material. There was another interview with more questions about how independent I was or wasn't. I had a complete physical including blood pressure, pulse, temperature, blood oxygen levels, a skin check, and weight. The weigh-in was interesting. They hooked me up to a sling fitted with a scale and lifted me out of my chair, like weighing a big fish. The scale read 205 pounds, which was a full 30 pounds above my pre-injury weight. I *had* gotten chubby at the old folks home, and that extra weight had to be pushed around with my arms. I did, over a couple of years, lose the extra weight and I'm back to 170 pounds now, but the distribution of those pounds is much different and not nearly as attractive as my pre-injury shape.

Mickey Cheers Me Up

On Tuesday afternoon I had my appointment with Mickey Ginsberg. I liked Mickey when we had chats during my stay at Craig when I was first injured and I was looking forward to seeing him again, even though I didn't expect our talk would be very much fun. I rolled up to his desk and settled in.

He smiled and said, "I see you've done really well with your rehabilitation work."

I was stunned, speechless, and for a moment could only stare at him. For months I had been depressed about my lack of progress, the months lost due to pain, and Mickey is telling me I've been doing really well? Finally I stammered out, "But ... but I lost months, almost a year, to the pain problem. I should be much farther along."

"No, no," he said, looking at the opened file in front of him. "Let's see. You're living by yourself in an apartment with minimal help, doing your own shopping and cooking, driving yourself around, and you're working six hours a day. You even came here from Oregon by yourself. For a man your age with the injuries you had, this is quite remarkable."

Wow. This was good news, although I'm not sure about his "a man your age" comment. I could stop feeling bad about losing time, but I was still having some trouble believing it. "What would you have expected?" I asked.

"Well, most men in your situation would need more personal assistance, and would never have returned to work," he replied.

Son of a gun. Maybe I was not as much of a slacker as I thought. For the rest of the appointment we chatted about this and that, but I recall leaving in a much lighter mood than when I arrived.

Sadly, I never saw Mickey again. He died before my 2003 trip to Craig of a sudden heart attack. It was a shock to everyone who knew him and a real blow to the hospital staff. He was way too young and is missed by many people.

Other Re-Eval Results

In summary the other findings of my first Craig re-eval were:

- The attempt to fix the left index finger failed. The problem wasn't binding scar tissue as they thought, but some nerve damage.

- I should be doing some range of motion and mild strengthening exercises.

- I should find more active recreational activities.

- My internal organs all seemed in good condition.

- They fixed my wheelchair so it went straight.

Meeting Dee Granger

My wife and I tell people we met in the handicapped parking lot at work. It was summer of 2002 and I had parked in the van-accessible slot at work and had rolled down the ramp. I was in a hurry because I was just barely on time for a meeting. As I held the switch to raise the ramp, a woman approached me. She was walking with a cane from the direction of the motorcycle parking area. I noticed she was carrying a helmet and wearing a riding jacket.

"Hi, I'm Dee," she said.

"Hello, I'm Paul. I'd like to stay and chat, but I've got to rush to a meeting right now."

"Do you work in this building?"

"Yes, on the third floor. You too?"

"I work on the first floor," Dee replied.

By then the ramp had folded up into the van and the door shut. "I gotta run. Hope to see you around," I said as I started rolling toward the front door.

"What's your last name?"

"Ritter!" I shouted back over my shoulder as I hit the button to open the building door. I barely made it to the meeting on time and pushed the whole episode to the back of my mind.

A couple of days later I remembered. *She seemed pretty nice,* I thought. I remembered her first name and that she worked on the first floor. The floors were typical office cubicle farms, and the names of the cubicle residents in the cross-hall were posted in the main hallway. I went down the main hallway reading each set of names until in the next to last cross-aisle I saw the name Dee Granger. I went down the aisle and found her cubicle, but no one was there.

Once I knew her last name, I knew her work e-mail address, so I went back to my cubicle and sent her an e-mail. In the message I re-introduced myself and passed on the e-mail address of some local motorcycle groups, including one for motorcyclists who worked for HP, adding that they could be a source of activities and resources.

The very next day Dee was on her way to work when she got a flat tire. She parked her bike as concealed as possible and called a co-worker to come pick her up. Once she got to work, she used the e-mail addresses I had given her and asked if there was anyone who could help her retrieve the bike.

The HP group swung into action. A co-worker, Dave, got Dee's key. The bike was picked up; the wheel with the flat was taken to the local motorcycle shop where they found the leak and patched the tire. Dee found them in the motorcycle parking area next to building, one putting the wheel back on her motorcycle. She didn't have to do a thing–she was a motorcyclist in need and the group gave her a hand. Motorcyclists do that sort of stuff for each other. And, of course, I earned some big points with Dee.

Collateral Benefits

Statistics aren't good for romance after an SCI. Most couples who were married before the accident get divorced, not being able to handle the extra strain of the SCI. Single people in chairs don't have much luck either. People tend to see the chair and fail to see past it to the person inside. After my breakup with ToTB, I figured I would be single and girlfriend-less for the rest of my life.

———

Dee told me later she had recently gone to Europe. She knew it would involve a lot of walking and wore a brace to support the ankle she had injured in a motocross race in the 1970s. She found that people treated her differently when they saw she was wearing a brace, and she didn't like it. Sometimes they would grab stuff out of her hands "to help," or talk very loudly or very slowly, as if she was hard-of-hearing or stupid. She promised herself that she would never act that way, so when she saw me getting out of a van that had a motorcycle bumper sticker (it read "Start SEEING Motorcycles"), she ignored the fact I was in a chair. She figured we could be friends.

After the motorcycle rescue, Dee suggested a movie night. Her place wasn't accessible, so it would be at my apartment.

"But I don't have a DVD player," I said.

"No problem, I'll bring one over," she said.

So Dee came over with a DVD player that she hooked up to my ancient (1978) TV, and we watched *October Sky*, a good movie about reaction to the Russian launch of the Sputnik satellite.

After the group rescued Dee's motorcycle and repaired the flat tire, she had made a thank-you note to all in the form of a collage, photos of herself on motorcycles through the years, going back to the 1970s when she was an active motocross racer in Southern California. It was a nice single-page-size poster.

After the movie was over I said, "That was a nice little poster you made. Now I get to show you mine." I went back into the bedroom and got my framed copy of the 2-foot-by-3-foot poster Ducati had made after my win at the first Sears Point AMA National.

"Oh, wow," she said. "How lucky that Ducati chose your picture to put on their poster ... um ... what? ... wait a minute." She got very quiet as she carefully examined the poster.

"You *won* an AMA National Superbike race?" she finally asked.

"I won two, actually. That poster was for the 1977 race. I won again in 1978, but they didn't make a poster of that."

Dee was racing motocross in the late 1970s and no longer followed road racing, but she had heard of the new Superbike class and wondered what all the fuss was about. She knew who Cook Neilson was and had heard of Reg Pridmore, and she certainly knew the significance of an "AMA National." Dee had originally thought we would be friends, but after seeing the poster she began to think of me in a different way. She calls the poster "The Aphrodisiac." After a couple of months getting to know each other, we fell in love and I had a girlfriend again. Life was starting to look a lot better.

CHAPTER FIFTEEN

Back in the Saddle?

Having owned my own home, I found it difficult to live in an apartment: rules about nearly everything, no pets and, worst of all, no garage. It was always a temporary solution. The long-term objective was to be a homeowner again. It's still the American Dream after all, to own your own home. My other dream was to ride a motorcycle again.

By summer of 2002, after being in the apartment for two years, I was ready to become a homeowner again, and started looking for a house to buy. I got lucky when I found an under-construction house on Caribou Street in the large new development off 53rd Avenue in Albany.

The development's lots were small and most of the houses felt cramped with smallish front and back yards and minimum separations on the sides. The Caribou St. lot had a big advantage— it was on the western edge of the development and the backyard butted up to a city-owned greenbelt and walking path. Instead of a neighbor's fence, the view from the master bedroom window was a row of mature oak and maple trees on the far side of the walking path.

I found the lot after the foundation was poured and the subfloor was installed, but before any walls were up. The builder and I went over the plans and made some accessibility modifications: ramps in place of steps, changes in the kitchen counters, putting a roll-in shower insert in the master bathroom, and a few other changes. It was a small three-bedroom, two-bath house with a three-car garage that suited my situation well: one bedroom for me, one for my office, and a guest bedroom. The garage had room for my van and plenty of room for my bike and a workshop area; I could get my motorcycle and all my other personal belongings out of storage.

One of the ironic things about depression is it prevents people from doing the things that could help drive the dark clouds away. The effort to get out and do things, meet people, get involved with something, be active, felt so overwhelmingly huge that I did almost nothing.

Not having a girlfriend really added to the feelings of loneliness. There were e-mail lists that helped some, but they didn't really fill the need for play or actual human contact. I started thinking about new ways to have fun. The recreational therapy department at Craig Hospital had lots of helpful suggestions, and I tried a few things, but I needed someone to push me, to get me past that initial feeling of ennui. I did experiment with riding again, but the real successes came after I met Dee Granger. Dee had many ideas that, with her encouragement and support, I was willing to try.

"He'll Never Ride Again." Oh Yeah?

I thought I could ride again. All I needed was some sort of training wheels that extended when speed fell below a certain amount and retracted when above that speed. With that in mind, I found and bought a Moto Guzzi V1000 Convert. This was a bike Moto Guzzi introduced in 1975 with a torque converter instead of a gearbox. It was sarcastically called, "The answer to a question nobody asked." Perhaps Guzzi was aiming for the police market, but it seemed motorcycle patrolmen didn't mind shifting gears. The Convert never sold well and was discontinued in 1982.

But I thought it'd be perfect for me. Motorcyclists shift gears with their feet, and the Convert didn't have gears. I had heard about a guy who had developed the sort of training wheels I had imagined, only instead of being automatic they were controlled by a button.

Before getting too deep into that project, I wanted to see if I could ride at all. As a rider I had always gotten lots of information from my feet and from my butt in the seat of the bike that would now be unavailable.

So I enlisted the aid of three good motorcycle pals, Dustin, Derek, and Keith, and early one Sunday morning in March of 2002, we took the Convert to a large empty parking lot at the local junior college for a test ride.

The guys had to help me get onto the saddle, which wasn't a great start, but something I thought I could figure out in due time. The Convert had floorboards, not foot-pegs, so getting my feet tucked in was easy. My knees splayed outward, so a strap was passed over the tank to hold the knees in snuggly. I fired up the bike and the guys pushed it off the center-stand. I gave it some throttle and it moved forward.

Whew! I didn't drop it immediately. At first I was moving very slowly in wide ovals around the perimeter of the lot. I was staring at the patch of asphalt 10 feet in front of the wheel and the ride was erratic–lots of little steering corrections. Then I remembered, *look ahead–look where you're going*. It's one of fundamentals of the New Rider class. So I looked up, not down, and the ride smoothed out.

This was good. I upped my speed some and realized my helmet visor was still open. This was not good. Without leg or lower torso muscles, my arms supported all my upper body weight. If I took a hand off the handlebars, I would immediately fall towards the tank. I needed a really tall tank bag or something like that to lean my chest against. Finally I pushed backward with my left hand, quickly reached up and snapped the visor closed, and then caught the left handlebar before I had dropped very far. It resulted in a bit of a wobble, but it corrected itself quickly.

This was fun. I started doing tighter circles, figure-eights, weaving, circling the light post standards. I tried a big handful of throttle and got lots of noise, but not much acceleration. It was not a fast bike and the torque converter acted like insulation between the throttle and the rear wheel. The motor responded quickly, but the message to the rear wheel was delayed. The wheel would eventually catch up, but acceleration was feeble. Still, more speed was available than I could get in this parking lot, as big as it was. For a moment I contemplated the idea of leaving the lot and taking off down the road, but didn't.

Riding the Moto Guzzi Convert in the parking lot.

Enjoying the afterglow of the moment. *Keith Underdahl*

After some 30 minutes or so, I signaled to the guys and I drove in and they caught me. After a little fuss, I was back in my wheelchair, soaking in the good feelings of the moment.

In the end, after much thought, I decided to scrap the idea of riding solo on two wheels again. The fact that I needed to keep two hands on the handlebars at all times, and that so much weight was transferred onto my wrists gave me second thoughts. The parking lot pavement was smooth, but what if there had been rough spots? Riding stiff-armed across bumpy road is no way to control a motorcycle. I decided to use the Convert for a different project, a sidecar rig.

Laguna Seca Regained

I had been going to the motorcycle races at Laguna Seca every year since 1972 as a spectator, then three years as a competitor before I quit racing and drifted away from the scene. After reviving my interest in motorcycles in 1996, but before the accident at Steamboat, I had been to the AMA National race at Sears Point a couple of times and was planning on returning to Laguna Seca to watch the World Superbike races.

After the accident I figured Laguna Seca was lost to me forever. My memories of the track included lots of dirt paths, lots of hills, and pedestrian bridge crossings with steps. No part of that is OK for a pavement-oriented wheelchair.

Then I heard through the Bevelheads e-mail list that the late Dan Neff, then a quadriplegic living in British Columbia, Canada, had gone to the World Superbike Races in 2001. I found a phone contact and talked to him, asking him, "How did you do that?"

Dan told me about the golf-cart vehicles they had at the track. They were designed to help the handicapped get around, and they would take you wherever you asked to go. A couple of the carts could carry a person in a wheelchair. He was very enthusiastic about his adventure and encouraged me to go. With his positive results, I made plans to attend in 2002 and see for myself.

As the date approached, I contacted some friends from the Bevelheads e-mail list. I got an accessible room in the same Pacific Grove motel where several of them were staying and they agreed to give me a ride to the track each day. I also found someone to pick me up at the San Jose Airport and take me to the motel.

It's nice to have friends.

The carts worked as Dan had described. All I needed to do was find a track worker with a radio and ask for a wheelchair cart. One would show up in a few minutes, the driver would help me up the steep ramp, and take me where I asked. I was able to get to viewing areas on the outside of turns 2 and 5, to the paddock area, and to Ducati Island.

I went every year after that until some recent shoulder problems made travel difficult. In fact Dee and I took our first plane trip together to see the World Superbike races there in 2003, and we saw some of the later MotoGP races. We were able to watch the famous Stoner-Rossi battle of 2008. People still talk about that one.

The Power Trike

Dee found this great new British invention called a Power Trike–a mountain-bike-style front wheel with an electric motor in the hub. It attached to my manual wheelchair and allowed me to go up to 12 mph on the flat pavement, and also move over rougher terrain. There are two parts to it. The first part is a tube with hardware to mount the tube beneath the wheelchair seat. The second part includes the front wheel, battery, and handlebars, with a shaft that was inserted into the tube and clamped in place. The wheelchair's front caster wheels are lifted off the ground so the whole thing becomes a three-wheeler.

We had tried it out on the streets around home, but wanted to test its off-road worthiness, so we took it to the beach at Newport. We found a

Racing the waves on the Power Trike and Nye beach. *Dee Granger*

parking area, attached the Power Trike to my chair, and then discovered the beach access had steps. I started dashing about the streets trying to find an access ramp, with Dee following me in the van. She remarked later it was hard to keep up.

I did find a ramp. I pushed through a bit of dry sand, to get to the firmer wet stuff. Once on the firmer sand, I just took off, chasing the waves the way I did before the accident. It was thrilling! It was a beautiful, clear, cold winter day and the chill caused us to stop after about an hour. If it had been warmer, I would have kept going.

We dismounted the Power Trike front end and celebrated with an excellent seafood dinner at the coast, watching the sunset. It was a good day.

I took the trike lots of places: WetLeather dinner parties, a local U-pick blueberries site, and camping at the Paradise Campground along the McKenzie River, for example. The added length of the trike meant I couldn't take it everywhere, but there were lots of places where it fit in nicely. I took it with me to visit my son on his 13th birthday. Steven hung onto the back of my chair and got a long birthday ride on his skateboard through Bidwell Park in Chico, California. There is so much you can do with enough imagination and an adventurous heart!

Picking blueberries with the Power Trike. *Dee Granger*

Camping

Dee and I really enjoy camping. I knew my sleeping-on-the-ground-in-a-tent days were over, but Dee had a Chalet camping trailer, the kind with a top that opened up into an A-frame. It was pretty basic, with a sink and a one-burner propane cook top, a small refrigerator, a few cabinets, and a couch that converted into a bed. It could be hooked up for water and electricity, but there was no lavatory. The door was too narrow for my wheelchair, but I thought if I could get inside we could make it work so we did a test run while it was sitting in the driveway. I could transfer into it using my long board, but then I was sitting on the floor and getting from there to the bed was a real struggle.

Dee went into research mode and discovered the company that made the Chalet A-frames had moved from California to Albany, Oregon. What a stroke of luck! We contacted them in the spring of 2003 and they were quite willing to widen the door. With the wider door, we were able use a ramp so I could roll into the trailer. There wasn't room inside to let me move about, but I could transfer from the chair onto the bed, a much easier process than the struggle to get off the floor. We made several camping trips with it in 2003 and 2004, to the Oregon coast, the McKenzie River, and the Metolius River.

Camping with the world's smallest wheelchair accessible trailer. *Dee Granger*

The Chalet A-frame was fun, but it had some deficiencies. Because the top had to move up and down, there were no overhead cabinets and not much storage beneath the counters. Getting ready for a trip was a lot of work because almost everything had to be packed into storage tubs and then unpacked when we got home. There was no bathroom. We needed to get dressed and dash to the cold camp potty the first thing each morning.

We went back to Chalet RV to see what they had to offer. There was a new guy in charge of design and production, Karl, and he had this new small platform called the Curv. It was a non-folding design, but small. His first one was only 15 feet long. We talked to him about the needs for accessibility and we (mostly Dee, actually) worked with him to design a version with a wheelchair user in mind. It ended up being an 18-foot trailer, but still light enough to be towed by my van.

There are overhead cabinets where stuff such as spare linens, camp clothes, and other lightweight stuff can stay, the lower cabinets get dishes and cooking pots and pans and camping gear such as a hatchet, fire grills, etc. There is an outside compartment that holds an EZ-up awning to augment the rollout awning mounted on the trailer itself. And it has a cassette toilet. No more need to get dressed and dash to the restroom first

Reading a book with the sound of a rushing river in my ears. It's a great way to spend a warm afternoon. *Dee Granger*

thing in the morning. We've taken it camping in the Cascade Mountains and to the Oregon coast several times. It's been to the MotoGP races at Laguna Seca twice.

Scuba!

Dee was an avid scuba diver when she lived in Southern California, with more than 800 dives in her logbooks, diving around the Channel Islands with occasional trips to warm water dive sites in the Caribbean Sea. She thought scuba diving would be a sport I could enjoy. I was quite willing to try, but first I had to learn to swim without using my legs. I had tried once in the small pool at Craig Hospital and it was a total failure. I couldn't keep my head above water. I was pretty unhappy about that, as I had always enjoyed swimming.

Re-Learning to Swim

This time I wanted to be sure there was enough time to try different things. I scheduled some 50-minute sessions with a physical therapist that specialized in water therapy. Dee wanted to come along and neither I nor the therapist, Scott, objected.

We started in the kiddie pool, maximum depth 4 feet and warmer water than the big pool. In the first session we started using two of those long closed-cell foam tubes (noodles) as flotation devices. I ran them across my chest and under my arms and found I could stay afloat with my face out of the water. I could even move a little by paddling with my hands, being careful not to let the tube get away. So far so good.

I ditched one of the tubes. This caused me to sink a little, but my face was still above water. Again I tried to paddle around so I wasn't just sitting in one spot. Still doing OK.

When I tried it without the floatation tubes, it was not so good. I couldn't keep my face above water and Scott on one side and Dee on the other had to lift me up, spluttering a bit. I couldn't take a full breath anymore because of the lack of the lower abdominal muscles to help, so I couldn't stay under very long.

"Let me think about this for a minute," I said, so they parked me at the edge of the pool to think. This line of approach wasn't going very well.

"Let's try something else," I said. "Let's see if I can float on my back."

I had never been able to float on my back before. I would get horizontal to the surface, face up with my head barely out of water and my lungs full of air, and relax. Immediately my feet would start to sink, then my legs. My body would slowly go from horizontal to vertical at which point my face would go under as I continued to sink to the bottom of the pool. In those days I was rather slender, but with strong leg muscles. Muscles sink, fat floats. I didn't have enough body fat to keep me up.

But that was then, this was later. My lower body muscles had long since gone soft from disuse, and I had gained weight at the assisted living home. True, my shoulder muscles had built up with all the pushing I had done, but still I had a lot more body fat than before.

It worked. I could float on my back and keep my face out of water. Finally, some success. I could even swim, after a fashion, using my arms to pull myself from one side of the small pool to the other.

Scott suggested I had done some good work for the day, but there was still some time left. I had another idea. We had brought a mask and snorkel. "Let me try the mask and snorkel," I said.

I put them on and, holding to the edge of the pool, stuck my face in the water. I started breathing through the snorkel, then slowly, carefully, let go of the pool edge. I knew Dee and Scott were at my sides, ready to lift me up if the snorkel went under. Not only did I not sink, I floated high enough that the snorkel stayed out of the water. As long as I kept looking mostly downward toward the bottom of the pool, I could breathe.

I kept going, building one step at a time upon what I had managed to do. By the end of the session I was swimming from one side of the pool to the other, switching from being on my back free breathing to swimming face-down breathing through the snorkel, then back to swimming face-up. Each time I switched from face-up to face-down I had to take a deep breath, then blow hard through the snorkel to clear out all the water. The timing was tricky, but I managed it.

I had a couple more water therapy sessions to refine the technique, and by the time we finished, I felt I knew how to swim again.

Scuba Certification

I needed to get a certificate from my local rehab doctor stating it was OK for me to go diving. I was taking all that pain medicine, including narcotics, and there was some worry the increased underwater pressure would enhance the effects of the drugs, and not in a good way. She did some research and decided it wouldn't be a problem and signed the certificate.

During the summer of 2003 I took the required PADI certification classes from a dive shop in Eugene. I passed the final test, completing the dry-land portion of the certification process. Dee and I signed up for an outing with the Handicapped Scuba Association (HSA) to the island of Bonaire in the Caribbean, one of the most spectacular diving destinations in the hemisphere. We made arrangements with Jim Gatacre of the HSA to meet a couple of days ahead of the main party so I could complete my in-water tests.

The initial wet test was in a swimming pool at the resort. The first part was to make sure I understood what all the gear was and how to use it. The compressed air in the scuba tank did a bunch of stuff besides provide air to breathe. There was a buoyancy compensator, the regulator and mouthpiece, and a pressure gauge that showed how much air was left in the tank. There was a secondary mouthpiece and regulator called an octopus in case another diver needed to share your air. The mask, snorkel, and weight belt had to be fit in a particular way. I didn't use fins, of course, but I had a pair of gloves with webbing between the fingers that gave my arm strokes a little extra power.

In addition to the equipment familiarization, Jim made sure I remembered the hand signals that were taught during the dry land class.

Dee warned me that one of the exercises many new divers have trouble with is removing the mask, then putting it back on and clearing the water out of it. She told me many people fail certification because when the water gets in their face their instinct is to hold their breath, which is one of the things you are taught to *never* do while diving. Even a small change in depth can cause the air to expand enough to cause serious damage to the lungs if you are holding your breath. Jim and Dee watched me very carefully during this exercise, but it wasn't a problem for me. Dee claims I am a natural diver.

As we were going through the exercises, I suddenly felt resistance when I tried to draw a breath. I was surprised. I hadn't been watching my air pressure gauge, but neither Jim nor Dee appeared to be having any problems. I turned to Dee and gave her the "I'm out of air" hand signal and she came right over and we shared her regulator (called buddy breathing) while we moved to the edge of the pool to surface.

"Why did you do that?" asked Jim. "That wasn't part of the exercise."

I looked at my pressure gauge–it showed zero. "It wasn't an exercise. I'm out of air."

They both checked their gauges and they had close to 1,000 psi left. (A full tank is 3,000 psi and at 500 psi it's time to head for the boat or dock.) We concluded I must have gotten a tank that was a short fill, or one that had been used a little and then mistakenly put back in the section reserved for full tanks.

"Well, you did exactly the right thing," said Jim, smiling.

The next day I had to do the open water part of the certification process. This time I checked my pressure gauge before getting into the water and it read the full 3,000 psi. We worked off the dock, not from a boat, in about 10 feet of water in the open sea. Karl was my instructor this time and Dee was still there as my dive buddy. The exercises were similar to the ones we did in the pool. When we got to the mask removal step, Karl signaled for me to remove my mask and I did, and then waited for him to signal to replace it and clear it. And waited. After what seemed like plenty of time, I pointed to the mask, then to my face, and then signaled, "OK?" He signaled, "Yes," so I put the mask back on and cleared it. All the other tests went well.

Back at the surface I asked Karl, "Why didn't you signal me to put my mask back on?"

"You were just supposed to take it off, then put it right back on. I didn't expect you to wait for any signal," he said.

"Oh. What did you think when I sat there with the mask off?" I asked.

"I thought you were just showing off!" We got a good laugh from that.

At this point I was cleared for an HSA level-two dive certification, which allowed me to dive with two dive buddies. The reasoning here is if one of my buddies gets in trouble the other buddy can do the rescue. There was one more hurdle I had to jump to get to level-one certification.

They sent Dee to the ocean floor to act as an injured diver. My task was to get to her, remove her weight belt and inflate her buoyancy control vest and get her to the surface, give her mouth-to-mouth resuscitation, and then pull her to the dock that was simulating the boat.

It was all pretty easy except the transport part. Swimming with no fins and being able to use only one arm, even with the webbed glove, was very slow going. But I did it, even though it took a long time. So in September, 2003, two days before the fifth anniversary of my near-fatal racing accident, I became a handicapped level-one certified scuba diver.

Diving in Bonaire

Bonaire is one of the three Dutch Antilles islands, sometimes called the ABC islands as the other two are Aruba and Curacao. It's a desert island in the Caribbean Sea, 10 miles off the coast of Venezuela. There appears to be three sources of income for Bonaire: vacation homes, a mostly idle salt works, and diving. The waters around the entire island coastline are a marine reserve. There is no fishing, no hunting, and no gathering permitted. Divers are not allowed to wear gloves so they are less likely to harm the coral or pick up shells and such. They make an exception and let folks like me wear webbed gloves. With the special webbed gloves, I swim by splaying my fingers out and doing a breast stroke movement with my arms.

There are dozens of dive sites on the leeward side of Bonaire and around the small next-door islet called Klein Bonaire. The HSA has been bringing groups here for several years and the boat crews are well practiced in handling the handicapped.

The undersea world is amazing. The colors, the creatures, even the sounds are an experience like no other. Everywhere I looked there was something interesting to see: colorful parrotfish, saucer-sized angelfish, mean-looking moray eels, and dozens of different kinds of coral. If you're lucky, you might spot a sea turtle or a seahorse. There are trumpetfish everywhere; their camouflage is to try and look like strands of seaweed. I wondered why they are called trumpetfish as they are long and thin, not much like a trumpet at all. Then, later in the week I saw one open its mouth. It opens in a flair, very much like the bell of a trumpet. With the shape of the rest of their body, though, they should be called clarinetfish, but nobody asked me.

Myself (left) and Dee at a coral reef in Bonaire.
Russ Granger/Don Rorschach

Dee says I'm a natural diver and maybe that's so, because I was instantly comfortable underwater. Part of that is because the waters of the Caribbean Sea are warm enough that a wet suit isn't necessary. I wore a lycra dive skin that offered some protection, but it is thin nylon and easy to get on and off compared to a wet suit.

We could take three dives per day. The boats would visit two dive sites in the morning, return to shore for lunch, and then go out to one site in the afternoon, for a possible total of 15 dives over the 5 days. We skipped one of the afternoon dives to get some rest, but otherwise went under the sea.

CHAPTER SIXTEEN

Married Life

As I've mentioned, the statistics for romance for quads and paras aren't very promising. I was trying to accept the idea that I was going to be single for the rest of my life. It was not a cheering thought. I'm one of the lucky ones. Partially thanks to a certain Ducati Race poster, things turned out differently than I expected.

———

I proposed to Dee in the spring of 2004 and happily she accepted. We got married on Sunday of Labor Day weekend. I made a deal with Dee that our anniversary would be the Sunday of Labor Day weekend, an attempt to avoid having to remember an actual date. I'm lousy at remembering dates of events. It was a clever idea, but it kind of backfired. I do remember the date: September 5, 2004. We celebrate our wedding anniversary twice each year, the Sunday of Labor Day weekend and on September 5.

Our wedding was a very special event. *Marissa Ritter Reyes*

The newlyweds in front of the redecorated wheelchair van.

Caroline Gee Blauvelt

We had a lovely wedding ceremony in Peavey Arboretum, a facility of Oregon State University just north of Corvallis. There is a small building that can be rented for different events, including weddings. It is set amongst a wooded, park-like setting, with a big lawn and lots of trees. Our honeymoon was spent scuba diving for a week in Bonaire, with another HSA trip.

Torn Biceps Tendon

We were very happy being newlyweds, but only for four months. Bad things happened to us starting in January of 2005. In the middle of January of 2005, I completely tore a biceps tendon in my left arm, the long tendon that attaches at the shoulder. My shoulder had been sore for a while, but I couldn't rest it. It was needed for me to get around. One morning as I was getting dressed in bed and trying to pull myself into a sitting position, I felt something in my left shoulder go *snap*! and the pain stopped for the first time in months. Then, as I turned to tell Dee what had happened, the muscle cramped. Yow! That hurt a lot.

The cramp subsided slowly, but after a few minutes a dark bruise started to appear in my arm, and grew rapidly until it covered from my elbow halfway to my shoulder. It was impressive. My doctor had seen it before, and he explained there usually wasn't any need to repair it. "Other muscles will compensate and your left arm will just be a little weaker than before."

"Wait a minute, doc. I need my arms to get around and they will need to push this chair for many more years. What happens if these compensating muscles wear out?" I asked.

"Hmm. Maybe in your case repairing the tendon might be a good idea."

After talking it over with Dee and my doctor, we decided to get the tendon repaired. It ended up taking two surgeries and a donor tendon because mine was so shredded it couldn't be salvaged. During the next several weeks, I couldn't move my arm at all, which meant I could not do transfers from bed to wheelchair and vice versa, and I couldn't drive. Even after I was allowed to move my arm, I couldn't use it for transfers for six months. I had to take disability leave from work.

We had to hire someone to come every morning to help me dress, and use a lift to get me out of bed and into my old power chair, then be my van driver if I needed to go anywhere. Dee had to use the lift in the evenings to get me back into bed and it was hard on her. It was hydraulic, but it still required hand cranking, which hurt her arm and neck. It put a big damper on our first year of marriage.

Our New House Disaster

After we were married, we went looking for a house. Dee's house in Corvallis had accessibility problems and my house in Albany was too small. We saw some pretty nice places, but they all needed modifications for wheelchair use, which would add $10,000 to $20,000 to their price. We decided to try to build from scratch, so the accessibility features wouldn't be add-ons, but would be included in the original design. We found a house plan on the Internet we liked and discovered the designer's office was in Tigard, Oregon, a Portland suburb. We got together with him and we (Dee, mostly) altered the plans for accessibility. Then we found a lot in a nice neighborhood in North Albany and contracted with a builder to build the house. He broke ground in March 2005.

Things started going wrong almost immediately. The contractor failed to keep to the contract, we objected, he refused to correct his errors. With the house about 80 percent done, he quit and filed a lien on the house, demanding the full amount of the contract. Lawyers got involved.

We counter-sued, claiming breach of contract. Because there was a lien on the house, the bank froze the remaining part of the construction loan so we had no money to finish the house. It stood empty and unfinished for more than a year.

We were living in my little house on Caribou Street. Soon after we got married, Dee sold her house in Corvallis and put all her stuff into storage. We expected the new house would be done in a few months and the extended time in my small house was disappointing and stressful.

As the trial date approached, the contractor made some offers to settle, but they were mostly inadequate. Then, about 10 days before the trial, he made us an offer that was acceptable with a little tweaking. On the morning of the day he had promised he would sign the agreement, I got a phone call from one of his sub-contractors. Our contractor had died of a heart attack. A big strong man in his 40s dropped dead to avoid making a settlement with us.

After waiting a proper amount of time to allow the widow to grieve, we moved against the contractor's estate. In the end we got a judgment against his estate for $125,000, but he died broke. All we got was $15,000 from his contractor's bond.

There is a happy ending. When the lien was lifted, the bank unfroze the loan and we could finish the house. We had to borrow more money to fix all the things the contractor had done incorrectly. We finally moved into the completed house in September 2007, more than two years after construction started. It's a nice house and the accessibility modifications worked well. We did a minor remodel in 2010 to fine-tune a few things and that made it even better.

Between the torn tendon and the house disaster, our first year of marriage wasn't the joyful, fun time it's supposed to be, but the marriage and we survived. We're still looking for a do-over.

The CADREZ

One of the problems with narcotics for pain is that the body builds up a tolerance. By 2005 the pain medication I had been taking since 2001 was losing its effectiveness. I had switched from OxyContin to methadone in 2003 at my doctor's recommendation, but it had the same problem. The pain was beginning to win. Not only that, I was beginning to show outward signs of addiction. I would nod-off like a heroin addict, falling asleep for a short period, usually in the afternoon or evening, even while driving. I had two minor accidents because of nodding off and my family was afraid to ride with me. The methadone was also dulling my thinking, although it had happened so gradually I hadn't really noticed it.

Dr. Falci, a neurosurgeon at Craig Hospital, had developed a procedure called CADREZ that helped people with an SCI and the type of neurogenic pain I had. CADREZ is an abbreviation for Computer-Assisted Dorsal Root Entry Zone. It involves opening up the spinal cord's sheath and using a computer-controlled sensor to identify the nerves that are sending out the pain signals. Those nerves are then cauterized where they enter the back of the spinal cord (an area called the dorsal root entry zone). They then make another pass with the sensor to make sure they got all the rogue nerves.

It is not a simple procedure–it can take up to 10 hours and has a number of scary possible side effects, such as blindness. I had talked to Dr. Falci in 2004 and he described the procedure.

"That sounds like a last resort kind of action," I said. He agreed, suggesting it be considered only after all other pain relief attempts have failed. I wasn't to that point yet.

By 2006, however, my choices were more limited. I could increase the dose of narcotics or I could try CADREZ. It was time for Dee and me to make a trip to Englewood, Colorado.

The operation was a success. The ring of fire around my chest was replaced with a ring of numbness–a good trade–and I suffered none of the possible bad side effects. When I woke up after surgery and realized the pain was gone, tears started flowing down my face.

After some days in the hospital for the incision to heal, we headed home. Now it was time to wean myself from the narcotic. That was tough. It took six months and for much of that time my skin felt like it was itching from the inside. But as my body flushed out the drugs, I could feel my mind starting to work more like it used to before the meds. Dee was relieved to find I was a nice guy even when I wasn't on drugs.

The procedure was truly a life-altering operation. I was being forced down a dark path by the pain and the drugs and now I could change directions and not spend the rest of my life in a numbed, zombie-like condition.

The Sidecar Rig

After my accident and spinal cord injury, some of my friends sent articles on trikes and sidecar rigs designed for disabled people. I wasn't interested in a trike, but the idea of a sidecar rig with the motorcycle controls transferred to the chair was interesting to me. I could use my Moto Guzzi Convert as the motorcycle starting point.

Some rigs were built around a Honda CB750A, another motorcycle with an automatic transmission. One thing about them bothered me—they had all used a U.S. specification sidecar, which put the chair with the controls on the right side of the rig, making the driver's seat on the right and the passenger seat (the motorcycle saddle) on the left. To me it looked like a vehicle designed for places where they drive on the left, such as England or Japan. I wanted to drive from the left of the rig, facing oncoming traffic, with the passenger on the right, just like it would be in a car.

I contacted Dauntless Motors, a company near Seattle that sold and installed sidecars on motorcycles. They didn't specifically produce sidecar rigs for the disabled, but they did a lot of custom work and they agreed to try to put something together for me. They didn't have any business connections with British sidecar companies, but they spent some time looking for a British-spec sidecar already in the U.S. and had no luck. They would have to start from scratch, building a sidecar for the left side. Dauntless had installed a number of sidecars on Moto Guzzi motorcycles and were up to the task.

Barry, the lead design engineer on the project, delivered the rig in October 2006. It wasn't quite the way I had visualized it, but it did the job. Barry said it was pretty neat to ride. With the driver in the chair, it was a lot more stable than having the driver in the motorcycle's saddle.

"It handles like a little slot car," Barry claimed.

I took my first runs in it at Christmas when Dee's son Russ came to visit. It was just around the neighborhood because it wasn't registered in Oregon and I didn't have the required endorsement on my driver's license. We got it registered in the spring. Dee had to drive it to the DMV because she was the one in the family with a motorcycle endorsement. A couple of weeks later I took the test and got an endorsement on my driver's license—I can now legally drive a car equipped with hand controls and a three-wheel motorcycle.

I rode it a fair amount during the summer of 2007, getting to understand its unique handling characteristics. It's very different from a motorcycle. It doesn't lean into turns, obviously, but there's more to it than that. A two-wheel motorcycle turns by leaning, so there is a progression. The motorcycle starts vertical and not turning, and then as it leans into a turn, the more it leans the tighter the turn, then the turn is finished as the

Test sitting the newly delivered sidecar rig with the transferred controls.
Dee Ritter

bike returns to vertical. Done correctly a turn is a smooth transition from going straight to carving around the corner to going straight again. With my sidecar rig, when I turn the handlebars, it turns *right now*. There is no progression. It took some getting used to.

It is like a motorcycle in one very important way, however. In the rig, unlike in a car, you are *in* the environment you're passing through. The important wind-in-your-face feeling is very much the same.

Unfortunately the rig has been idle for a couple of years. The Convert drives the rig OK, but even with a 1,000cc motor it strains a bit to pull all the extra weight. Dee and I started to take it on an extended trip, both of us on board, and after about an hour on the freeway, the motor went onto one cylinder, and it is way too much weight for a 500cc single. We got off the freeway and turned for home on the back roads, and after about 30 minutes of plodding along, it started running on both cylinders again. It has an aftermarket electronic ignition instead of the original points and there seems to be some sort of overheating problem. There are some other minor problems I want to tackle. Life seems to keep throwing things at me, unexpected and unscheduled things that need to be handled right away, and finding the time to work on the Moto Guzzi has proven difficult.

The Ducati Sport Lives (Sort Of)

Every year the Oregon Vintage Motorcyclists (OVM) club has their vintage bike show and swap meet in May, the Sunday of the weekend before the Memorial Day weekend, at the Benton County Fairgrounds in Corvallis. Each year a different brand is highlighted, and in 2007 the featured marque was Ducati and I wanted to take my 1974 Ducati 750 Sport.

Dee's son, Russ, who has a fair amount of mechanical skill, was staying with us for a couple of weeks at the time. He thought it was a good idea, so he helped me get the electrics hooked up. We put fresh oil and fuel in the appropriate places and he tried to start it.

I can't claim it fired on the first or second kick, but it did start, and the garage echoed with the booming sound from the Conti mufflers for the first time in 20 years. I was *very* pleased. The bike wasn't running well. The horizontal cylinder was blowing out oil smoke and kept cutting out at odd intervals, but it was running. I was *very* pleased. Oh, wait, I already said that, didn't I?

Russ Granger on my Ducati Sport and me in the Moto Guzzi sidecar rig about to leave for the 2007 Oregon Vintage Motorcycle show. *Dee Ritter*

Russ rode the Sport to the fairgrounds, a distance of about 15 miles. Dee and I followed on the Moto Guzzi rig. I remarked that Russ looked really good on the bike. That means I must have looked really good too back then, because he looked just like I used to look. He had to rev the heck out of the Sport a couple of times to clear the spark-plug and keep it running on two cylinders, but both bikes made it to the fairgrounds.

There were a half dozen or so Ducati bevel-drive twins in the assembled bikes, and we parked the Sport with them. Many other bikes were on display as well. For a relatively small organization, the OVM gets a pretty good showing. There were lots of bikes from the 1950s and '60s, U.S., British, and Japanese brands mostly, with a few European bikes. This year there were quite a few old Ducatis, both single-cylinder bikes from the '60s and early '70s, and twin-cylinder models from the late '70s and early '80s.

We did eventually figure out what the problem was with the Ducati's motor. On a later visit Russ and I got additional help from Quentin, a pal of Russ' who now works for Ducati as the western regional dealer representative. I told Quentin about the oiling problem and he thought it was likely either valve guide seals, or valve guides, or piston rings. Quentin is a better mechanic than most people, and as we took the top end off the motor, he checked things out. The valve seals and valve guides looked OK.

"It feels like you've got some cylinder wall scoring," he said as he felt the inside of the horizontal cylinder.

"Really? Show me, please." I couldn't tell by visual inspection, but if I closed my eyes and ran my fingertip across the area he indicated, I could feel the very slight irregularities in a small spot on the cylinder wall. Yep, that would allow oil to sneak past, especially while accelerating briskly. We all wondered what could have caused the scoring.

A few nights later I was looking at the pistons as they sat on the workbench and noticed the ring gap of the middle ring of one was way too big. I looked carefully and discovered the ring had a problem—a small piece of the ring adjacent to the gap had broken off. The broken off piece, which was missing, must have been short enough that it could turn slightly sideways in the ring groove, allowing the sharp edge to scrape the cylinder wall. It must have broken during that last race I ran in 1980.

I had new rings, but I did not have a pair of good cylinder sleeves, so we couldn't replace the damaged sleeve before Quentin's visit was up. I have since found some and will be able to get the Ducati running well again, someday. When I can find the time, after all the other projects I need to get done around the house.

You know, you would think now that I am no longer working I would have plenty of time to spend on house projects, but it seems like the list of things to do just keeps growing and keeps me really busy. There was a time, in fact, I thought about getting a new job just so I could get some rest!

CHAPTER SEVENTEEN

A Ducati Legend?

As the years since my 1977 and 1978 successes with Ducati have increased, the events from that time have gained importance. When I was racing for Dale Newton, I was only vaguely aware I was doing something historic. As the Superbike class grew and became internationally popular, my and the other Superbike pioneer's efforts in those early years have grown in stature. Phil Schilling has described the racing from that time as "legendary," and the fact remains Cook Neilson is still the only racer to win an AMA Superbike race at Daytona on a Ducati. Likewise, I'm the only one to win an AMA Superbike race at Sears Point Raceway (now Sonoma Raceway) on a Ducati. I find that fact amazing. There have been some really good racers on Ducati motorcycles who have won numerous AMA Superbike races since 1978, but none at Sears Point and none at Daytona.

Since then I've been able to use my past success to some advantages. I'm not good at self-promotion, but I would like my accomplishments to be more widely known.

———

In early 2001 Ducati announced they were going to throw a party in the U.S. They called it "Ducati Revs America" and it would be similar to the popular World Ducati Week bashes they held in Italy. It was scheduled for October 2001 at the Las Vegas Motor Speedway, which overlapped with the visit of the Guggenheim Museum's "The Art of the Motorcycle" exhibit to Las Vegas.

When I first heard about the DRA, I called the office of Ducati North America and suggested having Cook Neilson and myself as part of the show. We could answer questions, swap stories, and sign autographs. Frankly, I was hoping they would fly me to Las Vegas and put me up at a swell hotel in exchange for the entertainment Cook and I would provide, although I said nothing about that at the time. The guy I ended up talking to said he would take it under advisement.

Weeks went by and I heard nothing, so I made arrangements to go as an average Ducati fan, booking a flight, renting a car, and reserving a hotel room. Then, not long before the event itself, I got a call from Dan Van Epps. He said he was a Ducati employee and they were planning on having a panel of old racers for some Q and A sessions and they wanted me to participate.

I asked Dan if he worked for Ducati North America and he said no, he worked for Ducati in Italy, the parent company. He offered to pay for my hotel room. I told him to count me in.

The old racers panel was pretty comprehensive. Frank Scurria represented the racing successes of the Ducati 250cc singles back in the 1950s and 1960s. Frank also had a lot to do with the development of the 350cc and 450cc singles.

Most Ducati fans know about Paul Smart. He was the winner in the one-two Ducati finish at the Imola 200 race in Italy in 1972. Smart's success in the "Daytona of Europe" showed the world Ducati made a great twin-cylinder Superbike as well as nice little single-cylinder bikes.

Cook and I represented the racing success of the 750SS and 900SS bevel-drive twins in the United States from 1975 to 1978, and Giancarlo Falappa had helped develop the Ducati 916, racing it both in the European and the U.S. Superbike series.

It was great seeing Cook again. His knowledge of his own race bike was supplemented by a deep knowledge of the state of the industry in the U.S. in the 1970s, knowledge gained as the editor of *Cycle*. He added a lot to the discussion, having known Mike Berliner, one of the two brothers who were importers of Ducati and Moto Guzzi motorcycles. Cook had some interesting things to say about Berliner's personality.

I got to know Frank Scurria pretty well over the three days. He worked for the U.S. Ducati importer in the 1960s and had won many races in Southern California. He told of making the first 350cc single by stroking a 250cc motor and later boring a 350cc motor to make the first 450cc single. It seems the factory took a lot of clues from his one-off specials when they made the official production versions of the 350cc and 450cc motorcycles.

Paul Smart was really funny. He had the audience and other panel members laughing out loud with his stories of how he came to ride the

The Old Racers panel at DRA 2001 in Las Vegas. Paul Smart, the author, Frank Scurria, and Cook Neilson. Off photo right is GianCarlo Fallapa.

Imola race bike. He has a great, dry British sense of humor and is a good storyteller.

Giancarlo was more of a challenge. His English skills weren't very good and the only Italian I know is from watching Hollywood movies about the Mafia. I'm sure he was telling some great stories if only I could have understood him.

I was both intimidated and honored to be included in this panel. Cook helped me settle in by pointing out my accomplishments were a big part of Ducati's history in the U.S. and I had earned my spot in the group. "It is part of your personal history as well," he said, "and always will be. You were one of the top racers in your day and no one can take that away from you."

Have I mentioned that Cook is a classy guy?

By the end of the long weekend, I was exhausted, completely wiped out. The speedway is outside of town and I needed to drive there from the hotel. That meant getting in and out of the car at least twice a day, lifting the wheelchair across my body twice each time. My arms got quite a workout, hoisting that 25 or so pounds off the ground, up and over me and into the passenger seat every time I drove somewhere. I had a great time, reconnected with a bunch of old pals, and met some amazing people for the first time. I went back to the quiet, empty apartment, but I was glad to be home and able to use my ramp van again.

"The Ringer" Article in *Cycle News*

At the beginning of 2006, a fellow named Larry Lawrence contacted me. He explained he was an archivist working for the national motorcycle news weekly *Cycle News* and he was doing a weekly one-page history article in the newspaper. He wanted to do one about my inaugural AMA Superbike win at Sears Point in 1977. I agreed. Larry proceeded to interview me and asked if I had any photos from the event he could use. I e-mailed some scans of old photos.

The article, entitled "The Ringer," appeared in the May 31, 2006, issue. It was a good retelling of the race, emphasizing the fact I had won the first professional race I entered, and how rare that was, especially in a high-level class like Superbikes. There was a little bit at the end about the Steamboat Springs accident and the challenge of recovery from that and how I had fought back to build a different but satisfying life for myself.

Dee took a copy of the page, had it framed, and hung it in the hallway. I think she likes having a trophy husband.

The Pilgrimage

There is a racing museum in Bologna, Italy, inside the Ducati factory that contains displays and examples of Ducati racing history going all the way back to the 1940s when Ducati first started making motorcycles. The museum was started after the Texas Pacific Group purchased Ducati in the mid-1990s, took over management, and modernized production. The museum opened its doors to the public in 1998.

Along a wall inside the museum are a series of metal panels, containing the dates, names, and locations of all forms of Ducati racing success the world over. My name is on one of those panels, listing my two AMA Superbike race wins. Jon, a WetLeather pal, had been to the factory in 2005 and sent me a photo of the panel, and I noticed my name, and Cook Neilson's name, and thought, *Gee, that's nice of Ducati to remember the successes we had back in the day.*

Then a couple of years later Phil and Cook also visited the museum and e-mailed a photo of the panel to me. This time I took a closer look at the photo and noticed something that made the hair on the back of my neck stand up.

In the center of the plaque, under the year 1978, are the words "3/6 ENGLAND–TT Isle of Man Formula 1 World Championship, Hailwood, Mike, Ducati 900."

Holy shit! My name is on the wall at the Ducati Museum alongside Mike Hailwood's! Stanley Michael Bailey Hailwood, a.k.a. Mike the Bike, and me, on the same panel.

In 1966, when I was first reading motorcycle magazines, Mike Hailwood was a multi-time world champion, riding for makes such as MV Agusta and Honda. He was one of my early idols, and some still consider him the greatest motorcycle road racer of all time.

I immediately told Dee, showed her the photo, and explained the significance of it. She must have heard the excitement in my voice, because when I finished she said, simply, "We have to go see it."

I thought for a minute. "We do," I replied. We started making plans, referring to the trip as the Pilgrimage. It took a while getting an itinerary together and finding accessible accommodations at all the stops we wanted to make, but we finally flew to Italy in late May 2009. Besides the visit to Bologna and the Ducati factory, we planned stops in Milan, Venice, Rome, and Florence. As a special treat to ourselves, we timed our trip to match the date of the Italian MotoGP race at Mugello, a racetrack near Florence.

When we arrived at the factory Livio Lodi, the Ducati museum curator met us. I first met Livio in 2001 at the Ducati Revs America event in Las Vegas and was pleased to see him again. He was our host for lunch in the Ducati Cafeteria, with a guided factory tour and the museum tour in the afternoon.

At the end of the factory tour, Livio gave us a special treat—a visit to the MotoGP shop. This area is strictly off-limits to the usual visitor, but Livio had asked for permission in advance of our visit, a benefit of my past success as a Ducati racer. We got to see the bikes being prepared for the Italian GP at Mugello in 10 days time. We saw Nicky Hayden's carbon-fiber-framed Desmosedici with its fairing off. Very cool.

One of the important reasons for his trip was to see the plaque on the museum wall with my name on it, along with Cook's name, and especially Mike Hailwood's. There is a row of panels along the wall documenting Ducati's notable racing successes in many countries, starting back in the late 1940s. I won two AMA Superbike races, one in 1977 and one in 1978, and my name is on the wall for those years. Mike Hailwood is listed for winning the Isle of Man TT race and the TT World Championship in 1978. On the same panel!

When we entered the museum, the first thing we saw was a long curving row of race bikes from the earliest tiny singles up to the World

Superbike and MotoGP winners from 2008. The panels on the wall are behind the row of bikes, and Livio led us to the one we came to see. It was truly a thrilling moment for me.

Livio Lodi points to the panel with my name. *Dee Ritter*

UNITI/USA - Championship A.M.A. - 11/6, Daytona Beach, FL, SBK, Neilson Cook. Ducati - 16/7, Sonoma, CA, SBK, Ritter Paul, Ducati.
1978 - AUSTRIA - Meister Schaft Osterreich Osk Cup Serie Class, Wolfschlucker, Ducati 900 SS - Amstetten, S.C. Wolfschlucker, Ducati 900 SS - Salzburgring, S.C., Wolfschlucker, Ducati 900 SS - **INGHILTERRA/ENGLAND - TT Formula 1 World Championship, Hailwood Mike, Ducati 900 - TT Formula 1 Constructors World Championship, Ducati Meccanica, Ducati 900,** - 3/6, T.T. - Isle of Man, F/1, Hailwood Mike, Ducati 900 - 11/6, Mallory Park, F/1, Hailwood Mike, Ducati 900 - **SPAGNA/SPAIN** - 21/5, Subida S.Maria de Vitalba, 500, Coronilla Jose', Ducati - **STATI UNITI/USA - Championship A.M.A.** - 15/7, Sonoma, CA, SBK, Ritter Paul, Ducati.
1979 - ITALIA/ITALY - 26/8, Fontepetri-Montalcino, 250, Rossi Antonio, Ducati 250 - **STATI UNITI/USA - Championship A.M.A.** - 17/6, Loudon, NH, SBK, Schlachter Rick, Ducati.

My name is on the second line for 1977, then fourth from the bottom for 1978. Mike Hailwood's name is in the center in bold. *Jon Diaz*

Legends in Sonoma

In early spring of 2011 I heard Infineon (formerly Sears Point Raceway) was having a Legends in Sonoma promotion as part of its West Coast Moto Jam, a weekend where they have a number of events: a vintage motocross, a Supermoto race, and an AMA National road race. They were advertising the presence of Scott Russell, Rich Oliver, and Brad Lackey. I called the track and told them I should be a part of this as well.

"Who are you again?" the guy on the phone asked.

"Paul Ritter. I won the first two AMA Superbike races at your track, in 1977 and 1978, on a Ducati," I replied.

"You should talk to Hannah Philbin. She's our PR and promotions person."

So I talked to Hannah Philbin and she was happy to let me be part of the Legends. "It's too late for the press releases, but I'll make sure you get free admission and you'll be part of the autograph signing and the press conference."

"Thanks. You should know I use a wheelchair to get around and I'm going to have my son with me to help out. He'll need free admission too."

"No problem."

Normally Dee would accompany me on a trip like this, but her son Russ was turning 40 on that weekend and had invited her to his birthday party. She was conflicted but really wanted to help Russ celebrate. I enlisted my 21-year-old son to help me out. He lives in Chico, California, so I simply picked him up on my way to the motel in Vallejo.

During the Saturday autograph signing, I got to talk with Rich Oliver (five-time AMA 250cc Grand Prix champion) and briefly with Brad Lackey (U.S. and World Motocross champion). Later in the day I handed out the trophies for the AMA Superbike top three. As I handed the trophy to winner Josh Hayes, who had won the Superbike races in 2010, the announcer said, "The winner of the first two Superbike races at this track is handing out the trophy to the winner of the last two Superbike races at this track."

Saturday night at the motel I was checking my e-mail and saw a message from Mark, a racing pal from the 1970s. "Scott Russell just dropped your name big time during the Speed Network's coverage of the AMA race at Sears," he said. After I got home, Dee and I watched the Speed Network coverage of the event, which was available on the Internet. It seems Scott had wondered when the last time a non-Japanese bike had won the Superbike race at the track.

Surrounded by talent: Tommy Hayden, Martin Cardenas, and Josh Hayes, finished the 2011 Saturday AMA Superbike race in 2nd, 3rd, and 1st, respectively. *N. Jacobson*

"I had to go back to 1978 when Paul Ritter won on a Ducati," he announced.

I met Scott Sunday morning at the press conference. He came up to me and said he was really glad to meet me. I was a bit flustered. This was Scott Russell, World and AMA Superbike champion, the winner of five Daytona 200 races–his nickname is Mister Daytona–saying *he's* glad to meet *me*. I think I managed to blurt out, "Likewise, I'm sure," or something.

Steven and I watched the Sunday races from the top of the start/finish grandstands. The weekend was the first time he had watched a motorcycle road race. About midway through the Superbike race, he turned to me and said, "Boy, this sure beats NASCAR!"

Yes it does. It certainly does.

Ducstock

In October of 2011, NCR, the Italian specialist speed shop known for building some really fast Ducati-powered motorcycles, got together with Ducati North America to put together a party at the Barber racetrack and museum in Alabama called Ducstock. It was held in conjunction with an AHRMA event at the track. Dee and I were invited to join.

Ducati was featured this year and several Ducati celebrities had been brought to the event: Paul Smart, Cook Nielson, and Jason DiSalvo (who won the Daytona 200 that spring on a Ducati 848).

I had met Paul Smart at DRA in 2001, and Cook and I are old pals from the 1970s. There was an autograph session with these three and Alan Cathcart, the moto-journalist and noted author of several motorcycle books. Cook pulled a spare chair next to him and I got added to the end of the signature line. I had brought some copies of the Sears Point 1977 poster, in the 8.5x11-inch size, and Cook and I started autographing them and giving them to folks.

I gave one to Alan Cathcart who stared at it for a moment then said, "I remember this. It caused quite a stir at the time. Congratulations."

"Thank you, Sir Alan," I replied.

Toward the end of the session, a fellow picked up a poster and said, "I've got some 8mm film from the 1977 Laguna Seca race weekend. I know Cook is in it and you might be too. I can check when I get home if you want."

"Man, I would give my left nut to get a copy of that. One of my great regrets is never getting any video of my riding, and my wife has never seen me not in a wheelchair."

The gent's name was Buzz and he was true to his word. Not long after returning home from Ducstock, a small parcel arrived in the mail containing a CD with the movies on it. It was pretty cool and is a treasured item to me and to Dee.

In summary, during Ducstock I got to sign some autographs, meet Sir Alan Cathcart and Jason DiSalvo, scored some film of myself on the track and in the pits at Laguna Seca in 1977, and had a great conversation with Patrick Slinn, a member of the NCR crew working for Mike Hailwood during his 1978 Isle of Man triumph. And as icing on the cake Vicki Smith of Ducati North America gave me a neat magnetic name badge identifying me as a Ducati Legend. A very successful trip.

The "Ducati Legend" name badge presented to me at Ducstock in October 2011.

AFTERWORD

These days my life is a search for balance, both literally and figuratively. Literally, because without torso muscles I can fall over at the waist while in my chair if I get out of balance. When this happens, I need to find something to push against and use my arms to haul myself back upright. Figuratively, in that I need to balance fun activities with the mundane activities of daily living and the many chores and projects I hope to accomplish. I want to get my Ducati Sport running strong again and there's the pergola for the patio that is only partly complete–just two examples from a rather long list.

I've been asked, if I could do it over again, would I give up motorcycles if it meant I could avoid the SCI? My answer is, "No." Life in a chair, with all its limitations, is still life. However, I cannot imagine my life without motorcycles. I am, and always will be, a motorcyclist.

INDEX